37 f
43 f
48 ff
61 f
65 ff
77 ff
82 f
85 ff
89 ff
93

JOURNAL FOR THE STUDY OF THE OLD TESTAMENT
SUPPLEMENT SERIES
223

Sheffield Academic Press

Janus Parallelism in the Book of Job

Scott B. Noegel

Journal for the Study of the Old Testament
Supplement Series 223

For my wife Laurie

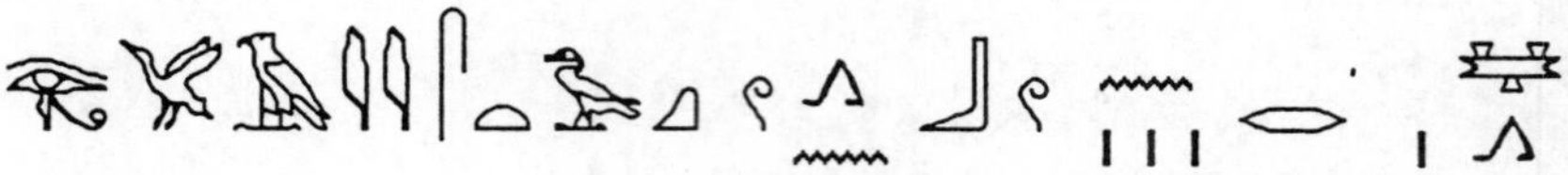

Published by
Sheffield Academic Press Ltd
Mansion House
19 Kingfield Road
Sheffield S11 9AS
England

Typeset by Sheffield Academic Press
and
Printed on acid-free paper in Great Britain
by Bookcraft Ltd
Midsomer Norton, Bath

British Library Cataloguing in Publication Data

A catalogue record for this book is available
from the British Library

ISBN 1-85075-624-4

CONTENTS

ACKNOWLEDGMENTS

Among the many contributors to my professional training in Semitic languages and literatures are Professors Alan Corré and Bernard Grossfeld of the University of Wisconsin–Milwaukee who first impressed on me a deep appreciation for Semitic literature. While in Milwaukee I also had the good fortune to study under visiting Professors Moshe Garsiel of Bar-Ilan University and Yair Hoffman of Tel Aviv University, whom I thank for their insightful classes and for staying in touch over the years. Other influential professors at the university include Robert Reinders, Abbas Hamdani, Carole Shammas, Bruce Fetter, Mary Wiesner-Hanks, Mel Lawrenz and Eldon Knoche.

I am also grateful for the generous support of the Wisconsin Society for Jewish Learning, Harry and Sara Platkin, George and Sylvia Laikin, and the Menahum Mansoor Fund, without which I could not have finished my BA degree.

The following individuals also must be recognized for their friendship and conversations which continue to inspire me: Michael DiMilo, Jim Sullivan, Dan Hintz, Greg Bowman, Jeremy Singer, Steve Witt, Voot Warnings, Richard Dietrich, and Professors Martin Bernal, Frederick Ahl, Hayden Pelleccia, Mike Shurman, David Powers, Angel Saenz-Badillos, and Larry Kant. I reserve special gratitude, however, for my wife Laurie Ramacci Noegel, whose love, encouragement, and humor I could not do without.

I am indebted also to Professors David I. Owen and Ross Brann, of Cornell University, whose erudite insights greatly aided in the preparation of this manuscript. Their warmth and encouragement helped to make the creation of this book a memorable project. Finally, I must acknowledge Professor Gary A. Rendsburg, also at Cornell, who, upon seeing my love for puns, first suggested the topic of this monograph. His originality and impeccable memory never cease to impress me. For his wisdom, guidance, and friendship I am eternally grateful.

ABBREVIATIONS

AB	Anchor Bible
AcOr	*Acta orientalia*
AfO	*Archiv für Orientforschung*
AGJU	Arbeiten zur Geschichte des antiken Judentums und des Urchristentums
AHw	W. von Soden, *Akkadisches Handwörterbuch*
AIOU	*Annali Instituto Universitario Orientale*
AJSLL	*American Journal of Semitic Languages and Literatures*
ALBO	Analecta lovaniensia biblica et orientalia
ANET	J.B. Pritchard (ed.), *Ancient Near Eastern Texts*
AnOr	Analecta orientalia
AOAT	Alter Orient und Altes Testament
AOS	American Oriental Series
ARM	Archives royales de Mari
ASTI	*Annual of the Swedish Theological Institute*
BA	*Biblical Archaeologist*
BARev	*Biblical Archaeology Review*
BDB	F. Brown, S.R. Driver and C.A. Briggs, *A Hebrew and English Lexicon of the Old Testament*
BHS	*Biblia hebraica stuttgartensia*
Bib	*Biblica*
BibOr	Biblia et orientalia
BJRL	*Bulletin of the John Rylands Library*
BJS	Brown Judaic Studies
BM	*Beth Miqra*ʾ
BSac	*Bibliotheca Sacra*
BZ	*Biblische Zeitschrift*
BZAW	*Beihefte zur ZAW*
CAD	*The Assyrian Dictionary of the Oriental Institute of the University of Chicago*
CBQ	*Catholic Biblical Quarterly*
CBQMS	*Catholic Biblical Quarterly*, Monograph Series
CdE	*Chronique d'Egypte*
CJ	*Classical Journal*
DISO	J.J. Hoftijzer, *Dictionnaire des Inscriptions Sémitique de l'Ouest*

EI	*Eretz Israel*
HAHAT[18]	D.R. Meyer, *Hebräisches und aramäisches Handwörterbuch über das Alte Testament* (Berlin, 18th edn).
GKC	*Gesenius' Hebrew Grammar*, ed. E. Kautzsch, trans. A.E. Cowley
HALAT	W. Baumgartner *et al.*, *Hebräisches und aramäisches Lexicon zum Alten Testament*
HAR	*Hebrew Annual Review*
HTR	*Harvard Theological Review*
HUCA	*Hebrew Union College Annual*
IBS	*Irish Biblical Studies*
IDB	*Interpreter's Dictionary of the Bible*
IDBSup	*IDB*, Supplementary Volume
JAAR	*Journal of the American Academy of Religion*
JAOS	*Journal of the American Oriental Society*
JETS	*Journal of the Evangelical Theological Society*
JBL	*Journal of Biblical Literature*
JBQ	*Jewish Bible Quarterly*
JCS	*Journal of Cuneiform Studies*
JEA	*Journal of Egyptian Archaeology*
JNES	*Journal of Near Eastern Studies*
JNSL	*Journal of Northwest Semitic Languages*
JPOS	*Journal of the Palestine Oriental Society*
JQR	*Jewish Quarterly Review*
JSOT	*Journal for the Study of the Old Testament*
JSOTSup	*Journal for the Study of the Old Testament*, Supplement Series
JSS	*Journal of Semitic Studies*
JTS	*Journal of Theological Studies*
KB	L. Koehler and W. Baumgartner (eds.), *Lexicon in Veteris Testamenti libros*
KUB	*Keilschrifturkunden aus Boghazköi*
LSJ	Liddell–Scott–Jones, *Greek–English Lexicon*
NABU	*Nouvelles assyriologiques bréves et utilitaires*
NTS	*New Testament Studies*
OLD	R.C. Palmer, *et al.* (eds.), *Oxford Latin Dictionary*
OTG	Old Testament Guides
PMLA	*Publications of the Modern Language Association of America*
RA	*Revue d'assyriologie*
RB	*Revue biblique*
REg	*Revue d'égyptologie*
Rel	*Religion*
REJ	*Revue des études juives*
SBLDS	SBL Dissertation Series
SBLMS	SBL Monograph Series
Sem	*Semitica*

SJOT	*Scandinavian Journal of the Old Testament*
TrinJ	*Trinity Journal*
UF	*Ugarit-Forschungen*
UT	C.H. Gordon, *Ugaritic Textbook*
VT	*Vetus Testamentum*
VTSup	Supplements to *Vetus Testamentum*
WBC	Word Biblical Commentary
WO	*Die Welt des Orients*
ZA	*Zeitschrift für Assyriologie*
ZAH	*Zeitschrift für Althebräistik*
ZAS	*Zeitschrift für ägyptische Sprache und Altertumskunde*
ZAW	*Zeitschrift für die alttestamentliche Wissenschaft*

Chapter 1

INTRODUCTION TO JANUS PARALLELISM

> The scroll of the Torah is (written) without vowels, in order to enable man to interpret it however he wishes... When it is vocalized it has but one single significance; but without vowels man may interpret it (extrapolating from it) several (different) things, many marvelous and sublime.[1]
>
> R. Baḥya ben Asher
> *Commentary on the Pentateuch* (thirteenth century)

The existence of word-play in biblical Hebrew and in the Semitic languages in general is well known and is commonly accepted.[2] Certain types of word-play have been studied well.[3] For example, paronomasia, or sound-play, is the subject of the classic work by I.M. Casanowicz,[4] of

1. Quoted in S. Parpola, 'The Assyrian Tree of Life: Tracing the Origins of Jewish Monotheism and Greek Philosophy', *JNES* 52 (1993), p. 206.

2. E.L. Greenstein, 'Wordplay, Hebrew', in D.N. Freedman (ed.), *The Anchor Bible Dictionary* (Garden City, NY: Doubleday, 1992), VI, pp. 968-71; J. Sasson, 'Word Play in the Old Testament', *IDBSup* (Nashville: Abingdon Press, 1976), pp. 968-70.

3. Compare the advances in Old English studies; for example P.F. Baum, 'Chaucer's Puns', *PMLA* 71 (1956), pp. 225-46; H. Kökeritz, 'Rhetorical Word-Play in Chaucer', *PLMA* 69 (1954), pp. 937-52; M.M. Mahood, *Shakespeare's Wordplay* (London: Methuen, 1957); R. Frank, 'Some Uses of Paranomasia in Old English Scriptural Verse', *Speculum* 47 (1972), pp. 207-26; in the classics; for example, M. Sulzberger, 'Onoma Eponymon: Les noms propres chez Homère et dans la mythologique Grecque', *Revue des études grecques* 183 (1926), pp. 381-447; C.J. Fordyce, 'Puns on Names in Greek', *Classical Journal* 28 (1932–33), pp. 44-46; A. Strus, *Nomen Omen* (Rome: Pontifical Institute, 1978); R.K. Johnston, *The Christian at Play* (Grand Rapids: Eerdmans, 1983); E. Richard, 'Expressions of Double Meaning and their Function in the Gospel of John', *NTS* 31 (1985), pp. 96-112; and in Far Eastern studies; for example, C.D. Orzech, 'Puns on the Humane King: Analogy and Application in an East Asian Apocryphon', *JAOS* 109.1 (1989), pp. 17-24.

4. I.M. Casanowicz, *Paronomasia in the Old Testament* (Boston, 1894).

numerous articles by a variety of scholars,[1] and of a recent book by M. Garsiel devoted to sound-play in biblical names.[2] But other categories of word-play have not been researched extensively or systematically.

Among the latter is the type of word-play known as polysemous parallelism, or more commonly, Janus parallelism.[3] The latter term was coined by Cyrus Gordon to describe a literary device in which a middle stich of poetry parallels in a polysemous manner both the line that precedes it and the line which follows it.[4] Gordon's initial discovery was in Song 2.12.

הנצנים נראו בארץ
עת הזמיר הגיע
וקול התור נשמע בארצנו

The blossoms have appeared in the land;
the time of זמיר has arrived,
the call of the turtledove is heard in our land. (Song 2.12)

Gordon observed that the word זמיר can be read both as 'song'[5] and as 'pruning'.[6] As 'song' it connects with the phrase קול התר, and as 'pruning' with נצנים. Gordon's discovery offered a new direction for scholars interested in the sophisticated literary devices of the biblical authors.

Since Gordon, others have contributed equally interesting examples of the device. For example, E. Zurro found the device at work in Job 9.25.[7]

וימי קלו מני רץ
ברחו לא ראו טובה

Now my days are swifter than a runner.
They ברחו they see no more good. (Job 9.25)

1. See Appendix 4.

2. M. Garsiel, *Biblical Names: A Literary Study of Midrashic Derivations and Puns* (Ramat-Gan: Bar-Ilan University Press, 1991).

3. I will employ both terms interchangeably throughout the book.

4. C.H. Gordon, 'New Directions', *Bulletin of the American Society of Papyrologists* 15 (1978), pp. 59-66.

5. So BDB, p. 274; KB, pp. 259-60; *HALAT*, I, pp. 262-63.

6. See BDB, p. 274; KB, p. 260; *HALAT*, I, p. 263.

7. Though Zurro's discovery, which appeared as 'Disemia de brḥ y paralelismo bifronte en Job 9, 25', *Bib* 62 (1981), pp. 546-47, was suggested by M. Dahood to C.H. Gordon. See Gordon, 'Asymmetric Janus Parallelism', *EI* 16 (1982), p. 80*.

As E. Zurro noted, the use of the word ברח in Job 9.25 constitutes a Janus parallel. In its meaning 'flees' (*brḥ*),[1] the word points above to 'runner', and as 'evil' (*brḥ*),[2] it faces 'they see no more good'.

To present just two more examples, we may utilize Gen. 49.26 and Gen. 15.1, noted by G. Rendsburg.[3]

ברכת אביך גברו
על ברכת הורי עד
תאות גבעת עולם

The blessings of your father surpass,
The blessings of הורי עד,
The delight of the eternal hills. (Gen. 49.26)

The pivot here is הורי עד in v. 26b, meaning both 'parents'[4] which connects it with 'your father' in v. 26a, and 'mountains'[5] which links it to 'the eternal hills' in v. 26c.

אל תירא אברם
אנכי מגן לך
שׂכרך הרבה מאד

Fear not, Abram,
I am a מגן to you,
Your reward shall be very great. (Gen. 15.1)

The Janus is מגן, which can be read as 'shield'[6] and therefore as a parallel with the previous expression of fear, or as 'bestow'[7] in which case it anticipates 'reward'. Though this Janus parallel might require the alteration of the vowels, it will be noted that the original consonantal text would have been ambiguous, and that by marking the vocalization, the later Masoretes would have been forced to remove the intended ambiguity.

1. So BDB, pp. 137-38; KB, p. 149; *HALAT*, I, p. 149; *HAHAT*[18], pp. 174-75.
2. The meaning of *brḥ* as 'evil' is derived from its use in Ugaritic and Arabic; *UT*, p. 376, nos. 514, 515. See *HALAT*, I, p. 149.
3. See G. Rendsburg, 'Janus Parallelism in Gen. 49.26', *JBL* 99 (1980), pp. 291-93; 'Notes on Genesis XV', *VT* 42.2 (1992), pp. 266-72.
4. From the root הרה. See BDB, pp. 247-48; KB, p. 242; *HALAT*, I, p. 245.
5. So BDB, pp. 249-51; KB, p. 241; *HALAT*, I, p. 244.
6. So BDB, p. 171; KB, p. 494; *HALAT*, II, p. 517; *HAHAT*[18], p. 225.
7. From the root מגן. See BDB, p. 171; KB, p. 190; *HALAT*, II, p. 517. The root is attested in Ugaritic, Hebrew, and Phoenician. For discussion, see M. O'Connor, 'Semitic **mgn* and its Supposed Sanskrit Origin', *JAOS* 109 (1989), pp. 25-32.

In the decade and a half since Gordon's brief article, roughly two dozen examples of polysemous parallelism have been proffered by scholars.[1] Nevertheless, even this rather scant evidence garnered thus far has led to the general acceptance of the device as utilized by the poets of ancient Israel. Thus, for example, standard works on Hebrew poetry such as those by W.G. Watson and A. Berlin[2] mention and illustrate the device.

A remaining desideratum, however, is a systematic study of polysemous parallelism, one which points out many more examples of the phenomenon and one which attempts to sub-categorize the different types of the device while explaining their function. These are specific tasks which I propose to undertake in this monograph. However, before doing so, it will be profitable to broaden the scope, and situate Janus parallelism within the larger context of scholarship. I also shall illustrate why one must take into consideration the ancient belief in the power of words when examining the device.

1. *Janus Parallelism within the Context of Scholarship*

The Assumption of Modern Scholarship

Though countless tomes have been written on the book of Job from a variety of angles, none has included an in-depth discussion on its widespread employment of word-play.[3] A few scholars have mentioned such devices, but only in passing or in brief footnotes.[4] Doubtless, this is due to an 'either/or' scholarly disposition when it comes to philological analysis. Modern exegesis proceeds on the assumption that a given lexeme or passage has but one meaning or interpretation. Yet, as a perusal of the early versions and rabbinic commentaries readily demonstrates, early exegesis recognized the multiplicity of meanings inherent in the biblical compositions.

1. These will be discussed in Chapter 2 and Appendix 3.

2. W.G.E. Watson, *Classical Hebrew Poetry: A Guide to its Techniques* (JSOTSup, 26; Sheffield: JSOT Press, 1984), p. 159; A. Berlin, *The Dynamics of Biblical Parallelism* (Bloomington, IN: Indiana University Press, 1985); *idem*, 'Parallelism', in D.N. Freedman (ed.), *The Anchor Bible Dictionary* (Garden City, NY: Doubleday, 1992), V, pp. 155-62.

3. See the bibliographic note at the end of Chapter 4.

4. See, for example, R. Gordis, *The Book of Job: Commentary, New Translation and Special Studies* (New York: Jewish Theological Seminary, 1978), who cites several examples of *talḥin*, 'word-play', and A. Guillaume, *Studies in the Book of Job* (Leiden: Brill, 1968), who also mentions word-play, albeit only intermittently.

The Failure of Modern Linguistic Approaches

Another factor contributing to the scholarly disposition toward a single interpretation of the biblical text is the traditional reliance upon the Masoretic vowels in order to elucidate difficult passages. Certainly, the Masoretic system is a reliable witness to one tradition of vocalization,[1] but it must be clarified that by developing a system of notating the vowels, the Masoretes committed an interpretive act. By pointing a word they were forced to remove the intended ambiguity. It is this lack of ambiguity which has become the goal of modern scholarship.

Another reason why modern scholars are disinclined to see multiple readings in the Bible comes from the Indo-European linguistic and non-semantic framework which governs Semitic philology today, specifically with regard to the rules of the semantic language system. As Ellen van Wolde states:

> This Greek–Latin orientation, which is essentially analytic and logically discriminating, has resulted in a Hebrew linguistics that is directed at discontinuity, at logical distinctions, and at classifications that rule each other out: something means x and can therefore not mean not-x at the same time. On the basis of this elementary binary principle one tries to construct a rule system or paradigm of that language.[2]

Thus, because the usual understanding of semantics in biblical Hebrew tends to be universalistic or lexicographic, in that it aims 'to formulate a general semantic lexicon of the Hebrew language system',[3] it tends to neglect the influence of the specific Hebrew language code in the analysis of the Hebrew text. A more text-semantic and holistic approach, on the other hand, has an advantage in that it can explain the elements of meaning not just in terms of 'conventional relationships in a system of logic', or 'purely on the basis of how words function in a discourse but on the basis of the interaction between both'.[4] The lack of appreciation for the complexities of interaction and the text-semantic uses of lexemes, I aver, has caused the modern reader to 'miss the point', and consequently, it has blinded the scholar to a plethora of internal references and a multiplicity of meaning which enlivens the ancient text.

1. See, for instance, the important work by Sh. Morag, 'On the Historical Validity of the Vocalization of the Hebrew Bible', *JAOS* 94 (1974), pp. 307-15.

2. E. van Wolde, 'A Text Semantic Study of the Hebrew Bible, Illustrated with Noah and Job', *JBL* 113 (1994), p. 22.

3. Van Wolde, 'A Text Semantic Study of the Hebrew Bible', p. 20.

4. Van Wolde, 'A Text Semantic Study of the Hebrew Bible', p. 23.

The inability fully to appreciate internal references and punful allusions applies not only to the modern philological approach within historical linguistics, but to the discipline of socio-linguistics as well. Specifically, socio-linguistic studies on polysemy begin with the assumption that puns are effective only when in close proximity.[1] While this certainly is true for those of us dependent on computer chips and calculators, it cannot be said of the ancients, whose well-practiced memories, without such aids, were far superior.

In addition, the book of Job portrays a heated debate, one which is stoked continually by its contestants. One can assume that, just as is the case in a real debate, contentious remarks stick in the memories of the participants. For this reason, proximity of the referent to the polyseme is not required for the pun to be effective in Job. Therefore, it should not surprise us to find the characters in Job referring to polysemous remarks several chapters later. Indeed, it is precisely this punful and referential

1. See, for example, J. Brown, 'Eight Types of Puns', *PMLA* 71 (1956), pp. 14-26; D.G. MacKay and T.G. Bever, 'In Search of Ambiguity', *Perception and Psychophysics* 2 (1967), pp. 193-200; J. Mehler and P. Carey, 'Role of Surface and Base Structure in the Perception of Sentences', *Journal of Learning and Verbal Behavior* 6 (1967), pp. 335-38; *idem*, 'The Interaction of Veracity and Syntax in the Processing of Sentences', *Perception and Psychophysics* 3 (1968), pp. 109-11; D.J. Foss, T.G. Bever, and M. Silver, 'The Comprehension and Verification of Ambiguous Sentences', *Perception and Psychophysics* 4 (1968), pp. 304-306; D.J. Foss, 'Some Effects of Ambiguity upon Sentence Comprehension', *Journal of Learning and Verbal Behavior* 9 (1970), pp. 699-706; P. Carey, J. Mehler, and T.G. Bever, 'Judging the Veracity of Ambiguous Sentences', *Journal of Learning and Verbal Behavior* 9 (1970), pp. 243-54; *idem*, 'When Do We Compute All the Interpretations of an Ambiguous Sentence?', in G.B. Flores d'Arcais and W.J.M. Levelt (eds.), *Advances in Psycholinguistics* (Amsterdam and London: North-Holland Publishing Company, 1970), pp. 61-75; L.G. Kelly, 'Punning and the Linguistic Sign', *Linguistics* 66 (1970), pp. 5-11; P. Farb, *Word Play* (New York: Knopf, 1973); *idem*, *Word Play: What Happens When People Talk* (New York: Bantam, 1975); M.K.L. Ching, 'The Relationship among the Diverse Senses of a Pun', *The Southeastern Conference on Linguistics Bulletin* 2.3 (Fall, 1978), pp. 1-8; *idem*, 'A Literary and Linguistic Analysis of Compact Verbal Paradox', in *idem*, *et al.* (eds.), *Linguistic Perspectives on Learning* (London: Routledge & Kegan Paul, 1980), pp. 175-81; W. Redfern, *Puns* (Oxford: Basil Blackwell, 1984), pp. 37-38, 177; G. Ulmer, 'The Puncept in Grammatology', in J. Culler (ed.), *On Puns: The Foundation of Letters* (Oxford: Basil Blackwell, 1988), pp. 164-89; J. Culler, 'The Call of the Phoneme: Introduction', in *idem* (ed.), *On Puns*, pp. 1-16.

character which the author of Job exploits in order to lend the debate an air of realism.

Moreover, such punful referencing must be seen in the light of the frequent use of internal quotations in Job. According to Gordis:

> the use of quotation in Job (as elsewhere in biblical and oriental literature) is a highly important element in the author's style, and by that token, a significant key to the meaning of the book.[1]

Polysemous references, therefore, should be seen in tandem with the use of quotations, as an intertextual device, and, by extension, as a means by which one character distorts the other's position.[2]

Modern Scholarship and Extra-Biblical Polysemy

To all who work with ancient Semitic languages it is clear that the initial progress which scholars made in the deciphering of the ancient Semitic languages (such as Akkadian and Ugaritic) relied heavily upon earlier advances in biblical studies. The early translators naturally gravitated to the Hebrew language in order to isolate phonemes and to establish the semantic ranges of lexemes. Consequently, we find the same faulty assumptions with regard to polysemy in place today in Assyriology, Ugaritology, and for that matter, Egyptology, Hittitology, and Sumerology. This lack of appreciation for word-play is most evident in the extremely sparse treatment of polysemy in critical editions of texts, and in the secondary literature.[3] Thus, the same criticisms apply to biblical linguistics and to scholarship in other ancient Near Eastern languages (see Appendix 2).

1. R. Gordis, *The Book of God and Man: A Study of Job* (Chicago: University of Chicago Press, 1965), p. 189.

2. For more on inner quotations and the rhetorical distortion of arguments in the debate see Gordis, *The Book of Job*, p. 373; J.C. Holbert, 'The Function and Significance of the "Klage" in the Book of Job with Special Reference to the Incidence of Formal and Verbal Irony' (PhD dissertation, South Methodist University, 1975); N.C. Habel, *The Book of Job: A Commentary* (Philadelphia: Westminster Press, 1985); J.E. Course, *Speech and Response: A Rhetorical Analysis of the Introductions to the Speeches of Job (Chaps. 4–24)* (CBQMS, 25; Washington, DC: Catholic Biblical Association of America, 1994).

3. See, for example, n. 1 in Appendix 2 in which only two of the authors listed provide an in-depth discussion of polysemy.

2. *Janus Parallelism and the Ancient Understanding of Words*

The Conception of Words as Found in the Book of Job

The vigor with which the characters in the book of Job constantly outwit each other must be seen within the larger context of how the ancients conceived of words. It is commonly accepted that the ancients, both in biblical Israel and in the Near East in general, believed words to be more than an extension of the spoken idea; they possessed the substance and form of that idea. Thus, once spoken, words were capable of affecting the observable reality.[1] In the words of Isaac Rabinowitz:

> In the culture of ancient Israel... while words indeed did constitute the medium of interpersonal communication and expression, the words were not perceived and thought of as exchangeable *symbols* or *representations* of their sensible referents, but rather as *those referents themselves*—the palpable objects, the 'real' and perceptible actions and events, the sensible relationships and interactions—in the *concentrated form* of words.[2]

Therefore, if we are to understand the use of polysemy in biblical Israel, or for that matter in ancient Near Eastern literature as a whole, we cannot do so without first taking into consideration this ancient mindset. Thus, if words possess power and essence, polysemes contain twice the power, twice the essence. This may explain why conventionally in literature belonging to the wisdom genre, such as the book of Job, one finds a concern with uncontrolled speech and a caveat to the uninitiated.[3]

Indeed, it is in examining the remarks made about words by each of the characters in the book of Job that the ancient belief in the power of words and Job's opponents' concern with his double-talk becomes evident. Moreover, within the context of a debate, such one-upmanship takes on the character of a highly charged poetry contest. As Elihu

1. See, for example, F.L. Moriarty, 'Word as Power in the Ancient Near East', in H.N. Bream, *et al.* (eds.), *A Light Unto My Path: Old Testament Studies in Honor of J.M. Myers* (Philadelphia: Temple University Press, 1974), pp. 345-62; and more recently I. Rabinowitz, *A Witness Forever* (Bethesda, MD: CDL Press, 1993). For an opposing and in my opinion unconvincing view see A. Thiselton, 'The Supposed Power in Words in the Biblical Writings', *JTS* 25 (1974), pp. 289-99.

2. Rabinowitz, *A Witness Forever*, p. 3. The italics are original.

3. See, for example, J.C. Thom, '"Don't Walk on the Highways": The Pythagorian *Akousmata* and Early Christian Literature', *JBL* 113 (1994), especially pp. 102, 107. I examine this point in greater detail in Chapter 4.

impatiently puts it in 33.5: אם תוכל השיבני ערכה לפני התיצבה, 'If you are able, respond to me, prepare for the contest, take your stand'. It is Job's attempt to answer this call which forces Bildad to bestow upon him the title קנצי למלין, 'word–hunter' (18.2).[1]

In 4.2, Eliphaz, the oldest speaker in the debate, asks Job: 'If one ventures a word with you, will it be too much? But who can hold back his words?' Yet, to Job, the words of his friends amount to little more than insult in the face of injury, as he states in 19.2: 'How long will you torment me, and crush me with words?'

In 34.2-3 Elihu exhorts: 'Hear my words, wise ones, and give ear to my knowledge, for the ear tests words as the palate tastes food'; and again in 34.16: 'Therefore, understand and hear this, listen to what I say'. In a similar vein are his words in 34.34-35: 'Men of understanding speak to me, wise man, hear me. Job speaks without knowledge, and his words are without prudence.'

Indeed, a perverse mouth was seen as a dangerous open trap, one which is best shut. Witness the remark of Eliphaz in 5.16: 'The mouth of wrongdoing is shut', and similarly, his rhetorical queries to Job in 15.2-6:

> Does a wise man answer with windy opinions, and fill his belly with the east wind? Should he argue with useless talk, with words that are of no worth? You subvert piety and restrain prayer to God. Your sinfulness dictates your speech, so you choose crafty language. Your own mouth condemns you—not I; your lips testify against you.

Again in 15.30, Eliphaz avers that the evil speaker 'will not escape from the wind of his mouth'. Job's and his friends' views of words seem to mirror each other. To each, the other's speeches are nothing but vanity. See, for example, Job's response to Eliphaz in 16.2-4:

> Is there no end to your words of wind; and what compels you to answer? I would also talk like you if you were in my place; I would compose for you with words, I would wag my head over you, I would encourage you with my mouth. My moving lips would bring relief. If I speak, my pain will not be assuaged, and if I do not, what have I lost?[2]

1. With Gordis, *The Book of Job*, p. 190. See also S.B. Noegel, 'Another Look at Job 18.2, 3', *JBQ* 23 (1995), pp. 159-61.

2. There might be a hint of irony in that though Job's friends frequently accuse him of speaking windy words, it is God who eventually does so from the whirlwind. I hope to develop this point further in a future article.

That the author of Job believed words to possess an unpredictable power when emitted from an unbridled mouth can be seen by the fact that though Job declares himself blameless, when God speaks from the whirlwind, Job's first reaction is to put his hand to his mouth (40.4). Shortly after this, God asks quite appropriately: 'Do you thunder with a voice like his?' (40.9). It is for this reason that Job cautions himself in 9.14: 'Can I answer him [God]? I will choose (carefully) my words with him.'

The Conception of Words in Other Ancient Near Eastern Literatures

The belief in the essence and form of words was held also by the other peoples of the ancient Near East.[1] It is not surprising, therefore, that we find a similar treatment of and attention to words in the texts which contain polysemy (see Appendix 2). This is seen clearly in the statement which Utu-napištim makes to Gilgameš before launching into his tale: 'I will reveal to you, Gilgameš, a thing that is hidden, a secret of the gods I will tell you!' (XI.9-10). The implication here is not merely that what Utu-napištim has to tell Gilgameš is secret, for when Utu-napištim speaks in tablet XI, it is clear that the event is *post facto*. Moreover, that Utu-napištim is helpless to make Gilgameš immortal suggests that if the information itself were secret, it would be inconsequential to Gilgameš anyway. On the contrary, it is the manner in which Utu-napištim speaks which is clandestine; which is, in essence, the manner in which the god Ea passed on to Utu-napištim the knowledge of the deluge. It will be remembered that Ea, the god of wisdom, was ordered by the assembly of gods not to tell anyone about the coming catastrophe, and that in order not to break his word to the assembly, he was forced to tell Utu-napištim through a reed hut, addressing his speech to that hut. Yet it was not only the subject of his address which Ea had to conceal, but also the language of that address. That Utu-napištim possessed the sagacity to understand Ea's veiled wisdom earned him the appelative 'Atra-ḫasis' (lit. 'Exceedingly Wise').

This explains why both Ea's instructions to build the boat and his news of the coming flood appear in polysemous statements (XI.14, 25-27). Moreover, this also explains the polysemy on Ea and his epithets in XI.16-20 (see Appendix 2). He is the wise one who speaks the mysteries of the gods, and so must himself possess a changeable name capable of

1. See, for example, Moriarty, 'Word as Power in the Ancient Near East', pp. 345-62.

containing hidden meanings. Indeed, even in the *Descent of Ištar* 89-92, Ea's craft requires punning quips. For in creating a man and ruse to trick Ereškigal into releasing Ištar, he does so utilizing the magic of polysemy.[1]

3. *References to Word-Play in the Book of Job*

As iron sharpens iron,
one sharpens the wit of his friend. (Prov. 27.17)

It is in the Jobian characters' expressed concern for words, their power, and their manipulation that we must look for references to sophisticated speech, for it is in these expressions that one finds oblique references to polysemy. For instance, in 6.3 Job states that his grief compels his manner of speech: על כן דברי לעו, 'On account of this have I spoken indistinctly'. What could Job mean by לעו, 'indistinct', other than words of uncertain or indefinable meaning, that is, polysemy?[2] The havoc which Job's polysemy wreaks on the ears of his friends becomes a source of contention between them. Hence, in 4.12, Eliphaz compares Job's subtlety to a nocturnal theophoric experience: 'A word came to me in secret, my ear caught a whisper of it'.[3]

Such secret and allusive linguistic subtleties are tied up with the characters' understanding of what constitutes wisdom. For example, Zophar reprimands Job in 11.2-6 by asking:

> Is a multitude of words unanswerable? Must a loquacious person be right? Your prattle may silence men; you may mock without being rebuked... but would that God speak, and talk to you himself. He would tell you the secrets of wisdom (תעלמות חכמה), for there are two sides to sagacity (כפלים לתושיה).

Wittily, Zophar remarks that just as Job has relied on double-talk, so too there are two sides to God's understanding, one of which Job does not understand. What makes Zophar's point so poignant is his polysemous wisecrack immediately afterwards: 'And know that God ישה [forgets/ demands payment for] your iniquity' (11.6c). To Zophar, then, the double side of God's wisdom is that he both forgets and demands

1. See, for example, S.N. Kramer and J. Maier, *Myths of Enki, the Crafty God* (New York: Oxford University Press, 1989).

2. Cf. Obad. 16 where this word appears in reference to the slurred speech of drunkards.

3. Cf. Job 26.14.

retribution, depending on the patron's perception.

Eliphaz too is aware of Job's penchant for word-manipulation, as he states: 'It is your guilt that teaches your mouth, and makes you choose crafty (ערומים) speech' (15.5). It would appear that at least to Eliphaz, crafty speech alone is not what is wicked, but rather the sinful intent behind the crafty speech.

To Zophar as well, it is not hidden language that is a threat, but rather the content of the hidden material. In 20.12-13, for example, Zophar accuses Job:

> If wickedness grows sweet in his mouth, he hides (יכחידנה) it under his tongue; if he loves it and does not let it go, and saves it in his mouth, his food in his stomach is turned into the gall of asps within him.[1]

The reason why Job and his friends view the intent and content of the language more cautiously than the act of concealment is perhaps the association of things hidden with things divine (cf. the Holy of Holies). The implication of this is that speech concealment, that is, polysemy, is an illocutionary, perhaps quasi-divine, act. It is in this light that we must understand Job, who though he admits to concealing his own language, denies hiding the secrets of God: 'Never have I hidden (כחד) the words of the Holy One' (6.10). A belief in the illocutionary nature of polysemy also explains Elihu's remark in 37.14, 'Give ear to this, Job, stand and consider the words of El', which follows upon a lengthy litany of polysemy and paronomasia.

Elihu's polysemous attack begins in 32.17: 'I will respond, even I, my portion (חלק)'. As Curtis observed, the root חלק also denotes 'smooth' or 'slippery' language.[2] In effect, Elihu declares that it is his turn to turn a phrase. Several of the characters drop the word חלק, 'portion, smooth speech', into their discourses. In 20.29 Zophar concludes his string of puns: זה חלק אדם רשע מאלהים ונחלת אמרו מאל, 'this is the wicked person's portion from God and the inheritance of his words from El'. That חלק alludes to the 'smooth words' of the wicked men in v. 29a can be seen by its use in conjunction with אמרו, 'his words'. Similarly, Job remarks in 24.18: 'You say to me "they perish quickly, like water their portion/smooth words (חלקתם) is/are cursed in the land".' Job uses חלק

1. Regarding the root כחד Gordis (*The Book of Job*, p. 216) noted: 'the piel carries the nuance of "conceal in speech"'.

2. See J.B. Curtis, 'Word Play in the Speeches of Elihu (Job 32–37)', *Proceedings of the Eastern Great Lakes and Midwest Biblical Societies* 12 (1992), pp. 23-24.

again in 27.13: 'This is the sinner's portion (חלק) from God'.[1]

Of all of the friends, it is Elihu who is most preoccupied with Job's manner of speaking and with what he believes to be a failure on the part of Job's friends to outwit him. Witness, for example, his angry remark in 32.15: חתו לא ענו עוד, 'they are beaten, they do not respond'. This is why in 35.4 he proclaims: 'I will return to you words, and to your friends with you'. It is perhaps this preoccupation which explains why most of Elihu's polysemous parallels involve plays upon speech and hearing, for example, אזין (32.11), מלל (32.17-18), and שרר (36.24-25) (see Chapter 3). His concern with speech also is transparent in 33.1-5: 'But now Job, listen to my words, give ear to all I say. Now I will open my lips; my tongue forms words in my mouth', and in 33.8: 'indeed, you have stated in my hearing, I heard the sound of your words (קול מלין)'. Elihu's use of the word קול, 'sound', in 33.8 and 24.16 is extremely suggestive of the manner in which Job speaks.

To Elihu, as to Zophar above, hidden speech is equated with wisdom. In 33.16 Elihu states: 'Thus, he reveals to men's ears, and in their chastisement, he terrifies them', and in 33.31-33 he continues:

> Pay heed, Job, and hear me, be silent, and I will speak; if you have anything to say, answer me; speak, for I am eager to vindicate you. But if not, you listen to me; be silent, I will teach you wisdom.

Elihu's equating of wisdom with concealment also finds support in 28.20, the Hymn to Wisdom: 'But wisdom, whence does it come, and where is the place of understanding? For it is hidden from the eyes of all living things, concealed even from the birds of the air.' Elihu believes that Job is speaking wisdom without knowledge, that is, without a pious intent, and so he deepens his insults in 35.16: 'Yet, Job keeps chirping (יפצה) empty talk; he multiplies words without knowledge'.

It is in such statements by Elihu that we may discern a subtextual doctrine regarding polysemy. For example, in 36.2 Elihu makes Job aware that despite his prowess at paronomasia and polysemy, it is God who is the grand manipulator: 'Wait a little, and I will declare; that moreover words belong to God'. According to Elihu, it is God who creates words, and thus he alone can exploit the relationships between words: מן החדר תבוא סופה וממזרים קרה מנשמת אל יתן קרח ורחב מים במוצק, 'the storm wind comes from its chamber, and the cold from its constellations; by the breath of God ice is formed, and the expanse of water

1. Gordis (*The Book of Job*, p. 291) attributes 27.13 to Zophar.

becomes solid' (37.9-10). Note that here it is the breathing of God which is credited with turning 'cold' (קרה) into 'ice' (קרח), a change which requires of a speaker only a harder breath.

Similarly, Elihu speaks indistinctly in 37.12-13, playing on the visual and aural closeness of ארצו, 'his land', and לא רצו, 'they do not obey': כל אשר יצום על פני תבל ארצה אם לשבט אם לארצו אם לחסד ימצאהו, '...all that he commands them through the inhabited earth, be it for chastisement, if they do not obey, or for kindness, he brings it all to pass'. Again, Elihu credits God as the source of such speech in 37.14: 'Give ear to this Job, stand and consider the words of El'.

God too is concerned with the power and intent of words. In 38.2-3 he thunders: 'Who is this who darkens my counsel by words without knowledge? I will ask, and you make [it] known to me'. In 12.22 Job declares that God 'reveals deep secrets (עמקות) from the darkness'. These 'deep secrets', as demonstrated above, must refer to secret speech acts, that is, polysemous usages. Therefore, if God brings to light concealed language, darkening counsel 'by words without knowledge' is tantamount to the suppression or abuse of polysemous language; this is why Job's friends are concerned with his manner of speech and why God exonerates Job in the end.

Further evidence for the equating of wisdom with words comes from Prov. 8.22-32, in which 'Wisdom' declares that she existed before the creation of the world. According to Genesis, little existed before the creation except for God and his word. In fact, creation takes place by fiat. Therefore, wisdom must be seen as an extension of, or equivalent to, God's spoken word.

In 41.4-5 God draws an analogy between a hippopotamus and humankind in order to underscore humankind's powerlessness before God. The gist of the analogy is that the mighty hippopotamus is powerless before God; how much more so a mere human. His reprimand, which we later learn is directed at Job's friends (42.7-8), conceals an allusion to crafty speech: 'I will not be silent concerning him and his martial exploits. Who can uncover (גלה) his garment (לבושו)? Who can approach his double jaws (בכפל רסנו)?' The latter half of this statement also can be read as 'Who can reveal his shame [reading לבושו as preposition ל + בוש + suffix pronoun ו]? Who can approach his double-talk?'

Indeed, in 38.36 it is God who asks: 'Who gave wisdom to the ibis (טחות); who gave understanding to the cock (שכוי)?' As noted by Pope and Gordis,[1] the ibis (טחות) has a long-standing association with wisdom and the scribal arts. Thus, it is interesting to note that God credits himself with having taught the ibis wisdom, and, by extension, the hidden scribal arts.

It is noteworthy that though Job's friends see his polysemy as unprofitable (for instance in 15.3), God exonerates Job in the end. In 42.7 God addresses Eliphaz as follows: 'I am incensed at you and your two friends, for you have not spoken to me correctly as did my servant Job'. Therefore, we may assume that Job's crafty speech was of some profit, at least in the eyes of God. Moreover, at the tale's end, Job receives 'double' for everything he lost. Does the principle of *lex talionis* operate here, with Job receiving double for speaking in doubles?[2]

4. *An Overview of the Contents of the Monograph*

At this juncture we must pause for an overview of the contents of this book. As scholarship always proceeds from the labor and observations of one's scholarly predecessors, I thought it appropriate to continue the study by discussing the already published Janus parallels. These will be arranged chronologically, in the order of their discovery, in Chapter 2.

In Chapter 3, the core of the volume, I will present 49 hitherto unrecognized examples of polysemous parallelism in the book of Job. I have chosen to focus on the book of Job because it is a lengthy poetic discourse with an extremely rich vocabulary, and thus a potentially ripe source for such word-play. Each of these polysemous parallels will appear in the Hebrew consonantal text and will be accompanied by an English translation with the Hebrew polyseme left untranslated (as in the examples above). I have done this in order to preserve the inherent ambiguity of the text.

Below the English rendering I will discuss the various ancient translations (that is, LXX, Targum,[3] Vulgate, Syriac, and, where extant, the

1. M. Pope, *Job* (AB, 15; Garden City, NY: Doubleday, 1965), pp. 302-303; Gordis, *The Book of Job*, pp. 452-53.

2. Cf. P.J. Nel, 'The Talion Principle in Old Testament Narratives', *JNSL* 20 (1994), pp. 21-29.

3. As the Targum to Job, as found in the printed editions, is often unreliable I have found it beneficial to consult C. Mangan, *The Targum of Job* (The Aramaic

fragments of 11QTgJob[1]) in reference to the polyseme in question. After listing this data, I will discuss the philological evidence for the proposed readings, and where available, I will provide support based on the argument that certain lexemes form established word-pairs.[2] I then will classify the polysemous parallel according to form: symmetrical and asymmetrical, and according to type: oral and visual, strictly visual, and semantic.[3]

I can briefly demonstrate the classification schema based on the examples presented at the start of this introduction. Since זמיר in Song 2.12 is pronounced and spelled the same whether it means 'song' or 'pruning', this example is both oral and visual. By contrast, since מגן in Gen. 15.1 is pronounced differently depending on whether it means 'shield' or 'bestow', this example is strictly visual. I will reserve the term 'semantic' for those polysemes which exploit the semantic range of a lexeme (that is, the two meanings are etymologically related). In addition, since the Janus parallel in Song 2.12 is accomplished in three stichs, and that in Gen. 15.1 in two, they are symmetrical and asymmetrical, respectively.[4]

Bible: The Targums, 15; Collegeville, MN: Michael Glazier, 1991) and Ms. Villa-Amil (ed.), *Targum de Job* (Madrid: Consejo Superior de Investigaciones Cientificas, Instituto Francisco Suarez, 1984).

1. I have found most useful the editions and commentaries of D.M. Stec, *The Text of the Targum of Job: An Introduction and Critical Edition* (AGJU, 20; Leiden: Brill, 1993); A.D. York, 'A Philological and Textual Analysis of the Qumran Job Targum (11QtgJob)' (PhD dissertation, Cornell University, 1973); R. Weiss, התרגום הארמי לספר איוב (Tel Aviv: Tel Aviv University Press, 1979); M. Sokoloff, *The Targum to Job from Qumran Cave XI* (Ramat-Gan: Bar-Ilan University Press, 1974); and J.P.M. van der Ploeg, *Le Targum de Job de la grotte XI de Qumrân* (Leiden: Brill, 1993). Also consulted were S.A. Kaufman, 'The Job Targum from Qumran', *JAOS* 93.3 (1973), pp. 317-27; J. Gray, 'The Massoretic Text of the Book of Job, the Targum and the Septuagint Version in the Light of the Qumran Targum (11QtargJob)', *ZAW* 86 (1974), pp. 331-50; B. Zuckerman, 'A Fragment of an Unstudied Column of 11QtgJob: A Preliminary Report', *Newsletter of the Comprehensive Aramaic Lexicon* 10 (1993), pp. 1-7.

2. See, for example, M. Paran, 'למשנה הוראה במקרא', *Beersheva* 1 (1973), pp. 151-61; Y. Avishur, *Stylistic Studies of Word-Pairs in Biblical and Ancient Semitic Literatures* (AOAT, 210; Neukirchen–Vluyn: Neukirchener Verlag, 1984).

3. The last three types are not mutually exclusive; that is, the category 'semantic' may apply both to the 'oral and visual' and to the 'strictly visual' types.

4. *Contra* the opposite classification scheme proposed by Gordon in 'Asymmetric Janus Parallelism', pp. 80-81*.

After classifying the polysemous parallel, I will survey the pertinent exegetical comments by medieval commentators[1] (namely, Rashi, Ibn Ezra, Yehiel Hillel Altschuler's *Metsudat David* and *Metsudat Zion*, Ralbag, Moshe Qimḥi, Minḥat Shai, and Saᶜadia) and modern commentators (namely, Yellin, Driver, Dhorme, Pope, Gordis, Tur-Sinai, Guillaume, Hartley, and Clines[2]), with an eye to the more philologically oriented. Each of the sections will conclude with a discussion of the polyseme's rhetorical and/or referential function in the book of Job (see also Chapter 4).

Chapter 4 contains a conspectus of the results of my research, including a discussion of: (1) the referential function of Janus parallelism in Job and in other Near Eastern literatures within the context of dialogue and debate; (2) the relationship of word-play to wisdom literature; (3) the continued importance of preserving polysemy in the ancient translations; and (4) other implications of this research, including (a) the biblical and (b) extra-biblical examples of Janus parallelism and their relation to other types of word-play; (c) the impact of Janus parallelism on textual criticism; (d) the compositional structure of polysemous parallelism; and (e) the implications of my research for the unity of the book of Job.

In addition, while researching this monograph I have collected some information which, while relevant to the thesis, properly speaking lies outside the study of the book of Job. This data I have placed in the three appendices described below.

Appendix 1 is a collection of hitherto unrecognized extra-Jobian Januses which I have discovered while undertaking general study. As these Janus parallels fall outside of the book of Job, I will present them briefly, without the versional witnesses and without philological analysis.

In my study of extra-biblical texts, notably Akkadian, Ugaritic, and

1. I am aware of the important commentary by Rashbam, but it has not been published yet. See S. Japhet, 'The Nature and Distribution of Medieval Compilatory Commentaries in the Light of Rabbi Joseph Kara's Commentary on the Book of Job', in M. Fishbane (ed.), *The Midrashic Imagination: Jewish Exegesis, Thought, and History* (Albany, NY: State University of New York Press, 1993), pp. 98-130. Also unpublished is the commentary of R. Samuel ben Nissim of Aleppo. See, for instance, W. Bacher, 'Le Commentaire sur Job de R. Samuel B. Nissim d'Alep', *REJ* 21 (1890), pp. 118-32. I am also aware of the important study of B. Richler, 'Rabbeinu Tam's "Lost" Commentary on Job', in B. Walfish (ed.), *Frank Talmage Memorial Volume I* (Haifa: University of Haifa Press, 1993), pp. 191-202, but have not found it useful for this work.

2. Please see the bibliography for references.

hieroglyphic Egyptian, I have kept my eye out for instances of polysemous parallelism. I noted several particularly interesting examples in extra-biblical literature, and have published brief notes on them.[1] In addition, I have gathered examples from a still wider range of ancient Near Eastern languages including Arabic, Hittite, and Medieval Hebrew. As these examples illustrate the continuity of the device from most ancient times until the medieval era I have included them in Appendix 2.

Of the 34 examples of polysemous parallelism published by scholars, I have rejected 13. Typically, my rejection is based on either a lack of philological evidence for the proposed readings or a lack of a referent in either of the adjacent stichs. Often, while I do see a pun at work in these passages, I do not see in them polysemous parallelism. For the sake of completeness, however, I discuss them in Appendix 3.

As I cannot demonstrate the presence of Janus parallelism and its function in the book of Job until I have presented all of the data, and because the presentation is quite lengthy and detailed, I beg the reader's indulgence.

1. S. Noegel, 'A Janus Parallelism in the Gilgamesh Flood Story', *Acta Sumerologica* 13 (1991), pp. 419-21; 'An Asymmetrical Janus Parallelism in the Gilgamesh Flood Story', *Acta Sumerologica* 16 (1994), pp. 10-12'; 'A Janus Parallelism in the Baal and 'Anat Story', *JNSL* 21 (1995), pp. 91-94; 'Another Janus Parallelism in the Atra–Ḫasīs Epic', *Acta Sumerologica* 17 (1995), pp. 342-44; 'Janus Parallelism Clusters in Akkadian Literature', *NABU* 71 (1995), pp. 33-34; W. Horowitz and Sh. Paul, 'Two Proposed Janus Parallelisms in Akkadian Literature', *NABU* 70 (1995), pp. 11-12.

Chapter 2

PREVIOUS RESEARCH REGARDING JANUS PARALLELISM

ימי קלו מני ארג
ויכלו באפס תקוה
זכר כי רוח חיי
לא תשוב עיני לראות טוב

> My days are more trifling[1] than a weaver's shuttle. They go without תקוה. Remember, my life is but a wind, my eyes will see no more good. (Job 7.6-7)

To my knowledge, the first scholar to note the presence of polysemous parallelism was David Yellin, who, in 1933, noted an interesting use of polysemy in Job 7.6-7.[2] As Yellin observed, the word תקוה in 6b means both 'thread'[3] and 'hope'.[4] As the former, תקוה parallels 'a weaver's shuttle' in line 6,[5] and as the latter, it parallels the expression of Job's failing hope in line 7: עיני לראות טוב. (An extended discussion of Job 7.6-7 will be found in Chapter 3.)

More than forty years later, C.H. Gordon, apparently unaware of Yellin's previous discovery, coined the term 'Janus parallelism' for what is tantamount to the same device.[6] Though Gordon's coinage is, more accurately, a specification of Yellin's discovery (that is, it specifies that the polyseme parallel both the preceding and following lines), the observations

1. With H.M. Szpek, 'The Peshitta on Job 7.6: "My Days Are Swifter than an ארג"', *JBL* 113 (1994), pp. 287-90.

2. D. Yellin, 'משנה ההוראה בתנ"ך', *Tarbiz* 5 (1933), p. 13. He was anticipated by Ibn Ezra.

3. As found in Josh 2.18, 21. See BDB, p. 876; KB, p. 1038; *HALAT*, IV, p. 1636.

4. BDB, p. 876; KB, pp. 1038-39; *HALAT*, IV, p. 1636.

5. It also may be connected to two roots in line 5: לבש, 'clothed', and עפר, 'dust', which may reflect the garment called *ǵpr* in Ugaritic. See *UT*, p. 465, s.v. *ǵpr*, (1106.7, cf. 24): '20 *ǵpr* garments'.

6. Gordon, 'New Directions', pp. 59-60.

by the two scholars are close enough to be classified as identical phenomena. Though I have discussed Gordon's find in Chapter 1, I include it here again for the sake of completeness.

הנצנים נראו בארץ
עת הזמיר הגיע
וקול התור נשמע בארצנו

The blossoms have appeared in the land;
the time of זמיר has arrived,
the call of the turtledove is heard in our land. (Song 2.12)

As Gordon noted, the word זמיר may be read both as 'song'[1] and as 'pruning'.[2] As 'song' it parallels קול התור, and as 'pruning', נצנים.

Since Gordon, others have contributed equally interesting examples of the device. For example, Walter Herzberg spotted the device at work in Ruth 1.21.[3]

למה תקראנה לי נעמי
ויהוה ענה בי
ושדי הרע לי

Why do you call me Naomi,
when Yahweh has ענה בי,
and Shaddai has brought misfortune upon me? (Ruth 1.21)

As noted by Herzberg, the words ענה בי may mean both 'answered me'[4] and 'afflicted me'.[5] As the former ענה בי parallels תקראנה לי, 'you call me', in the previous stich, and as the latter it parallels הרע, 'bring misfortune', in the next stich. The brevity of the stichs and the common use of the word-pair ענה//קרא includes Ruth 1.21 in the collection of known Janus parallels.

Following Herzberg's observation, G. Rendsburg found a Janus parallel in Gen. 49.26.[6]

ברכת אביך גברו
על ברכת הורי עד
תאות גבעת עולם

1. So BDB, p. 274; KB, pp. 259-60; *HALAT*, I, pp. 262-63.
2. See BDB, p. 274; KB, p. 260; *HALAT*, I, p. 263.
3. W. Herzberg, 'Polysemy in the Hebrew Bible' (PhD dissertation, New York University, 1979), pp. 63-65, 116.
4. From ענה I. So BDB, pp. 772-73; KB, pp. 718-19; *HALAT*, III, pp. 805-807.
5. From ענה II. See BDB, p. 776; KB, p. 719; *HALAT*, III, pp. 807-808.
6. See Rendsburg, 'Janus Parallelism in Gen. 49.26', pp. 291-93.

> The blessings of your father surpass,
> The blessings of הורי עד,
> The delight of the eternal hills. (Gen. 49.26)

As mentioned in Chapter 1, the pivot expression הורי עד in v. 26b means both 'parents',[1] connecting it with 'your father' in v. 26a, and 'mountains',[2] linking it to 'the eternal hills' in v. 26c.

Then came E. Zurro's discovery in Job 9.25 (already discussed in Chapter 1).[3]

וימי קלו מני רץ
ברחו לא ראו טובה

> Now my days are swifter than a runner.
> They ברחו they see no more good. (Job 9.25)

According to Zurro, the use of ברח in Job 9.25 constituted a Janus parallel. The lexeme, which can mean both 'flee' and 'evil', has referents in the adjacent stichs. As 'flee',[4] ברח faces 'runner', and as 'evil',[5] it looks toward 'they see no more good'.

Gordon then added to the list of Janus parallels by pointing to Gen. 1.31–2.2.[6]

וירא אלהים אתכל אשר עשה והנה טוב מאד ויהי ערב ויהי בקר
יום הששי
ויכלו השמים והארץ וכל צבאם ויכל אלהים ביום השביעי
מלאכתו אשר עשה...

> And God saw everything that he had made, and behold, it was very good.
> And there was evening and there was morning, a sixth day.
> Thus the heavens and the earth ויכלו, and all their host.
> And on the seventh day, God finished from the work which he did...
> (Gen. 1.31–2.2)

1. From the root הרה. See BDB, pp. 247-48; KB, p. 242; *HALAT*, I, p. 245.
2. So BDB, pp. 249-51; KB, p. 241; *HALAT*, I, p. 244.
3. Though Zurro's discovery, which appeared in his article 'Disemia de brḥ', pp. 546-47, was suggested by M. Dahood to C.H. Gordon. See Gordon, 'Asymmetric Janus Parallelism', p. 80*.
4. So BDB, pp. 137-38; KB, p. 149; *HALAT*, I, p. 149; *HAHAT*[18], pp. 174-75.
5. The meaning 'evil' is derived from its use in Ugaritic and Arabic; see *UT*, p. 376, nos. 514, 515. See *HALAT*, I, p. 149.
6. Gordon, 'Asymmetric Janus Parallelism', pp. 80-81*.

Gordon's Janus here revolves around the semantic range of the root כלה. According to Gordon the Janus was accomplished retrospectively in its meaning 'they were completed', referring to the first creation account in Genesis 1, and prospectively in its meaning 'they were destroyed'.[1] The latter paves the way for the second creation account in Genesis 2, where there is nothing left of the first creation.

To suit his new discovery Gordon coined the term 'asymmetrical Janus parallelism'. However, as his example relies on a tripartite division of stichs in which the second stich contains the pun, I respectfully refrain from applying this term to such constructions. Accordingly, as mentioned in Chapter 1, in this study I use 'symmetrical' to refer to those Januses which are comprised of three stichs in which the middle stich carries the pun; and reserve the term 'asymmetrical' for those Januses which are accomplished in two stichs.

ובשטף עבר
כלה יעשה מקומה
ואיביו ירדף חשך

But with an overflowing flood
he will completely destroy מקומה
and will pursue his enemies into darkness. (Nah. 1.8)

A Janus parallel in Nah. 1.8 then was noted by D.T. Tsumura.[2] The pivot word here is מקומה, which Tsumura reads both as 'its place' and as '(in) the rebel(s)',[3] that is, the city's rebels, a reading which is supported by the LXX. As 'its place' or, better rendered, 'its (the flood's) rising', מקומה parallels the notion of overflowing in the previous stich. As '(in) the rebel(s)' the polyseme anticipates the appearance of איביו, 'his enemies', in the following line.

In the same year that Tsumura's observation appeared, Duane L. Christensen published another Janus parallel from Jon. 3.7-8.[4]

1. Both from כלה. See BDB, pp. 477-78; KB, pp. 437-38; *HALAT*, II, pp. 454-55.

2. D.T. Tsumura, 'Janus Parallelism in Nah. 1.8', *JBL* 102 (1983), pp. 109-11.

3. Both from קום. See BDB, pp. 878-80; KB, pp. 831-33; *HALAT*, III, pp. 1015-18.

4. D.L. Christensen, 'Anticipatory Paronomasia in Jonah 3.7-8 and Genesis 37.2', *RB* 90 (1983), pp. 261-63.

האדם והבהמה הבקר והצאן אל יטעמו מאומה
אל ירעו ומים אל ישתו
ויתכסו שׂקים האדם והבהמה
ויקראו אל אלהים בחזקה

No man or beast—of flock or herd—shall taste anything!
They shall not ירעו and they shall not drink water!
They shall be covered with sackcloth—man and beast—and shall cry mightily to God. (Jon. 3.7-8)

As Christensen noted, the phrase אל ירעו can be read as 'they shall not feed' (from רעה)[1] and 'they shall not be evil' (from רעע).[2] The former parallels the mention of 'taste' in the previous stich, and the latter parallels the penitent actions of both man and beast in the next line.

אפך כמגדל הלבנון
צופה פני דמשק
ראשך עליך ככרמל
ודלת ראשך כארגמן

Your nose is as the tower of Lebanon which faces the face of Damascus.
ראשך upon you is as כרמל and the coiffure of your head is as purple wool. (Song 7.5-6)

In his book on the comparison of the Song of Songs with Egyptian love poetry,[3] Michael Fox spotted the presence of two additional Janus parallels in the Song of Songs, the first in 7.5-6 and the second in 7.12. As Fox noted,[4] both כרמל and ראשך have two meanings each. We may read the first as 'your head' and as 'your summit',[5] and the second as 'crimson'[6] and 'Carmel'.[7] If read as referring to a 'head of crimson' the stich precedes in a polysemous way the phrase 'the coiffure of your head is as purple wool'. If the expression ראשך עליך ככרמל is understood as 'your summit upon you is as Carmel' it follows upon the previous stich where the tower of Lebanon is mentioned alongside Damascus.

1. BDB, pp. 944-45; KB, pp. 898-99; *HALAT*, IV, pp. 1174-76.
2. BDB, pp. 947-48; KB, pp. 901-902; *HALAT*, IV, pp. 1184-85.
3. M.V. Fox, *The Song of Songs and the Ancient Egyptian Love Songs* (Madison, WI: University of Wisconsin Press, 1985), pp. 113, 160, 164.
4. Fox, *The Song of Songs and the Ancient Egyptian Love Songs*, p. 160.
5. Both from ראש. See BDB, pp. 910-11; KB, pp. 865-66; *HALAT*, IV, pp. 1086-89.
6. A by-form of כרמיל. See BDB, p. 502; KB, p. 455; *HALAT*, II, p. 474.
7. So BDB, p. 502; KB, p. 455; *HALAT*, II, p. 475.

לכה דודי נצא השדה
נלינה בכפרים
נשכימה לכרמים

Come my beloved, let us go to the field;
let us lodge in/among the כפרים,
Let us rise up early to the vineyards. (Song 7.12)

This Janus construction, according to Fox,[1] is accomplished with the word בכפרים, which can be read as 'in the villages',[2] which reminds us of נצא השדה, 'let us go to the field', in the previous line, and as 'among the henna plants',[3] which prepares us for נשכימה לכרמים, 'let us rise up early to the vineyards', in the next stich.

אתהלך לפני יהוה בארצות החיים
האמנתי כי אדבר אני עניתי מאד
אני אמרתי בחפזי כל האדם כזב

I walk before Yahweh in the land of the living.
I believed though אדבר, I was greatly afflicted.
I said in my consternation, 'Men are all a vain hope'. (Ps. 116.9-11)

Rendsburg added to the list of Janus parallels by citing Ps. 116.9-11.[4] The pivot word אדבר, derived from the root דבר, may be read as 'I will say'[5] and as 'I will go away'.[6] In its first meaning the word אדבר looks ahead to אני אמרתי בחפזי, 'I said in my consternation'. As 'I will go away' it follows nicely upon אתהלך לפני יהוה, 'I will walk before Yahweh'.

Rendsburg then eyed another polysemous parallel in Gen. 15.1.[7]

אל תירא אברם
אנכי מגן לך
שׂכרך הרבה מאד

Fear not, Abram,
I am a מגן to you,
Your reward shall be very great. (Gen. 15.1)

1. Fox, *The Song of Songs and the Ancient Egyptian Love Songs*, p. 164.
2. For general reference see BDB, p. 499; KB, p. 453; *HALAT*, II, p. 471.
3. So BDB, p. 499; KB, p. 453; *HALAT*, II, p. 471.
4. G. Rendsburg, *Linguistic Evidence for the Northern Origin of Selected Psalms* (SBLMS, 43; Atlanta: Scholars Press, 1990), p. 84.
5. So BDB, pp. 180-82; KB, p. 199.
6. So *HALAT*, I, p. 201.
7. Rendsburg, 'Notes on Genesis XV', pp. 266-72.

As mentioned in Chapter 1, the Janus word מגן can be read as 'shield'[1] and therefore as a parallel with the previous expression of fear, or as 'bestow'[2] in which case it anticipates 'reward'.

Following this discovery, Amos Frisch[3] illustrated the presence of the device in 1 Kgs 12.7.

וידבר אליו לאמר אם היום תהיה עבד לעם הזה ועבדתם
ועניתם ודברת אליהם דברים טובים
והיו לך עבדים כל הימים

> They answered him, 'If you will be a servant to those people and serve them, and if you ועניתם and speak to them with kind words, they will be your servants always.' (1 Kgs 12.7)

As Frisch noted, the author of 1 Kings has employed the root ענה for its polysemous ambiguity. As 'you will submit to them'[4] the phrase harks back to 'and serve them' just prior. As 'you will answer them'[5] it faces ahead to 'speak to them with kind words'. Thus, as Frisch rightly remarked, his example constitutes a Janus parallelism.

More recently, Shalom Paul[6] proposed examples of the sophisticated Janus construction in a variety of biblical texts including Isaiah,[7] Jeremiah, Hosea, Amos, Nahum, Zephaniah, Lamentations, and Job. These will be dealt with below in the order in which they appear in Paul's article.

1. So BDB, p. 171; KB, p. 494; *HALAT*, II, p. 517; *HAHAT*[18], p. 225.

2. From the root מגן. See BDB, p. 171; KB, p. 190; *HALAT*, II, p. 517. The root is attested in Ugaritic, Hebrew, and Phoenician. For discussion, see O'Connor, 'Semitic **mgn* and its Supposed Sanskrit Origin', pp. 25-32.

3. A. Frisch, 'ועניתם (I Reg 12,7): An Ambiguity and its Function in the Context', *ZAW* 103 (1991), pp. 415-18.

4. From ענה II. See BDB, p. 776; KB, p. 719; *HALAT*, III, pp. 807-808.

5. From ענה I. See BDB, pp. 772-73; KB, pp. 718-19; *HALAT*, III, pp. 805-807.

6. Sh. Paul, 'Polysensuous Polyvalency in Poetic Parallelism', in M. Fishbane and E. Tov (eds.), *'Sha'arei Talmon': Studies in the Bible, Qumran, and the Ancient Near East Presented to Shemaryahu Talmon* (Winona Lake, IN: Eisenbrauns, 1992), pp. 147-63.

7. I have not included Paul's discussion of Isa. 57.8 and 57.9, which he calls a 'Janus *entendre*' and a 'multiple *entendre*' respectively, because he seems to have distinguished them from his other proposed examples of Janus parallelism, and I do not see in them the required characteristics of Janus parallelism, i.e., a pivot word which polysemously plays both on what precedes it and on what follows it. (See pp. 155-56 of 'Polysensuous Polyvalency'.) I have rejected a few of his other examples for various reasons, and so I have included them in Appendix 3.

כי את על סבלו
ואת מטה שכמו
שבט הנגש בו החתת כיום מדין

For the yoke that they bore,
and מטה of their back,
the rod of their taskmaster,
you have broken as on the day of Midian. (Isa. 9.3)

Paul noted that the word מטה can be read both as 'staff'[1] and as the verbal participle of the root מטה, i.e., 'that which bends'.[2] As 'that which bends (the back)' מטה echoes the preceding verse 'for the yoke that they bore', and as the noun 'staff' it foreshadows 'the rod of the taskmaster' in the next stich.

והיה ביום ההוא יחבט יהוה
משבלת הנהר
עד נחל מצרים

On that day Yahweh will beat out
from the שבלת of the Euphrates
to the wadi of Egypt. (Isa. 27.12)

As Paul observed, and as was made famous by scholarship dealing with the incident at the fords of the Jordan in Judg. 12.1ff., the word שבלת may be understood both as 'fresh husks of grain'[3] and as 'torrents'.[4] As שבלת reflects back on יחבט, 'he will beat out' (normally said of grain), and looks forward to עד נחל מצרים, 'to the wadi of Egypt', it constitutes a Janus parallelism.

התנערי מעפר קומי
שבי ירושלם
התפתחו מוסרי צוארך שביה בת ציון

Shake off the dust, arise! שבי Jerusalem! Loose the bands of your neck,
O captive one, daughter of Zion. (Isa. 52.2)

Seeing in שבי an allusion to two separate roots, ישב and שבה, Paul[5] found reason to read שבי as 'sit!'[6] and as 'captive one'.[7] The former, as

1. BDB, p. 641; KB, pp. 515-16; *HALAT*, II, pp. 542-43.
2. BDB, pp. 639-41; KB, pp. 611-12; *HALAT*, III, pp. 654-55.
3. See BDB, p. 987; KB, p. 942; *HALAT*, IV, pp. 1296-97.
4. So KB, p. 942; *HALAT*, IV, p. 1297.
5. Though Paul does not cite him, Yellin anticipated his finds by nearly sixty years. See Yellin, 'משנה ההוראה בתנ"ך', p. 9.
6. From ישב. See BDB, p. 985; KB, pp. 409-10; *HALAT*, II, pp. 423-25.
7. From שבה. See BDB, pp. 985-86; KB, p. 939; *HALAT*, IV, p. 1294.

Paul rightly demonstrated, forms a word-pair with קומי, 'arise', and the latter anticipates שביה, 'O captive one', in the next line.

אם התרחצתי במו שלג
והזכותי בבר כפי
אז בשחת תטבלני

Even if I should wash my hands with nitre,
and clean my palms בבר,
You would still dip me in the pit. (Job 9.30-31)

According to Paul,[1] the poet in Job 9.30-31 cleverly displays his artistic skill in crafting this Janus. Here בר is used both as 'lye'[2] and as 'pit'.[3] The first of its meanings parallels במו שלג, 'with nitre', in the previous line and the second parallels בשחת, 'pit', in the following stich.

כי עמד מלך בבל אל אם הדרך בראש שני הדרכים לקסם קסם
קלקל בחצים שאל בתרפים ראה בכבד

For the king of Babylon has stood at the fork of the road, where the two roads branch off, to לקסם קסם. He has shaken arrows, consulted teraphim, and inspected the liver. (Ezek. 21.26)

Jack Sasson suggested the presence of a Janus device in Ezek. 21.24-26.[4] As he noted, the root קסם means both 'cut, divide' (cf. Arabic *qasama*) and 'practice divination'.[5] As the former, it refers back to the forked road on which the king of Babylon stood and as the latter it points forward to the three acts of divination in v. 26.

More recently Anthony Ceresko suggested that we see the famous *crux interpretum* לא אשיבנו in Amos 1.3 as an example of Janus parallelism.[6] It is repeated with variation in 1.6, 9, 11, 13; 2.1, 4, 6. For the sake of convenience I cite here only the first of these attestations.

1. Again, Paul did not cite Yellin's identical find. See Yellin, 'משנח ההוראה בתנ"ך', p. 16.

2. From ברר. So BDB, p. 141; KB, p. 146; *HALAT*, I, p. 146; *HAHAT*[18], p. 172.

3. From בור. See BDB, p. 92; KB, p. 105; *HALAT*, I, p. 102; *HAHAT*[18], p. 121.

4. J.M. Sasson, 'The Divine Divide: re FM 2.71.5', *NABU* 67 (1994), pp. 39-40.

5. BDB, p. 890; KB, pp. 844-45; *HALAT*, III, pp. 1041-42.

6. A.R. Ceresko, 'Janus Parallelism in Amos's "Oracles Against the Nations" (Amos 1.3–2.16)', *JBL* 113 (1994), pp. 485-90.

על שלשה פשעי דמשק
ועל ארבעה לא אשיבנו
על דושם בחרצות הברזל את הגלעד
ושלחתי אש בבית חזאל
ואכלה ארמנות בן הדד

> Because of three wicked acts of Damascus,
> For four לא אשיבנו!
> Because they threshed Gilead with threshing boards of iron.
> I will send down fire upon the palace of Hazael,
> and it shall devour the fortress of Ben-hadad. (Amos 1.3-4)

As Ceresko points out, the expression לא אשיבנו may be read both as 'I will not let him return (to me)' (from the root שוב) and as 'I will indeed fan/blow upon it (i.e., the fire [of my fury])' (from the root נשב). As the former, the expression parallels the previous mention of wicked acts not to be forgiven, and as the latter, לא אשיבנו faces ahead to the mention of a devouring fire.

בשומו לים חקו ומים לא יעברו פיו
בחוקו מוסדי ארץ
ואהיה אצלו אמון
ואהיה שעשעים יום יום
משחקת לפניו בכל עת

> When he assigned the sea its limits,
> so that its waters never transgress his command;
> when he fixed the foundations of the earth.
> I was with him as a אמון,
> a source of delight every day,
> playing before him at all times. (Prov. 8.29-30)

According to Avi Hurvitz[1] the Janus phenomenon is accomplished also in Prov. 8.30, where אמון can be read as 'architect, craftsman', and as 'one who raises a child' (cf. Isa. 60.4; Est. 2.20). As the former it parallels the cosmological building references in the previous stich, and as the latter it dovetails with the personification of Wisdom in the next line as one with whom a child plays and delights.

1. A. Hurvitz, 'לדיוקו של המונח "אמון" בספר משלי ח/ל', in S. Japhet (ed.), המקרא בראי מפרשו ספר זיכרון לשרה קמין (Jerusalem: Magnes Press, 1994), p. 648.

Chapter 3

JANUS PARALLELISM IN THE BOOK OF JOB

Job 3.23-24

לגבר אשר דרכו נסתרה
ויסך אלוה בעדו
כי לפני לחמי אנחתי תבא
ויתכו כמים שאגתי

To a man whose way is hidden, whom God has ויסך,
Instead of my food comes sighs, groans are poured out for me as water.

The root סוך is used here for its dual meaning 'fence in, enclose' and 'pour out'. Both roots are well-attested: סוך I, 'pour, anoint', can be found in Deut. 28.40; 2 Sam. 14.2; Ruth 3.3; Dan. 10.3, etc.; סוך II, 'hedge, fence in', in Job 38.8; and its variant שׂוך in Job 1.10; Hos. 2.8. When read as the former, לגבר אשר דרכו נסתרה ויסך אלוה בעדו reads 'to a man whose way is hidden, whom God has fenced in' in line 23.[1] As 'whom God has poured out' v. 23b anticipates ויתכו כמים שאגתי, 'my groans are poured out for me as water', in v. 24. That the root סוך as 'pour out' occurs in conjunction with water and washing in Ezek. 16.9 and 2 Sam. 12.20 supports the latter parallel. Further, this root can be found, as it is here, in sequential connection with the root בוא in 2 Sam. 12.20; 2 Chron. 28.15; and Dan. 10.3. As the polysemy occurs in the second of two stichs and is not differentiated in speech, it belongs to the oral, visual, and symmetrical categories.

Though the versions appear to take ויסך as 'hedge, fence in',[2] one must wonder if the LXX's συνέκλεισε, 'hedge (him) in',[3] for example,

1. The dictionaries read it as 'fence in'; BDB, pp. 691-92; KB, p. 651; *HALAT*, III, p. 704; *HAHAT*[18], p. 538.

2. *OLD*, p. 320, s.v. *circumeō*; J. Payne Smith, *A Compendious Syriac Dictionary* (Oxford: Clarendon Press, 1979), pp. 74, 251, s.v. המגן, סתר.

3. LSJ, p. 957, s.v. κλείω.

was selected because of its closeness in sound to συν + κλύζω, 'wash over, surge up, rinse',[1] that is, the other meaning of ויסך.[2] Moreover, as H. Orlinsky has noted,[3] the LXX's use of θάνατος generally is believed to stand for קבר in the previous verse (v. 22), but this is by no means certain. I would argue that the LXX used θάνατος to catch the nuance of ויסך, 'poured out' (i.e., to death). The same may be said of the Targum's use of וטלל, which, besides meaning 'hemmed in', may also be interpreted 'he sprinkled'.[4] Saᶜadiah Gaᵓon, Rashi, Ibn Ezra, Moshe Qimḥi, the commentaries *Metsudat David* and *Metsudat Zion*, Minḥat Shai, Driver, Dhorme, Pope, Gordis, Tur-Sinai, Michel, Guillaume, and Clines[5] also derive our Janus word from the root סוך II, 'hedge, fence in'. So, notwithstanding the lack of support from the versions, the Janus is cemented by the connection of the roots סוך I, 'pour', and מים in Ezek. 16.9 and 2 Sam. 12.20. According to Hartley:

> [Job's] complaint here functions as an ironic twist to the Satan's suspicion (1.10). The Satan argued that God had fenced Job in to keep him safe from any harm and thus Job grew prosperous without any hindrances. But now an anguished Job complains that God has fenced him about to keep any help from reaching him.[6]

1. LSJ, p. 962, s.v. κλύζω.
2. Yet, as noted by H. Heater, *A Septuagint Translation Technique in the Book of Job* (Washington, DC: Catholic Biblical Association, 1982), p. 65, there is no parallel with the previous line as the LXX ignores לגבר אשר דרכו נסתרה.
3. H.M. Orlinsky, 'Studies in the Septuagint of the Book of Job: Chapter III (Continued)', *HUCA* 32 (1961), p. 250 n. 59.
4. From טלל; *DISO*, p. 101; M. Jastrow, *A Dictionary of the Targumim, the Talmud Babli and Yerushalmi, and the Midrashic Literature* (New York: Judaica Press, 1989), p. 537; K. Beyer, *Die aramäischen Texte vom Toten Meer* (Göttingen: Vandenhoeck & Ruprecht, 1984), p. 590; M. Sokoloff, *A Dictionary of Jewish Palestinian Aramaic of the Byzantine Period* (Ramat-Gan: Bar-Ilan University Press, 1990), pp. 224-25.
5. S.R. Driver, *A Critical and Exegetical Commentary on the Book of Job, Together with a New Translation* (New York: Charles Scribner's Sons, 1921), I, p. 6; II, p. 39; P.A. Dhorme, *Le Livre de Job* (Paris: Lecoffre, 1926), p. 36; Pope, *Job*, p. 27; Gordis, *The Book of Job*, pp. 32, 39; N.H. Tur-Sinai, *The Book of Job: A New Commentary* (Jerusalem: Kiryath Sepher, 1967), pp. 12, 66; W.L. Michel, *Job in the Light of Northwest Semitic* (BibOr, 42; Rome: Pontifical Institute Press, 1987), pp. 39, 74; Guillaume, *Studies in the Book of Job*, p. 20; D.J.A. Clines, *Job 1–20* (WBC, 17; Dallas: Word Books, 1989), p. 68.
6. J.E. Hartley, *The Book of Job* (Grand Rapids: Eerdmans, 1988), p. 99.

Perhaps this explains the polysemy here as well. The poet, wishing to drive home the connection between Job's protection and his suffering, chose a deliberately ambiguous word and placed it in such a fashion as to create a tension with its intended meaning.

The referential nature of the polysemous parallel in Job 3.23 can be seen by comparing this verse to Job 3.10. Here we find the expression כי לא סגר דלתי בטני ויסתר עמל מעיני, 'because it did not block my mother's womb, and hide my trouble from my eyes'. In 3.23 the poet plays upon the expectation created by the paronomastic word-pair סגר/סתר. By inverting the pair and placing סתר first, readers, or more contextually speaking, Job's friends, expect to hear סגר again, but instead get ויסך. Though ויסך does convey the idea of 'closing, fencing in', its ambiguity demands that we interpret the word as 'pour out' as well. The reader is then edified in the next line (v. 24) where we find the mention of water being poured out. The twist allows Job to invert his own words and to subvert the expectations of his friends.

God's speech from the whirlwind in Job 38.8 is probably a retort to Job crafty tongue in 3.23. Note how ויסך occurs there with דלתים as it does in 3.10 and that it alludes to water as well, via ים and גיח. In effect, God has the last crafty word.

Job 3.25-26

כי פחד פחדתי ויאתיני
ואשר יגרתי יבא לי
לא שלותי ולא שקטתי
ולא נחתי ויבא רגז

> That which I have feared has come upon me, and that which יגרתי has come to me,
> I have no rest, no quiet, no repose, but continual agony.

יגרתי in line 25 may be understood in two ways: as 'I have dreaded' or 'I have stirred up, striven, quarreled with'. Both roots are well attested: גור II, 'stir up strife', occurs in Isa. 54.15; Ps. 56.7; Hos. 7.14; and גור III, 'dread', a by-form of the root יגר, can be found in Num. 22.3; 1 Sam. 18.15; Deut. 18.22; and Job 41.17.[1] As 'I have dreaded' it echoes the phrase פחד פחדתי, 'I have feared', and as 'I have stirred up', it parallels לא שלותי ולא שקטתי, 'I have no rest, no quiet, no repose', in the following line. Though the roots פחד and גור III are not parallel elsewhere, they

1. גור I, 'sojourn', is not applicable here: BDB, pp. 158-59.

have a word parallel in common: ירא. For גור with ירא see Ps. 22.24; 33.8. For פחד with ירא see Deut. 2.25; 11.25; 28.67; Ps. 27.1; Isa. 44.8.

The versions are in agreement as to the meaning of יגרתי, deriving it from גור III, 'dread'.[1] As with Job 3.22-23 above, one must question whether the ancient versions attempted to capture the pun. The LXX uses ἐδεδοίκειν, '(that) which I had feared', which is derived from δείξω.[2] Yet, like the Hebrew original, δείξω carries two meanings: 'fear, dread', and 'flee from', in the sense of being 'stirred up' or 'alarmed'.[3] Similarly, the Targum translates with the root דלח, either 'fear, dread' or 'stir up, make turbid, trouble';[4] and the Syriac uses זאע from the root זוע, 'fear, quake', and 'stir up, set in motion'.[5] The Vulgate's *verebar*,[6] the sages,[7] and modern commentators,[8] on the other hand, restrict their understanding to 'fear, dread'. In sum, the polysemous nature of the root גור and its connection elsewhere with the root פחד suggests that it was chosen for both of its meanings in Job 3.25. We have here, therefore, another symmetrical polysemy of the oral and visual types.

The poet undoubtedly selected the polysemous גור to contrast the previous object of 'stirring' (ערר, 3.8), the לויתן, with Job, who now 'stirs' in 'fear'. This is similar to the above connection between the 'doors' of Job's mother's womb in 3.10 and the 'doors of the womb of Yam' in 38.8. In addition, that Job now 'stirs' contrasts with the lack of peace for which he now laments. This contrast is brought out by the previous mention of the roots שקט and נוח which appear in both 3.13 and 3.26.

1. As are the dictionaries: BDB, p. 158; KB, p. 176; *HALAT*, I, p. 177; *HAHAT*[18], p. 135.

2. LSJ, p. 373.

3. See this secondary use in the *Iliad*, 5.556, 17.242, 22.251; LSJ, p. 373.

4. *DISO*, p. 58; Jastrow, *A Dictionary of the Targumim*, p. 309; Sokoloff, *A Dictionary of Jewish Palestinian Aramaic*, p. 150.

5. Payne Smith, *A Compendious Syriac Dictionary*, pp. 113-14.

6. *OLD*, pp. 2035-36, s.v. *vereor*.

7. Saʿadiah Gaʾon's rendering is a puzzle: 'what I guarded against'. See L.E. Goodman, *The Book of Theodicy: Translation and Commentary on the Book of Job by Saadiah ben Joseph Al-Fayyumi* (New Haven, CT: Yale University Press, 1988), p. 181.

8. Driver, *Job*, I, p. 39; Dhorme, *Le Livre de Job*, p. 36; Pope, *Job*, p. 27; Gordis, *The Book of Job*, p. 30; Tur-Sinai, *The Book of Job*, p. 68; Michel, *Job in the Light of Northwest Semitic*, p. 39; Guillaume, *Studies in the Book of Job*, p. 20; Hartley, *The Book of Job*, p. 100; Clines, *Job 1–20*, p. 68.

Job 4.2-3

הנסה דבר אליך תלאה
ועצר במלין מי יוכל
הנה יסרת רבים
וידים רפות תחזק

If one tried a word with you, would you not be offended? Yet who can refrain from speaking?
Behold, you have יסרת many, and have strengthened weak hands.

The root יסר in line 3 affords us two possible readings: 'chastise, admonish'[1] and 'bind'. Though the root יסר means 'bind' only in Aramaic,[2] and possibly also in Isa. 8.11, the numerous Aramaic dialectal tendencies in the book of Job suggest that the additional meaning would have been picked up by the hearer (note that the Aramaic מלין occurs here as well).[3] As 'you have chastised' the stich echoes דבר and מלין, 'words', in the previous line. As 'you have bound', the stich anticipates תחזק, 'you will strengthen, bind', in line 3. Textual support for the latter parallel comes from Hos. 7.15 where the roots חזק and יסר appear as a hendiadys and Isa. 8.11 where they occur as word-pairs (also in connection with יד, 'hand'). Again, this example is of the symmetrical as well as oral and visual types.

The versions, rabbis, and most moderns,[4] with the exception of Hoffman and Clines,[5] do not appear to have perceived the secondary meaning of the word here, 'bind'. The LXX and Vulgate use, respectively, ἐνουθέτησας and *docuisti*, both 'you have instructed'.[6]

1. BDB, pp. 415-16; KB, p. 387; *HALAT*, II, p. 400; *HAHAT*[18], p. 305.

2. Jastrow, *A Dictionary of the Targumim*, p. 583.

3. S.A. Kaufman, 'The Classification of the North West Semitic Dialects of the Biblical Period and Some Implications Thereof', in *Proceedings of the Ninth World Congress of Jewish Studies, Panel Session: Hebrew and Aramaic Languages* (Jerusalem: World Union of Jewish Studies, 1988), pp. 55-56; G. Rendsburg, '*Kabbîr* in Biblical Hebrew: Evidence for Style-Switching and Addressee-Switching in the Hebrew Bible', *JAOS* 112 (1992), pp. 649-51.

4. Driver, *Job*, I, p. 42; II, p. 23; Dhorme, *Le Livre de Job*, p. 39; Pope, *Job*, pp. 34-35; Tur-Sinai, *The Book of Job*, p. 76; Michel, *Job in the Light of Northwest Semitic*, p. 79; Guillaume, *Studies in the Book of Job*, p. 20; Hartley, *The Book of Job*, pp. 104-105.

5. Y. Hoffman, 'The Use of Equivocal Words in the First Speech of Eliphaz (Job IV–V)', *VT* 30 (1980), p. 114; Clines, *Job 1–20*, pp. 106, 109.

6. LSJ, pp. 1182-83, s.v. νουθετέω; *OLD*, p. 568, s.v. *doceō*.

Similarly, the Targum and the Syriac render, respectively, with כסנתא and רדית, both 'chastised'.[1] The only commentators to pick up on the other meaning of יסרת are Yellin[2] and Gordis; the latter suggested that 'the verb here is a metaplastic form of אסר',[3] for which he cited ample analogies in biblical Hebrew. Though a metaplastic form cannot be ruled out, there is no need to see one here, for יסר occurs in Aramaic with the sense 'to bind'. Though Tur-Sinai arrived at a similar translation, he did so by way of an unnecessary emendation.[4]

Eliphaz opens his discourse in 4.3 with a veiled accusation of Job's guilt; veiled in order to soften the blow which he feels compelled to deliver. In essence, Eliphaz remarks that 'though you think you have strengthened many, you must have bound them up in reality'. The polyseme יסרת which serves Eliphaz's agenda in 4.3 also serves the poet's agenda as a referential device. This can be seen by comparing our polysemous statement with Eliphaz's allusive accusation in 5.15: וישע מחרב מפיהם ומיד חזק אביון, '(God) saves the needy from the sword of their mouths and from a strong hand'. Note how both חזק and יד appear here to remind the reader of the contrast between Job, who claims to have 'encouraged many and strengthened (חזק) the hands (ידים) of the weak', and God, who alone can save the weak. A few verses later (5.17-18), Eliphaz again exploits the polysemy of his opening statement: 'Behold, happy is the man whom God reproves; hence do not despise the chastisement (מוסר) of Shaddai. For he wounds, but binds up (חבש); he strikes, but his hands (ידו) bring healing (תרפינה).' Not only is the notion of 'binding', the other meaning of יסרת in 4.3, made explicit, but the connection is bound by repeating the root רפה from 4.3 (i.e., רפות).

Job 5.24

וידעת כי שלום אהלך
ופקדת נוך ולא תחטא

You will know that your tent is at peace, when you ופקדת your home.
You will find nothing amiss.

1. From כסנתא. *DISO*, p. 124; Jastrow, *A Dictionary of the Targumim*, p. 654; Payne Smith, *A Compendious Syriac Dictionary*, pp. 529-30, s.v. רדא.

2. His rendering may have influenced Gordis. See D. Yellin, איוב־חקרי מקרא (Jerusalem, 1927), p. 110.

3. Gordis, *The Book of Job*, p. 46.

4. To יסדת; Tur-Sinai, *The Book of Job*, p. 76.

The root פקד has a variety of meanings,[1] and doubtless at least two of these alternatives were in the poet's mind when composing this passage. That a pun exists here already was noted by Gordis,[2] though he did not identify it as a Janus parallelism. As 'you visit'[3] ופקדת goes with וידעת, 'you will know', in line 24. As 'you will miss' it harkens to תחטא, 'you will miss', in the following line. For this meaning see Judg. 20.16; Prov. 8.36; 19.2; 20.2; and Hab. 2.10. That the root פקד may mean 'miss' is evident also from 1 Sam. 20.18 where Jonathan tells David: 'Tomorrow will be the new moon and you will be missed (ונפקדת) when your seat remains vacant (יפקד)'.[4] Further, the roots פקד and ידע are parallel in 2 Sam. 24.2; Jer. 6.15; 15.15; 44.29; Amos 3.2; and Job 35.15.[5] The root חטא occurs alongside the root פקד in Lev. 6.4, but only in its meaning 'sinned'. Therefore, that they are used as word-pairs here should not surprise us. Job 5.24, therefore, is a an oral, visual, and symmetrical polysemy of the semantic type.

As for the versions, the LXX renders as δίαιτα, itself a word with a plethora of meanings: 'mode of life, dwelling, abode, room, state, condition, investigation, etc.'.[6] Nevertheless, it seems that the LXX sees the Hebrew as meaning 'visit'. Could it be that the LXX translators chose δίαιτα because they wanted to take advantage of its closeness to διαισσω/-ᾳττω? The latter means 'rush through, dart through',[7] a meaning which פקד has in 1 Sam. 20.18. The Targum's expansion מזמין מדור בית משכנך ולא תזניק, 'you will visit (prepare) the dwelling of your sanctuary and you will not be injured', likewise can be explained as a means of bridging the two meanings of פקד here. The notion of 'visiting' is translated with 'visit the dwelling', while 'you will prepare your dwelling'[8] covers the second meaning of פקד, 'miss'; i.e., 'you will

1. B. Grossfeld, 'The Translation of Biblical Hebrew פקד in the Targum, Peshitta, Vulgate and Septuagint', *ZAW* 96 (1984), pp. 83-101.

2. Gordis, *The Book of Job*, p. 60.

3. So BDB, pp. 823-24; KB, pp. 773-74; *HALAT*, III, pp. 899-902; *HAHAT*[18], pp. 654-55.

4. Grossfeld, 'The Translation of Biblical Hebrew פקד in the Targum, Peshitta, Vulgate and Septuagint', pp. 87, 100-101.

5. Avishur, *Stylistic Studies of Word-Pairs*, pp. 153, 390-91, 653.

6. LSJ, p. 396, s.v. δίατα.

7, LSJ, p. 396, s.v. διάσσω.

8. *DISO*, p. 78; Jastrow, *A Dictionary of the Targumim*, p. 404; Beyer, *Die aramäischen Texte vom Toten Meer*, p. 569; Sokoloff, *A Dictionary of Jewish Palestinian Aramaic*, pp. 178-79.

provide so that nothing is "missing"'. The Peshitta similarly renders תהפוך, 'you will return'.[1] Commentators, ancient[2] and modern, like the Vulgate's *visitans*,[3] translate as 'visit, inspect' or the like.[4]

That פקד and חטא carry the added nuance of 'missing', especially in reference to arrows, may explain Job's reply in 6.3-4: על כן דברי לעו כי חצי שדי עמדי אשר חמתם שתה רוחי, 'On account of this I have spoken indistinctly. For the arrows of Shaddai are in me and my spirit drinks their poison (wrath).'[5] In other words, Job tells Eliphaz that 'though you say that if I were righteous I would miss nothing, it is God who did not miss me when he fired the arrows of his wrath'.

Two compositional features should also be observed in relation to Eliphaz's polysemous quip. First, 5.24-25 immediately follows a list of troubles from which God saves the righteous. These woes, which Gordis defines as 'famine, war, fire, flood, drought, rocks, and wild beasts',[6] are listed according to the common Semitic typology x, x + 1. That the polysemous stich comes at the end of the x + 1 device serves to underscore its importance. Secondly, that a polysemous parallel occurs both at the start and at the end of Eliphaz's discourse bespeaks the deliberateness of the device.

Job 6.20-21

בשו כי בטח
באו עדיה ויחפרו
כי עתה הייתם לא
תראו חתת ותיראו

They are ashamed because they trusted. They came to it and ויחפרו.
For now you have become nothing, you see distaste and fear.

The poet again displays his talent for polyvalence with the root חפר, both 'search, dig' and 'be ashamed'. That the roots would have been

1. Payne Smith, *A Compendious Syriac Dictionary*, pp. 105-106, s.v. הפך.
2. Saʿadiah may have attempted to render both meanings with 'you seek after'.
3. *OLD*, p. 2077, s.v. *vīso*.
4. Driver, *Job*, I, p. 58; Dhorme, *Le Livre de Job*, p. 65; Pope, *Job*, pp. 41, 46; Gordis, *The Book of Job*, p. 44; Tur-Sinai, *The Book of Job*, pp. 106-107; Michel, *Job in the Light of Northwest Semitic*, p. 104; Guillaume, *Studies in the Book of Job*, p. 23; Hartley, *The Book of Job*, pp. 124, 127 n. 23.
5. חמתם is also polysemous.
6. Gordis, *The Book of Job*, p. 59.

distinguished in speech, i.e., 'search, dig' = *ḫpr*; 'be ashamed' = *ḥpr*, suggests that the pun is purely visual.[1] With the meaning 'be ashamed', ויחפרו echoes בשו, 'they are ashamed', in line 20. As 'they searched' it faces forward to both הייתם לא, 'you have become nothing', and especially תראו, 'you see', in the following line. Though the roots חפר and ראה are not parallel elsewhere in the Bible they have a word-pair in common, the root נבט, 'behold'.[2] The difference in pronunciation demands that we categorize this example as a strictly visual and symmetrical polysemous parallel.

The LXX is significantly different from the MT, adding 'in cities and riches' in v. 20 and rendering the Hebrew חתת as τὸ ἐμὸν τραῦμα, 'my wound'. In light of such differences it is difficult to assess the relationship between the LXX and MT. One may only suggest that חפר was rendered with ἀνελεημόνως, 'without mercy',[3] i.e., as one who is (should be) 'abashed, ashamed'. The Targum's *ithpael* of כסף, 'ashamed', and the Vulgate's *pudore cooperti sunt*, 'they are covered with shame', suggest that only the primary meaning of חפר, 'ashamed', was perceived by their respective translators.[4] Interestingly, the Peshitta expands: ומטו לקתה ואחפרו, 'they came to gaze steadfastly and they were ashamed'. Is ומטו לקתה an attempt to catch the secondary meaning of the Hebrew original 'search, stare'?[5] The ancients as well as the moderns (Driver, Dhorme, Pope, Gordis, Tur-Sinai, Michel, Guillaume, and Hartley) understood the word as 'be ashamed'.[6]

Elsewhere in Job the root חפר occurs only as 'dig, search' (3.21; 11.18; 39.21, 29). That חפר should carry the additional meaning of 'ashamed' in 6.20 when in the last place it appeared (3.21) it meant only 'search' is a testament to the poet's skill in setting up expectation. In addition, before employing the polyseme the poet suggested the meaning

1. See BDB, pp. 343-44, s.v. חפר I and חפר II. The dictionaries prefer to read here *ḥpr*: BDB, p. 344; KB, p. 322; *HALAT*, I, p. 327; *HAHAT*[18], p. 250.

2. Avishur, *Stylistic Studies of Word-Pairs*, pp. 269, 295, 639, 659. See also Job 39.29.

3. LSJ, p. 131, s.v. ἀνελεημόνως.

4. Jastrow, *A Dictionary of the Targumim*, p. 655; Sokoloff, *A Dictionary of Jewish Palestinian Aramaic*, pp. 265-66; *OLD*, p. 442, s.v. *cooperiō*.

5. Payne Smith, *A Compendious Syriac Dictionary*, pp. 154, 523, s.v. חפר, מט.

6. Driver, *Job*, I, pp. 64-65; Dhorme, *Le Livre de Job*, p. 80; Pope, *Job*, p. 49; Gordis, *The Book of Job*, p. 64; Tur-Sinai, *The Book of Job*, p. 124; Michel, *Job in the Light of Northwest Semitic*, p. 132; Guillaume, *Studies in the Book of Job*, p. 24; Hartley, *The Book of Job*, p. 137; Clines, *Job 1–20*, p. 156.

of 'look' in 6.19: הביטו ארחות תמא הליכת שבא קוו למו, 'caravans of Tema look to them; processions from Sheba count on them'. This subtle suggestion sets up the reader for the unexpected twist, which, in turn, contrasts the 'hope' (קוה) of the caravans to 'see' (נבט) water with their false 'trust' (בטח) which turns to 'shame' (חפר). Again we see how dependent polysemous parallelism in Job is on such poetic referencing, for it forces a comparison between usages, and consequently, it dupes the reader into one interpretation upon which the poet can play.

References to the use of חפר continue in God's speech from the whirlwind (39.21), wherein he comments on the horse: יחפרו בעמק וישיש, 'He paws with force and rejoices'; and again, antanaclastically, in 39.29: משם חפר אכל, 'from there he spies out his food'.

Job 6.30–7.1

היש בלשוני עולה
אם חכי לא יבין הוות
הלא צבא לאנוש עלי ארץ
וכימי שכיר ימיו

Is there any iniquity upon my tongue? Cannot my palate discern הוות?
Is not toil for man upon the earth? As the days of a hireling are his days.

Normally, chapter divisions appear logical. Periodically, however, a division cannot be maintained for textual or other reasons. Such is the case here, where the lines 6.30 and 7.1 both begin with the interrogative *he*, suggesting that the two are a couplet. (For similar examples of interrogative *he*, see Isa. 40.21; Job 31.3-4; 39.11-12.[1]) The word הוות in 6.30 has been read in three different ways, two of which concern us here. It may be translated as 'words',[2] as 'ruin, destruction',[3] and as 'deceit, falsehood'.[4] The first meaning does not concern us at the present; the second meaning also is attested in Job 6.2; and the third meaning is

1. That the LXX does not translate the interrogative here is merely a stylistic trait of the translator. See, for example, H.M. Orlinsky, 'Studies in the Septuagint of the Book of Job: Chapter III', *HUCA* 30 (1959), pp. 153-67; 'Job: Chapter III (Continued)', pp. 239-68.

2. Akin to the Ugaritic *hwt*; *UT*, p. 389, s.v. *hwt*. See also M. Lubetski, 'The Utterance from the East: The Sense of *hwt* in Psalms 52.4, 9; 91.3', *Rel* 20 (1990), pp. 217-32.

3. The word is used in Job 6.2. So BDB, p. 217; KB, p. 228; *HALAT*, I, pp. 231-32.

4. BDB, p. 217; *HALAT*, I, p. 232.

found in Deut. 13.15; 17.4; Mic. 7.3; Ps. 5.10; 52.4; and in Job 42.7, 8. As 'deceit, falsehood' הוות echoes עולה, 'iniquity', in 6.30. As 'ruin, destruction' it foreshadows צבא, 'toil, war', in 7.1. Support for the former parallel comes from Ps. 5.10; 38.13; 52.2; and 55.11, where הוות occurs in connection with deceitful speech (for instance, with לשון and רמה). In Prov. 19.13 the word plays upon both meanings present in Job 6.30, 'deceitful words' and 'ruin': הות לאביו בן כסיל ודלף טרד מדיני אשה, 'A foolish son is ruin (deceit) to his father, and a wife's quarreling is a continual dripping of rain'. Though the roots צבא and הות are not parallel elsewhere, the synonym to הוות, רמה, can be found in parallelism with עולה in Job 13.7 and 27.4 and in parallelism with עון in Ps. 32.2. That צבא occurs in parallelism with עון in Isa. 40.2 further illustrates the interconnection between הוות and עולה in Job 6.30. This Janus parallel, therefore, is both oral and visual as well as symmetrical.

The LXX renders oddly, with μελετᾳ, 'understanding'.[1] This reflects neither of the two meanings of the Hebrew. Perhaps, again, it was selected to translate the Hebrew because it would provide a punning connection with μέλεος, 'miserable ruin',[2] the second meaning of הוות. This provides little help, however, because, if μελετᾳ translates יבין, σύνεσιν still lacks an explanation. Similarly, is it possible that the Targum uses רגושא to convey both senses of הוות, because, aside from meaning 'feeling', it also means 'moan' (reflecting 'word') and 'tremble, agitate' (reflecting 'ruin')?[3] The Syriac takes our Janus word as קושתא, 'justice, truth'.[4] The Vulgate translates *stultitia*, 'folly, stupidity', apparently understanding the lexeme as 'deceit, falsehood'.[5] Most of the rabbis take הוות as 'falsehood', as found in Mic. 7.3; Ps. 5.10; Deut. 13.15; 17.4, etc. Ralbag may have attempted to squeeze all three possible meanings out of the word: דברי רשע ושבר, 'words of wickedness and destruction'.[6] Though many modern commentators read '(false) words',[7] Driver,

1. LSJ, pp. 1096-97, s.v. μελετᾳ.
2. LSJ, p. 1096, s.v. μέλεος.
3. *DISO*, p. 275; Jastrow, *A Dictionary of the Targumim*, p. 1450; Beyer, *Die aramäischen Texte vom Toten Meer*, p. 692; Sokoloff, *A Dictionary of Jewish Palestinian Aramaic*, p. 516.
4. Payne Smith, *A Compendious Syriac Dictionary*, p. 499.
5. *OLD*, p. 1831, s.v. *stultitia*.
6. Saʿadiah Gaʾon translates as 'my hurt'.
7. Yellin, איוב־חקרי מקרא, p. 117; Pope, *Job*, pp. 49, 56; Gordis, *The Book of Job*, pp. 66, 78; Tur-Sinai, *The Book of Job*, pp. 130-31; Michel, *Job in the Light of Northwest Semitic*, pp. 132, 153; Clines, *Job 1–20*, p. 156.

Dhorme, and Guillaume see in הוות 'calamities'.[1] Though he did not comment extensively on the polysemy of הוות, 'deception' and 'ruin', Heater remarks: 'No doubt this word was chosen for both nuances.'[2]

Job's exploitation of the polyseme הוות enables him to contest his guilt while simultaneously pointing out the ruin of his situation. To Job, what his friends perceive as 'deception' (הוות) is in reality random 'ruin' (הוות). Whereas Eliphaz framed his discourse in chs. 4 and 5 with polysemous parallels, Job plays on Eliphaz's artistry by bookending his outpourings in ch. 6 with the polyseme הוות. The poet has used הותי in 6.2 (Q) only as 'calamity, ruin' in order to create an expectation once the word is heard again. When it occurs in 6.30, this expectation is subverted. It serves Job well to play on הוות here, for while his friends would have been quick to refute Job's claim that 'there is no iniquity on my tongue' (6.30a), they would have hesitated to deny the calamity which befell him. The ambiguity forces his friends to distinguish between the cause of his troubles, that is, his supposed iniquity, and its supposed consequence, that is, his ruin. Job's pun, therefore, subtly forces his friends to disconnect the two things.

Job 7.6-7

ימי קלו מני ארג
ויכלו באפס תקוה
זכר כי רוח חיי
לא תשוב עיני לראות טוב

> My days are more trifling than a weaver's shuttle. They go without תקוה.
> Remember, my life is but a wind, my eyes will see no more good.

Here the word תקוה means both 'thread' and 'hope'. As the former, it parallels 'a weaver's shuttle' in line 6.[3] The words עיני לראות טוב, in line 7, stand as a parallel expression of Job's failing hope. Cementing the connection is the fact that טוב appears in conjunction with תקוה in two other places: Prov. 11.23 and Job 17.15. Moreover, תקוה is used with the root ראה also in Prov. 26.12 and Ezek. 19.5. Job 7.6-7, therefore, is an oral, visual, and symmetrical Janus parallel.

1. Driver, *Job*, I, p. 67; Dhorme, *Le Livre de Job*, p. 95; Guillaume, *Studies in the Book of Job*, p. 25.

2. Heater, *A Septuagint Translation Technique in the Book of Job*, p. 142.

3. It may also be connected to two roots in line 5: לבש, 'clothed', and עפר, 'dust', which may reflect the garment called *ģpr* in Ugaritic. See *UT*, p. 465, s.v. *ģpr* (1106.7, cf. 24): '20 *ģpr* garments'.

The LXX's κενῇ ἐλπίδι and Vulgate's *spe* both reflect only 'hope'.[1] However, the Vulgate's addition in 7.6a of *quam a texente tela succiditur*, '(more) than the web is cut by the weaver', suggests an attempt to render the Hebrew allusion to thread. The Targum, however, finds a circumlocution to capture the pun: מחי ופסקו מדלית סברא, 'they wear out and are cut off without hope'. Note here that מחי also can mean 'weave',[2] and that מדלית, aside from meaning 'without', also may allude to דלת, 'thread',[3] meanings which the reader was to catch, especially after noticing the extra verb פסק, 'cut'. Rashi, Moshe Qimḥi, Y. Altschuler's *Metsudat David*, and Ralbag all appear to have been aware of the pun and virtually every modern commentator who has defined this word has noted the presence of a word-play.[4] Both Ibn Ezra and Immanuel Frances (seventeenth century)[5] noted this lexeme as an example of *tawriyya*, but appeared unaware of the more specific working of Janus parallelism per se. Though aware of the pun, Michel and Clines, perhaps following Dhorme,[6] render the word 'thread'.[7]

The referential nature of polysemous parallelism can be well illustrated by the shifting contexts in which the poet uses the noun תקוה. Prior to the Janus usage in 7.6-7, we have heard תקוה in 3.9; 4.6; 5.16 and 7.2. In 3.9 Job laments his birth as one who יקו לאור ואין, 'hopes for light and there is none'. In 4.6, it is Eliphaz who asks Job: 'Is not your hope (תקותך) your integrity?' 5.16, also in the mouth of Eliphaz, reads: ותהי לדל תקוה, 'there is hope for the poor'. That the word דל, 'poor', may also be read as 'hanging', i.e., from דלל, which can be used of thread,[8] may explain why Job chose to pun on it in 7.6. In 7.2 we find Job lamenting as follows: וכימי שכיר ימיו כעבד ישאף צל וכשכיר יקוה פעלו,

1. LSJ, p. 537, s.v. ἐλπίζω; *OLD*, pp. 1803-1804, s.v. *spes*.

2. Jastrow, *A Dictionary of the Targumim*, p. 760.

3. See BDB, p. 195. The Peshitta renders similarly with the expression בדלית סברא, but בדלית does not mean 'thread' in Syriac. Cf. לדל תקוה (Job 5.16) for a similar play.

4. Yellin, איוב-חקרי מקרא, pp. 118-19, 266; Pope, *Job*, pp. 57, 60; Gordis, *The Book of Job*, pp. 66, 80; Tur-Sinai, *The Book of Job*, pp. 136, 138; Guillaume, *Studies in the Book of Job*, pp. 25, 86.

5. I. Frances, ספר מתק שפתים, in H. Brody (ed.), *Hebraeische Prosidie von Immanuel Frances* (Krakau, 1892), p. 37.

6. Dhorme, *Le Livre de Job*, p. 91.

7. Michel, *Job in the Light of Northwest Semitic*, p. 154; Clines, *Job 1–20*, pp. 157, 164.

8. See for example דלה in Isa. 38.12.

'as the days of a hireling are his days, as a servant who pants for the shade, and as a hireling who hopes for his wage'. The use of יקוה, ימיו and כימי serve to establish an expectation for the polyseme in 7.6.[1] Note also that 7.6 begins with ימי. As such, תקוה in 7.6 is an antanaclastic Janus.

That Job intended both meanings in 7.6 can be seen by Bildad's equally referential reply in 8.14-15. There he states: ותקות חנף תאבד אשר יקוט כסלו ובית עכביש מבטחו, 'the hope of the godless will perish; his confidence is a mere gossamer thread; his trust, but a spider's web'. Bildad, in an effort to get 'one up' on Job, not only utilized both meanings of תקוה, but turned the ארג, 'weaver's shuttle', of 7.6 into an עכביש, 'spider'. That the root ארג occurs in connection with a spider in Isa. 59.5 illustrates the skill with which both Job and Bildad weave their remarks. The root קוה will be used again for its association with 'marking' in 17.13 (by Job), and by God in 38.5 when he thunders: מי נטה עליה קו, 'Who measured it [the earth] with a plumbline?'[2]

Job 9.9-11

עשה עש כסיל
וכימה וחדרי תמן
עשה גדלות עד אין חקר
ונפלאות עד אין מספר
הן יעבר עלי ולא אראה
ויחלף ולא אבין לו

> He makes the Bear and Orion, the Pleiades and the constellations of Teman,
> עשה great things beyond understanding, and wonders without number.
> Lo, he passes by me, and I do not see him.

In Job 9.9-11 the word עשה, normally 'he makes',[3] conceals a theologically significant expression. The root עשי may also be read as if derived from the Arabic *ġašawa*, 'hide, conceal'. The presence of this root in the Hebrew Bible has long been recognized in such passages as Obad. 6;

1. This may also explain the polysemous line in 9.25, which rests on the expectation built up by the use of וימי.

2. Moreover, one wonders if there is an allusive play on תקוה in Job's words a few verses later: חדל ממני כי הבל ימי, 'Desist from me, for my life is but a vapor' (7.16). One can hear the words דל, 'thrum' (in חדל, 'desist'), and ימי, 'my days', as well as a subtle hint of חבל, 'cord', in הבל, 'vapor' (the replacement for רוח in 7.7).

3. So BDB, pp. 793-95; KB, pp. 739-41; *HALAT*, III, pp. 842-45.

Job 23.9; Prov. 12.23; 13.16; Isa. 32.6, and as the etymology of the name עשו in Gen. 25.26.[1] As 'he makes' עשה reminds the reader of Yahweh's formation of the celestial bodies in line 9. As 'he hides, conceals', the poet anticipates Job's bewilderment at the ineffable and invisible attributes of God in line 11. In one breath, we are told that 'the creator' is also 'the concealer' of his creation. Job 9.10, therefore, is a strictly visual and symmetrical polysemous parallel.

One might explain the LXX's addition of ἐξαίσια, 'beyond what is ordained or fated, extraordinary',[2] as a means of incorporating both of the meanings of the Janus word into the Greek translation. Otherwise, one is hard pressed to explain the addition, other than by theorizing the existence of a variant *Vorlage*.[3] The Vulgate translates with a similar addition: *inconprehensibilia et mirabilia*.[4] If one avers a one-to-one word correspondence between the Hebrew original and the Targum or Syriac version it is clear that the Aramaic דעבד means 'he who makes'.[5] However, could it be that because Aramaic could not capture the pun the Targum and Peshitta's translators inserted פרשן, both 'wonders' and 'withdrawal, abstinence, separation?'[6] Medieval and modern commentators did not see in עשה anything but 'he makes'.[7] Nevertheless, Michel believes that 'this verse expresses praise, and so seems to present a difficulty'.[8] In an attempt to resolve this 'difficulty' Gordis remarks: 'What has not been observed is the ironic tone it bears here—after the destructive praise of God has been hymned by Job, "Yes, indeed, God

1. See for example *HALAT*, III, p. 845.

2. LSJ, p. 582.

3. For a deeper discussion see H.M. Orlinsky, 'Studies in the Septuagint of the Book of Job: Chapter I', *HUCA* 28 (1957), pp. 53-74.

4. *OLD*, pp. 872-73, s.v. *inconprehensibilis*.

5. *DISO*, pp. 198-202; Jastrow, *A Dictionary of the Targumim*, p. 1035; Beyer, *Die aramäischen Texte vom Toten Meer*, pp. 649-51; Sokoloff, *A Dictionary of Jewish Palestinian Aramaic*, pp. 391-92; Payne Smith, *A Compendious Syriac Dictionary*, pp. 396-97.

6. *DISO*, p. 237; Jastrow, *A Dictionary of the Targumim*, p. 1242; Beyer, *Die aramäischen Texte vom Toten Meer*, pp. 671-72; Sokoloff, *A Dictionary of Jewish Palestinian Aramaic*, pp. 451-52.

7. Yellin, איוב־חפרי מקרא, p. 123 (though Yellin notes the paronomasia of עשה and עש in v. 9); Pope, *Job*, pp. 68, 71; Gordis, *The Book of Job*, pp. 96, 104; Tur-Sinai, *The Book of Job*, p. 162; Michel, *Job in the Light of Northwest Semitic*, pp. 200, 208; Guillaume, *Studies in the Book of Job*, p. 27; Heater, *A Septuagint Translation Technique in the Book of Job*, p. 168; Clines, *Job 1–20*, p. 213.

8. Michel, *Job in the Light of Northwest Semitic*, p. 162.

does great things beyond understanding".'[1] While Gordis is undoubtedly correct in noting the irony here, it should be pointed out that such irony is all the more underscored by the duality of the verb עשׂה.[2]

Why Job should choose to use both meanings of עשׂה in 9.10 can be explained only by comparing 9.10 with Eliphaz's verbatim contention in 5.9: עשׂה גדלות ואין חקר נפלאות עד אין מספר, 'He makes great things without limit, and wonders beyond number'. It is clear from the comparison that Job's outcry in 9.10 is a direct quote of Eliphaz in 5.9. Yet it is from this very reference that Job's pun on עשׂה derives its impact. He has put words in Eliphaz's mouth without adding anything to his original statement. Elihu appears to concede Job's point in 37.5, where he referentially admits: עשׂה גדלות ולא נדע, 'He makes great things, but we do not know (them)'.

Further support for reading עשׂה as 'conceal' here appears in 22.13-14, where Eliphaz accuses Job of perceiving God as unable to see through the clouds, that is, as unconcerned with mortal affairs. Strengthening this reference is the mention of the heavens and constellations in both: כסיל, כימה, חדרי תמן (9.9) and כוכבים (22.12), חוג שמים (22.14).

References to עשׂה as 'conceal' continue in God's whirlwind speech in 40.19, where God states about the hippopotamus: העשׂו יגש חרבו, 'only his maker can draw the sword on him', and again, in 41.25: העשׂו לבלי חת, 'made as he is without fear'.

✓

Job 10.7-8

על דעתך כי לא ארשע
ואין מידך מציל
ידיך עצבוני ויעשׂוני
יחד סביב ותבלעני

> Though you know that I am not wicked, there is no one who can deliver me from your hand.
> Your hands עצבוני me, they have made me, altogether, yet now you swallow me.

The form עצבוני may be derived from two different roots: from עצב I (cf. Arabic *ġaẓaba*), 'hurt, pain, grieve', or from עצב II (cf. Arabic

1. Gordis, *The Book of Job*, p. 104.
2. The author of Job uses עשׂה, 'conceal', again in 23.9: 'In the North, he is concealed (בעשׂתו), and I do not behold him, in the South, he is hidden (יעטף), and I cannot see him.' This passage refers to Eliphaz's remarks in 22.13-15 as well.

ʿ*aẓaba*), 'shape, fashion',[1] both of which are employed in the Bible. That the Hebrew represents both roots with the same orthography provides the poet's pen with a visual pun. We may read the phrase ידיך עצבוני either as 'your hands hurt me' or as 'your hands fashioned me'. With the sense of 'hurt' the stich follows nicely upon the expression of grief in v. 7b, ואין מידך מציל. That the latter expression refers to destruction can be seen in Job 5.4 where אין מציל occurs alongside וידכאו בשער, 'may they be crushed at the gate'. As 'fashioned' עצבוני parallels equally well ויעשׂוני, 'they have made me', in v. 8a. Such expressions of Job's wit befit the label 'crafty word-hunter' which is placed on him later by Bildad in 18.2.[2] As the two lexemes involved with the polysemy are differentiated in speech, and as it is accomplished in two stichs, I group it with the strictly visual and asymmetrical types.

Does the LXX's ἔπλασάν με, 'have formed me', from πλάσσω,[3] represent another attempt to render the pun into Greek? Note the similarity between πλάσσω and πλήσσω, 'smite, strike',[4] and the documented confusion between the two roots.[5] The Targum is able to render the pun perfectly into Aramaic with צירוני, both 'fashion, form', from צור and 'vex, harm', from צרר.[6] That the second meaning of עצבוני was known to the ancients is suggested also by the Syriac which renders אידיך לאיבי, 'your hand troubles me'.[7] Yet the Vulgate translates עצבוני with *plasmaverunt me*, 'they have fashioned me'.[8] The rabbis are divided on this word. Rashi and Ralbag opt for the meaning 'form, make', whereas Ibn Ezra and Y. Altschuler (in both *Metsudat David* and *Metsudat Zion*) take it as 'harm, grieve'.[9] Interestingly, Saʿadiah Gaʾon rendered both meanings of עצבוני via paraphrasis: 'your blows have cut me and bruised me'. On the other hand, the moderns

1. So BDB, pp. 780-81; KB, p. 725; *HALAT*, III, p. 818.
2. See Chapter 4. See also Noegel, 'Another Look at Job 18.2, 3', pp. 159-61.
3. LSJ, p. 1412.
4. LSJ, p. 1421, s.v. πλάζω.
5. See for example *Iliad* 21.269 and *Odyssey* 5.389.
6. *DISO*, p. 245; Jastrow, *A Dictionary of the Targumim*, pp. 1270-71, 1305; Beyer, *Die aramäischen Texte vom Toten Meer*, p. 675; Sokoloff, *A Dictionary of Jewish Palestinian Aramaic*, pp. 461, 471.
7. Payne Smith, *A Compendious Syriac Dictionary*, p. 233.
8. *OLD*, p. 1388, s.v. *plasma*.
9. Moshe Qimḥi attributes to the verb עשׂה in 10.8 a negative, indeed abusive tone, as on a par with Ezek. 23.3.

invariably derive the word from עצב, 'shape, form'.[1]

In 10.7 Job switches to using יד instead of כף for 'hand' (cf., for example, 10.3). That כף had been used in a Janus construction previously (Job 9.30) may point to the importance of the change here. The switch would have been noticeable to his friends, and thus would have drawn attention to his remark. This would also explain why ידיך is fronted here. The change in lexemes piques the listener's interest in what follows, namely עצבוני. Furthermore, until this point Job has lamented his treatment at the hand (כף) of God, so עצבני immediately suggests the meaning 'pain me'. It is not until Job speaks the following word ויעשוני, 'made me', that one contemplates the other meaning of the root עצב, 'fashion'. The connection of עצבוני with 'pained me' is strengthened further by Job's antanaclastic exclamation only two lines prior (9.28): יגרתי כל עצבתי, 'I dread all my pains'. Therefore, the Jobian poet has set the reader up to think 'pain' when the root עצב occurs, only to play upon this expectation. The word-play in 10.8 also serves to prepare the reader for 10.9: זכר נא כי כחמר עשיתני ואל עפר תשיבני, 'Remember that you fashioned me like clay, and to dust you will return me'.

Job 13.22-23

וקרא ואנכי אענה
או אדבר והשיבני
כמה לי עונות וחטאות
פשעי וחטאתי הדעני

Then you may call and I will respond, or I will speak and והשיבני.
How many are my sins and iniquities? Make me know my transgression and my sin.

The Janus in this passage exploits the semantic range of the root שוב which means both 'reply' and 'repent'.[2] As the former, it echoes אענה, 'I will respond', in line 22. As the latter, it prepares us for the question כמה לי עונות וחטאות, 'How many are my sins and iniquities?' The Janus

1. Pope, *Job*, p. 78; Gordis, *The Book of Job*, pp. 98, 112; Tur-Sinai, *The Book of Job*, pp. 176-77; Michel, *Job in the Light of Northwest Semitic*, p. 235; Guillaume, *Studies in the Book of Job*, pp. 29, 89; Hartley, *The Book of Job*, p. 185; Clines, *Job 1–20*, p. 215 (mentions both roots). Note that though Tur-Sinai remarks that 'there is no connection between this word and עצב "grief"' (p. 177), he does not explain why.

2. So BDB, pp. 996-1000; KB, pp. 951-53; *HALAT*, IV, pp. 1326-31.

is bolstered further by the clever use of עונות, 'sins' (from the root עון), in line 23, which may also have been read in the consonantal text as 'retorts' (from the root ענה). The root שוב forms a word-pair with ענה in Gen. 16.9; Ps. 35.13; and Judg. 5.29, and is found in a non-parallelistic connection with the root in Exod. 19.8; Ruth 2.6; 11.21; 1 Sam. 12.3; 2 Sam. 19.43; 1 Kgs 2.30; 8.35; 13.6; 2 Kgs 1.11; Prov. 5.1; Hos. 7.10; and Zech. 10.6. The use of שוב in conjunction with פשע in Ps. 51.15; Isa. 44.22; 46.8; 59.20; Ezek. 18.28, 30; 33.12; Amos 1.3, 6, 9, 11, 13; 2.1, 4, 6 and with חטא in Exod. 32.31; Lev. 5.23; Num. 22.34; Deut. 24.4; 1 Sam. 15.30; 26.21; 1 Kgs 8.33, 47; 18.14; 2 Chron. 6.24, 26, 37; Neh. 9.29; Ps. 51.15; Jer. 2.35; Lam. 1.8; Ezek. 18.24; 33.12; and Dan. 9.16, binds the parallel relationship between שוב and the next stich even closer. Moreover, שוב also occurs with עון, as it does here, in Gen. 15.16; 2 Sam. 16.12; Ps. 78.38; Jer. 11.10; 36.3; Lam. 2.14; Ezek. 3.19; 7.13; 18.17, 30; 33.9; Dan. 9.13, 16; Hos. 8.13; 14.2, 3; Mic. 7.19; and Mal. 2.6. Therefore, Job 13.22-23 is an oral and visual symmetrical polysemous parallel of the semantic type.

The LXX uses the first person singular future active of the root δίδωμι in combination with the noun ἀνταπόκρισιν. The first person usage, different from the MT, perhaps reflects a tendency away from representing Job as placing demands on God.[1] It also may be explained as an attempt to convey the double meaning in the text: ἀνταπόκρισιν means both 'a reply' and 'a retrial, rejudgment'.[2] As the latter, it suggests the notion of Job receiving a second chance of sorts, that is, 'repentance'. The Aramaic and Syriac cognate תוב carries both meanings of the Hebrew root שוב,[3] making it unclear whether the Targum and Peshitta translators were aware of the pun.[4] Only the Vulgate explicitly refers to a 'reply': *tu responde mihi*.[5] Though only a few of the

1. However, I agree with the contrary view set forth by H.M. Orlinsky in 'Job: Chapter I', pp. 53-74; 'Studies in the Septuagint of the Book of Job: Chapter II', *HUCA* 29 (1958), pp. 229-71.

2. LSJ, p. 150, s.v. ἀνταποκρίνομαι.

3. *DISO*, p. 324; Jastrow, *A Dictionary of the Targumim*, pp. 1649-50; Beyer, *Die aramäischen Texte vom Toten Meer*, pp. 721-22; Sokoloff, *A Dictionary of Jewish Palestinian Aramaic*, pp. 576-77; Payne Smith, *A Compendious Syriac Dictionary*, p. 606.

4. This is less true of the Peshitta which adds פתגמא, 'answer'; Payne Smith, *A Compendious Syriac Dictionary*, p. 469.

5. Though the word also may mean 'reward the efforts (of)', it does not necessarily mean 'forgive'; *OLD*, p. 1634, s.v. *respondo*.

rabbis comment on the Hebrew here, there is reason to believe that the medieval exegete Y. Altschuler was cognizant of both its meanings: או קרא לומר מה פשעי ואני אשיב לך אדבר אני יושר דרכי ואתה תשיב לי, 'or call out and say what my sin is and I will reply to you, or I will straighten my ways and you will restore me'. None of the modern translators of Job has commented on the duality of meaning here.[1]

Not only does this Janus construction follow upon multiple arguments by Job, proclaiming that if only he were allowed to present his case before God, he would be vindicated (for example 13.15-16, 18), but the previous arguments are couched in the familiar Semitic poetic rubric x, x + 1. 'But two things do not do to me', cries Job in 13.20, suggesting that the second item which follows (i.e., that God not frighten him) should be highlighted. This naturally underscores the importance of the stich which immediately follows in 13.22. That this punful stich provides a summation of Job's claim enables him to connect his vindication polysemously with God's response, and in so doing, pivot his exoneration on God's reply.

Job 17.6-7

והצגני למשל עמים
ותפת לפנים אהיה
ותכה מכעש עיני
ויצרי כצל כלם

God has set me up as a by-word among the people, I am one in whose face men spit.
My eyes have תכה from grief, and all my limbs are as a shadow.

The root כהה has two meanings in biblical Hebrew, 'rebuke'[2] and 'grow dim'.[3] Therefore, we have reason to read ותכה מכעש עיני both as 'my eyes have grown dim from grief' and as 'my eyes have been rebuked by grief'. The former aligns with the first stich in line 6

1. Pope, *Job*, p. 97; Gordis, *The Book of Job*, pp. 130, 145; Tur-Sinai, *The Book of Job*, p. 228; Michel, *Job in the Light of Northwest Semitic*, pp. 217, 311; Guillaume, *Studies in the Book of Job*, p. 34; Hartley, *The Book of Job*, p. 224; Clines, *Job 1–20*, p. 277.

2. The word occurs with this meaning only once in the Bible, 1 Sam. 3.13. Nevertheless, its Syriac and Mandaic cognates argue for its existence as a separate root;. BDB, p. 462, s.v. כהה.

3. So BDB, p. 462; KB, p. 424; *HALAT*, II, p. 440.

where Job complains that he is a by-word and that men 'spit in his face'. With its second meaning, 'grow dim', the stich anticipates the phrase ויצרי כצל כלם, 'all my limbs are as a shadow'. We have here, then, an oral, visual, and symmetrical Janus parallel.

To render תכה, the LXX uses πεπώρωνται, 'harden, become blind', the Targum the cognate כהית, and the Vulgate *caligavit*, 'blind, dim'.[1] On the other hand, the Syriac, apparently to render the other meaning of our polyseme, translates with כאבת, 'I am grieved, in pain'.[2] None of the ancient versions reflects any awareness of polysemy here, nor do the rabbis or modern commentators.[3]

The expectation created by the previous stichs, לחלק יגיד רעים ועיני בניו תכלנה, 'He informs on his friends for a portion (חלק), and his children's eyes pine away' (17.5), and והצגני למשל עמים ותפת לפנים אהיה, 'He has set me up as a by-word among the people; I am one in whose face men spit' (17.6), persuades the reader to hear in the root כהה 'rebuke'. Equally suggestive of this notion are Job's words in 17.2: 'Surely mocking men keep my company, and my eye must abide their provocations'. What makes 17.2 so suggestive of 'rebuke' is not only the use of עיני, 'my eye', in conjunction with התלים, 'mockers', but also the use of the root לון which means both 'lodge' and 'murmur, complain'.[4] The point of Job's pun here is that his physical condition (i.e., dimmed eyes) is enough of a rebuke. Consequently, there is no reason for his friends to add to his misery by mocking him.

Job 18.4-5

טרף נפשו באפו
הלמענך תעזב ארץ
ויעתק צור ממקמו
גם אור רשעים ידעך
ולא יגה שביב אשו

1. LSJ, p. 1561, s.v. πωρόω; Jastrow, *A Dictionary of the Targumim*, pp. 614-15; Sokoloff, *A Dictionary of Jewish Palestinian Aramaic*, p. 252; *OLD*, p. 259, s.v. *caligavit*. Note that the Targum may also be read as 'rebuked'. See Jastrow, *A Dictionary of the Targumim*, p. 615.

2. Payne Smith, *A Compendious Syriac Dictionary*, p. 201, s.v. כאב.

3. Pope, *Job*, p. 127; Gordis, *The Book of Job*, pp. 172, 183; Tur-Sinai, *The Book of Job*, p. 278; Guillaume, *Studies in the Book of Job*, p. 39; Hartley, *The Book of Job*, pp. 266, 269; Clines, *Job 1–20*, pp. 368, 373.

4. This root is also used for a polysemous parallelism in Job 31.31-32.

> You, who tear yourself to pieces in anger. Shall the earth be forsaken on your account? Or the צור be removed from its place?
> In due course the light of the wicked is put out. The flame of his fire does not shine.

The polysemy at work here hinges on the word צור, normally translated 'rock'.[1] In the purely consonantal text, one might have read צור, 'adversary, enemy', as well, as a *qal* infinitive construct derived from צרר, 'show hostility toward'. Middle *waw* verbs often have geminate by-forms, and such is the case with the pair posited here. As 'rock' אור parallels 'the earth' in the previous stich, and as 'enemy' it anticipates 'the wicked' in the following stich. Support for the former parallel comes from Deut. 32.13 and Ps. 61.3. The root צור/צרר also occurs in conjunction with the noun ארץ, as it does here, in Deut. 2.9, 19 and 1 Chron. 20.1. Cementing the latter connection is the fact that the middle *waw* verb צור is found parallel to אויב, 'foe', in Exod. 23.22. In this way, the poet accomplished the desired polysemous effect. Therefore, Job 18.4-5 must be grouped with the strictly visual and symmetrical polysemous parallels.

LXX translates with ὄρη, 'mountain(s)',[2] perhaps, like Rashi, with the epithet for God in mind. The Targum again expands the verse in a way which may attempt to collect both meanings of the pair צרר/צור: 'And the mountain be removed from its stead?...or is it possible that, for your sake, the earth would be lifted up from (its) dwelling and the mighty removed from his stead?' Outwardly, the Targum seems to have translated our word with טינר, 'mountain'.[3] Yet the lexeme תקיפא, while possibly a representation of the Godhead, is nonetheless a blatent addition. If God were implied here, why not use המקום or השם? Therefore, I suggest that תקיפא probably does not refer to God, but to a person in general.[4] This being the case, we must ask why the Targum added this. I posit that it was added to capture the second meaning of צור, 'enemy, vexer', that is, one who is 'mighty'.[5] Support for this reading also

1. So BDB, p. 849; KB, p. 799; *HALAT*, III, pp. 952-53.

2. LSJ, p. 1255.

3. Jastrow, *A Dictionary of the Targumim*, p. 533; Sokoloff, *A Dictionary of Jewish Palestinian Aramaic*, p. 224.

4. Note that שהתקיף in Qoh. 6.10 may mean simply 'that which is mightier', without reference to God necessarily.

5. *DISO*, p. 333; Jastrow, *A Dictionary of the Targumim*, p. 1690; Beyer, *Die aramäischen Texte vom Toten Meer*, pp. 726-27; Sokoloff, *A Dictionary of Jewish Palestinian Aramaic*, p. 590.

comes from the fact that 'wicked' in v. 5 is left untranslated, implying that the 'light' refers back to the תקיפא, 'mighty', in v. 4.[1] The Vulgate chooses *rupes*, 'rocky cliff',[2] to translate צור. One cannot help but wonder if *mons*, 'mountain'[3] was avoided in order to produce an allusion to *rupex*, 'a coarse, uncivilized person'.[4] The Syriac, on the other hand, makes not so much as a hint of its meaning 'enemy', rendering with טורא, 'mountain'.[5] Commentators both ancient and modern have not picked up on the polysemy in this verse,[6] though if Dhorme[7] is correct in seeing our verse as a reaction to אפו טרף וישטמני, 'He has torn me in his anger and has been my enemy', in 16.9, then we have more support for reading צור as 'enemy'.

In accordance with the referential nature of Janus parallelism is 18.4, which must be seen in the light of Job's previous remark in 14.18-19 in which he compares his friends to water.[8] The analogy he puts forward portrays his friends wearing away his hope as water wears away stones. His simile compares the impermanence of mortal affairs with the impermanence of topographical features. According to Job: ואולם הר נופל יבול וצור יעתק ממקמו, 'mountains fall and crumble; rocks are dislodged from their place'. First, in 18.3, Bildad challenges Job's insult: 'are we regarded as brutes; are we stupid in your eyes?' Afterward (18.4), Bildad plays on Job's words by changing the object of his previous insult to Job himself. Because Job insulted his friends, the destroyers of hope, by comparing them to removers of stones, Bildad retorts that 'no

1. This is a most unusual omission in the light of Job 5.16; 6.10; 14.12; 30.3, etc., where 'wicked' is added to the text! See Mangan, *The Targum of Job*, p. 51 n. 3.

2. *OLD*, pp. 1669-70, s.v. *rūpēs*.

3. *OLD*, p. 1131, s.v. *mons*.

4. *OLD*, p. 1670, s.v. *rupex*. The Vulgate uses *rupex* only in Jer. 4.29; 14.6; Ezek. 6.3; 31.12; Job 18.4; 39.28; and Ps. 113.8. Elsewhere it translates צור, 'rock', with *mons*.

5. Payne Smith, *A Compendious Syriac Dictionary*, p. 170.

6. Driver, *Job*, I, p. 158; Dhorme, *Le Livre de Job*, p. 235; Pope, *Job*, p. 132; Gordis, *The Book of Job*, p. 134; Tur-Sinai, *The Book of Job*, pp. 286-87; Guillaume, *Studies in the Book of Job*, p. 40; Hartley, *The Book of Job*, pp. 273-74; Clines, *Job 1–20*, pp. 403, 405.

7. Dhorme, *Le Livre de Job*, p. 235. See also Heater, *A Septuagint Translation Technique in the Book of Job*, p. 65.

8. *Contra* Clines, *Job 1–20*, p. 412, who remarks: 'Such intertextual references do not necessarily imply that the character Bildad is deliberately referring to Job's speech and satirizing it.'

rock will ever be removed on his account'.[1] Bildad's cleverly calculated misquote combines into one reply a twofold message: first, that humans are less than God and, therefore, should not expect partial treatment; and secondly, that the wicked are eventually brought to ruin, just as rock structures naturally collapse.

Job 18.11-13

סביב בעתהו בלהות
והפיצהו לרגליו
יהי רעב אנו
ואיד נכון לצלעו
יאכל בדי עורו יאכל בדיו בכור מות

Terrors will make him afraid on every side, and will drive him to his feet.
His strength shall be רעב, and destruction shall be at his side.
It will devour the strength of his skin: even the first-born of death will devour his strength.

As A. Guillaume noted, the word רעב, 'hungry' (*rǵb*),[2] in line 12 occurs in Arabic with the meaning 'cowardly'.[3] Though aware of the pun on the semantic range of this word, Guillaume did not notice that it is possible to read רעב both as 'coward', in which case it mirrors the image given in the previous line, and as 'hungry', in which case it points to the next verse where the root אכל, 'eat', is used twice. That the roots רעב and אכל occur opposite each other in Isa. 65.13 and Ps. 50.12 illustrates their interrelatedness here. Though רעב has not been discovered elsewhere with the meaning 'cowardly', its connection to actions of רגלים also appears in Ezek. 6.11. Again, this example constitutes an oral, visual, and symmetrical Janus parallel.

The LXX perhaps shows an awareness of the pun here as it translates רעב אנו with λιμῷ στενῷ, 'distressing hunger'.[4] Might λιμῷ pun on λῆμα, 'will, mind, spirit', which when accompanied by an adjective

1. The word אבן, 'stone', is continually cast about in the debate, for instance in 24.18 and 34.7.

2. So BDB, p. 944; KB, p. 898; *HALAT*, IV, p. 1172.

3. A. Guillaume, 'The Arabic Background of the Book of Job', in F.F. Bruce (ed.), *Promise and Fulfillment: Essays presented to S.H. Hooke* (Edinburgh: T. & T. Clark, 1964), p. 114. See also Guillaume, *Studies in the Book of Job*, p. 40; H. Wehr, *A Dictionary of Modern Written Arabic* (Ithaca, NY: Cornell University Press, 1976), p. 347.

4. LSJ, pp. 1051, 1638, s.v. λιμῷ, στενῷ.

comes to mean 'cowardice'?[1] Such an adjective does indeed occur in στενῷ, 'difficult, meagre, thin'. All the other versions translate quite transparently 'hunger',[2] as do the rabbis and modern commentators,[3] with the exception of Guillaume, as mentioned above.

The poet has used the root רעב twice earlier only as 'hunger' (5.5, 20). That he should use it in 18.12 for 'cowardice' again demonstrates how dependent the Janus device is on earlier references. Here again the earlier usage establishes an interpretation which the poet can manipulate to surprise the reader. Nevertheless, the poet has hinted at the association of רעב with 'cowardice' in 5.20-23 in which Eliphaz lists the seven woes from which God saves the righteous:

> In hunger (רעב) he will redeem you from death (מות); in war, from the sword. You will be sheltered from the scourging tongue; you will have no fear (ולא תירא) when violence comes. You will laugh at violence and starvation (כפן), have no fear (אל תירא).

Note also how מות, 'death', occurs in 5.20 and again in 18.13b: יאכל בדיו בכור מות, 'death's first-born consumes his tendons'.[4]

Job 19.11-12

ויחר עלי אפו
ויחשבני לו כצריו
יחד יבאו גדודיו
ויסלו עלי דרכם
ויחנו סביב לאהלי

> His anger was kindled against me. He has considered me כצריו.
> His troops come forth together. They have paved their road against me, and encamp around my tent.

1. LSJ, pp. 1044-45, s.v. λῆμα. Note such a use in Aeschylus's *Septem contra Thebas*, line 616.

2. From כפנא; *DISO*, p. 125; Jastrow, *A Dictionary of the Targumim*, p. 660; Beyer, *Die aramäischen Texte vom Toten Meer*, p. 609; Sokoloff, *A Dictionary of Jewish Palestinian Aramaic*, p. 267; Payne Smith, *A Compendious Syriac Dictionary*, p. 222; *OLD*, p. 674, s.v. *famēs*.

3. Driver, *Job*, I, p. 160; II, p. 119; Dhorme, *Le Livre de Job*, p. 238; Pope, *Job*, p. 131; Gordis, *The Book of Job*, pp. 188, 191; Tur-Sinai, *The Book of Job*, p. 290; Hartley, *The Book of Job*, p. 277; Clines, *Job 1–20*, p. 406.

4. Eliphaz may also allude to his earlier speech in 22.7 in which he parallels רעב with לחם, 'food'. Note how רעב parallels מלחמה, 'war', in 5.20.

The pivot word here, צריו, may be derived from two different roots: צרר, in which case it means 'one of his enemies';[1] or צור, in which case it means 'one of his besiegers'. If read as the former, it directs us back to the line ויחר עלי אפו, 'his anger was kindled against me', in line 11. Support for this parallel comes from Ps. 7.7 where God's anger (אף) is lifted against the enemy (צוררי). If read as 'one of his besiegers' it leads us forward to the amassing and encampment of troops in line 12. That צרר occurs in a parallel relationship with the noun דרך in Ps. 10.5 demonstrates the appropriateness of the parallel here. The roots represented by צריו are different (צרר/צור, 'besiege', = Arabic *ṣrr*, whereas צרר, 'enemy', = Arabic *ẓrr*) and so there would have been a difference in the way the two were pronounced. Therefore, we may catalog this example with those Januses which are strictly visual and symmetrical.

The LXX's translation ἐχθρόν, 'enemy',[2] suggests that its translators derived our word from the root צרר (= Arabic *ẓrr*). If the translators did see in כצריו another possible reading, it is not evident in the rendering. The Targum, however, is able to render both meanings of the Janus word with the Aramaic root עוק, 'oppress, squeeze'.[3] Further, it renders ויסלו, 'they paved', in v. 12 with וכבשו, 'they pressed',[4] probably in an effort to capture the pun. The Syriac's בעל דבבא shows an awareness only of the interpretation 'enemy'.[5] The Vulgate's *hostem sum*, 'his enemy',[6] suggests the same, but its use of *obsederunt*, 'they have besieged',[7] in v. 12 stands as a specific reference to the kind of enemy hinted at in the Hebrew original, that is, one that 'squeezes, besieges'. Nevertheless, no definitive conclusion can be made on this basis. The use of the plural instead of the singular has bothered some commentators, inducing Gordis to suggest that we read כצריו as a distributive.[8] Yet this may be the author's way of connecting the Janus with the plural forms

1. So BDB, p. 865; KB, pp. 815, 818; *HALAT*, III, pp. 984-85.
2. LSJ, p. 748.
3. Jastrow, *A Dictionary of the Targumim*, p. 1056; Beyer, *Die aramäischen Texte vom Toten Meer*, p. 655; Sokoloff, *A Dictionary of Jewish Palestinian Aramaic*, p. 400. The Targum from Qumran is too fragmentary to be of service.
4. *DISO*, p. 115; Jastrow, *A Dictionary of the Targumim*, p. 611; Beyer, *Die aramäischen Texte vom Toten Meer*, pp. 602-603; Sokoloff, *A Dictionary of Jewish Palestinian Aramaic*, pp. 249-50.
5. Payne Smith, *A Compendious Syriac Dictionary*, p. 51, s.v. בעל.
6. *OLD*, p. 808, s.v. *hostis*.
7. *OLD*, p. 1724, s.v. *sedeō*.
8. For a brief discussion on this see Hartley, *The Book of Job*, pp. 284-85 n. 3.

in the next line. Few of the sages comment on כצריו, and of those who do, only 'enemy' is understood. The same goes for modern commentators, who have translated as 'enemy', 'foe', 'adversary', and the like.[1]

The play in 19.11-12 expresses Job's anguish at being treated as an enemy (צרר) by God and blamed for laying siege (צור) to God by his friends. The latter is suggested by 'his troops' (19.12) and the use of the plural. The polysemous usage also reinforces Job's previous claim in 19.6: 'Yet, know that God has wronged me; he has laid up siege works around me (ומצודו עלי הקיף)'.[2] Yet Job's words in 19.11-12 also respond to Eliphaz's accusation in 15.24: 'Anguish (צר) and agony (ומצוקה) terrify him; they besiege him (תתקפהו) like a king ready for the attack.'

Job 20.23-24

יהי למלא בטנו
ישלח בו חרון אפו
וימטר עלימו בלחומו
יברח מנשק ברזל
תחלפהו קשת נחושה

To fill his belly to the full. He will send his wrath against him. And rain down upon him בלחומו.
If he flees from an iron weapon, a bronze arrow will pierce him.

The word בלחומו typically has been understood as 'in his battle-fury', as if derived from the root לחם, 'do battle'.[3] However, as the phrase follows upon 'to fill his belly to the full', the reader is invited to understand בלחומו as 'for his bread, food', with לחום as a by-form of לחם, 'bread' (cf. the segholate noun גבר and its derived nominal form גבורה [albeit feminine]; or perhaps the related words קדם and קדומים).[4]

1. Driver, *Job*, I, p. 166; II, p. 123; Dhorme, *Le Livre de Job*, p. 249; Pope, *Job*, p. 138; Gordis, *The Book of Job*, pp. 196, 201; Tur-Sinai, *The Book of Job*, p. 298; Guillaume, *Studies in the Book of Job*, p. 41; Hartley, *The Book of Job*, pp. 284-85 n. 3; Clines, *Job 1–20*, pp. 427, 429.

2. ומצודו in 19.6 may also pun on מצוד, 'net, trap' (see, for example, Qoh. 7.26).

3. So BDB, p. 535.

4. Along with *HALAT*, II, 499. Others choose to emend the word; see for example KB, p. 478. For relationship of segholates to *qetûl* forms see C.W. Gordon, 'Qetûl Nouns in Classical Hebrew', *Abr-Nahrain* 29 (1991), pp. 83-86.

Note a semantically similar word-play in the *Epic of Gilgameš*, Tablet XI.45-47:[1]

> He will bring you a harvest of wealth:
> in the morning *kukki*-cakes,
> and in the evening, he will shower down a rain of wheat (*kibāti*).

Noteworthy here is the use of the Akkadian words *kukki* in line 46, both 'a type of cake' and 'darkness', and *kibāti* in line 47, both 'wheat' and 'oppression, calamity'.[2]

Consequently, there is reason to see two meanings in בלחומו in Job 20.23-24. With the meaning 'with his food' בלחומו reminds us of יהי למלא בטנו, 'to fill his belly'; with the meaning 'in his battle-fury', the polyseme foreshadows the remark: יברח מנשק ברזל תחלפהו קשת נחושה, 'if he flees from an iron weapon, a bronze arrow will pierce him'.[3] Note that the former parallel is bolstered by the use of לחם as 'food' in conjunction with the verb מלא in Prov. 20.17. As 'fighting' לחם parallels מלא in Jer. 33.5. Note also that the root לחם means 'fight' in Job 15.23-24, 26, and may have provided the poet with the impetus for the pun here. The connection of בלוחמו with the weapons of war in v. 24 is also strengthened by a contrast between לחם, 'bread', and קשת, 'bow', in 2 Kgs 6.22. As the two lexemes involved with the polysemy are not distinguished in speech, we categorize Job 20.23-24 as an oral, visual, and symmetrical Janus parallel.

Though the LXX renders our Janus as ὀδύνας, 'grief', it translates חרון אפו as θυμὸν ὀργῆς, 'torrent of pain (lit. anger)'.[4] Is it possible that this expression was chosen because θυμός also means 'appetite, desire for food and drink?'[5] With a slightly different accent (not required for puns to be effective),[6] we may also read θύμον as 'a mixture of thyme

1. A similar play on the polyvalent root *lḥm* may adhere in Ugaritic. See *UT*, ʿAnat IV: 67-68: [*barṣ*].*mlḥmt* [*aš*]*t.bʿprm ddy*[*ym*] *ask* [*šlm*] *lkb arṣ ar*[*bdd*] *lkb*[*d š*]*dm.yšt*, 'Shall I put bread (war) in [the earth]? Shall I set mandrakes in the dust? I shall pour [peace] in the midst of the earth, a plethora [of lovely things] in the mids[t of the fi]elds.'

2. *CAD* K, p. 498, s.v. *kukki*. Carl Frank, 'Zu den Wortspielen *kukku* und *kibāti* in Gilg. Ep. XI', *ZA* 36 (1925), p. 216.

3. לחם may mean 'battle-fury' in Job 15.23 as well.

4. Note that θυμόω means 'make angry, provoke'; LSJ, p. 810.

5. LSJ, p. 810. See for example *Iliad* 4.263 and *Odyssey* 17.603.

6. See the comments of F. Ahl, *Metaformations: Soundplay and Wordplay in Ovid and Other Classical Poets* (Ithaca, NY: Cornell University Press, 1985), pp. 35-40.

with honey and vinegar',[1] i.e., food. Note also that θῦμα, 'an animal slaughtered for food',[2] is used by the LXX in Gen. 43.16.

The Targumist rendered the pivoting lexeme with בשלדיה, 'into his burnt (decayed) carcass', or 'flake of flesh', suggesting an awareness of both meanings.[3] The Syriac, on the other hand, like the LXX, seems to favor the meaning 'battle-fury', rendering the term with בקרב תנותה, 'with war-like strength'.[4] Similar is the Vulgate's *bellum suum*, 'his warfare'.[5]

Saʿadiah Gaʾon, Rashi, and Y. Altschuler's *Metsudat David* and *Metsudat Zion* render as 'battle-fury', whereas Ibn Ezra and Ralbag translate בבשרו, 'on his flesh'. Moshe Qimḥi renders בשרו או מאכלו, 'his flesh' or 'his food'. Of the modern commentators, Yellin, Pope, and Gordis[6] render with the LXX and Vulgate, whereas Driver, Dhorme, and Clines follow the Targum's 'flesh, bread'.[7] Tur-Sinai and Guillaume differ greatly, the former giving the reading 'upon their cheeks' (requiring him to emend and to revocalize),[8] and the latter opting for 'into his very bowels' without comment.[9] Of special interest is Hartley's remark (even though he does not note the forward parallel to the weapons of war):

> With its first meaning MT is understood as 'on his flesh'. This affords a good parallel with 'his belly' in the first line. With the second meaning MT reads 'in his wrath'; the parallel is then with 'his burning anger'.[10]

1. LSJ, p. 810.
2. LSJ, p. 809.
3. This is how the Targum translates מפלי in Job 41.15; Jastrow, *A Dictionary of the Targumim*, pp. 1577-78. At least one manuscript translates with בקרביה which might be a play on 'innards'.
4. Payne Smith, *A Compendious Syriac Dictionary*, p. 517, s.v. קרב. Though קרב, as in the Targum, might play on 'innards'.
5. *OLD*, pp. 228-29, s.v. *bellum*.
6. Yellin, איוב-חקרי מקרא, p. 144; Pope, *Job*, pp. 150, 153; Gordis, *The Book of Job*, pp. 210, 219.
7. Driver, *Job*, I, p. 180; II, p. 141; Dhorme, *Le Livre de Job*, p. 274; Clines, *Job 1–20*, pp. 472, 477.
8. Tur-Sinai, *The Book of Job*, p. 318.
9. Guillaume, *Studies in the Book of Job*, p. 43.
10. Hartley, *The Book of Job*, p. 303 n. 20. L.L. Grabbe, *Comparative Philology and the Text of Job: A Study in Methodology* (SBLDS, 34; Missoula, MT: Scholars Press, 1977), p. 77, also finds support for both meanings.

The divergence between the LXX,[1] Vulgate, and Peshitta on the one hand, and the Targum, Ibn Ezra, and Ralbag on the other, demonstrates that Job 20.23-24 was understood in multiple ways.

The significance of this Janus is largely dependent upon the context of ch. 20. Previously, in Job 20.12-16, Zophar described the evildoer as follows:

> Though evil is sweet to his mouth, and he conceals it (יכידנה) under his tongue; though he saves it; (and) does not let it go, (he) holds it inside his mouth. His food (לחמו) in his bowels turns into asps' venom (מרורת) within him. The riches he swallows he vomits; God empties it out of his stomach (מבטנו). He sucks the poison of asps; the tongue of the viper kills him.

The evildoer to whom Zophar refers is Job, whose dangerous words are compared to a serpent's venom, which though concealed (probably by way of polysemy), will devour him eventually. Zophar's discourse should not be separated from his use of the pivot בלחומו in 20.23 only a few verses later. Support for this connection comes from בטן, 'stomach',[2] and the root מרר, here 'venom, gall', which appear again in the same context in 20.23-25.[3] Contextually, then, the 'food' suggested by בלחומו is not 'bread' per se, but the wicked words which the evildoer (Job) conceals under his tongue and which become the agents of God's wrath. In essence, Zophar is telling Job that his own words will destroy him.

Finally, we should note that the context of God's storm-like wrath in this section echoes another concealed reference to rain in 16.12-13, where Job cries: 'He has set me up as his target (מטרה); his bowmen (רביו) surrounded me...' Both words in the parentheses are polysemous. מטרה means 'target' and 'rain' and רביו means 'bowmen' and 'copious rains'.[4] Thus, these allusions prepare us[5] for Zophar's two polysemous parallels, the first in 20.23 utilizing בלחומו, 'food/fury', and the second in 20.25 (dealt with below) on ברק ממררתו, 'flashing as it passes/through the gall', both of which occur in the context of God's storm-like wrath.[6]

1. Even the LXX may be seen as between the camps. See the comments above.

2. Note that בטן also appears antanaclastically in 20.20 as 'children'. For this usage, cf. Hos. 9.16. Such key words help to underscore the lines which contain them, for instance 20.23.

3. Note that Zophar also exploits the root מרר for its polysemy in Job 20.25.

4. Deriving רביו also from רביבים, 'showers', in Deut. 32.2; Mic. 5.6; Ps. 65.11; 72.6. Cf. Ugaritic *rbb* which often parallels 'dew'; see *UT*, p. 482.

5. In Job 36.28, Elihu makes a similar allusion to rain in the expression אדם רב, 'and shower upon all humankind'.

6. See also Job 38.23 where צר, 'siege' or 'distress', is used in the context of

Job 20.25

שלף ויצא מגוה
וברק ממררתו
יהלך עליו אמים

Brandished and run through his innards. And (like) lightning ממררתו.
It casts terror upon him.

In v. 25 the poet plays on the expression ממררתו, which has been translated in several different ways depending on the commentator or version. I posit that two of its meanings, 'gall, intestines',[1] and 'in its passing' (from another root, מרר),[2] make this a Janus-type stich. As 'gall, intestines', ממררתו parallels the previous stich in which mention is made of 'his innards'; as 'its passing', ממררתו parallels 'it casts upon him', in the next stich. The former parallel finds support from the following correspondences: Job 16.13, in which the words מררה, 'gall', and כליות, 'kidneys', occur in parallelism; and *Targum Onqelos* to Exod. 29.13, which translates קרב (which occurs in a list of entrails including כליה) with גו. For the latter parallel between מרר and יצא see Dan. 11.11, and less clearly Ruth 1.13. Thus Job 20.25 belongs to the oral, visual, and symmetrical categories.

The LXX's reading of the Hebrew stich diverges greatly: ἄστρα δὲ ἐν διαίταις αὐτοῦ, 'let the stars be against his dwelling place',[3] in which διαίταις αὐτοῦ, 'his dwelling place',[4] appears to translate the Hebrew root מרר. The Targum uses the cognate ממירירתה, which can be read both as 'in its passing' and as 'from its gall'.[5] The Syriac takes our word only to mean 'gall'.[6] Curiously, the Vulgate not only renders it

rain-like war, and also 27.14 where לחם and חרב both play on 'warfare, battle'.

1. So BDB, p. 601; KB, p. 569; *HALAT*, II, pp. 603-604.

2. See BDB, p. 601; *HALAT*, II, p. 603.

3. Dhorme (*Le Livre de Job*, p. 303) explains this as from ἀστραπή (= ברק). See also H.M. Orlinsky, 'Studies in the Septuagint of the Book of Job: Chapter IV', *HUCA* 33 (1962), p. 142.

4. LSJ, p. 396, s.v. διαίτα.

5. *DISO*, p. 168; Jastrow, *A Dictionary of the Targumim*, p. 843; Beyer, *Die aramäischen Texte vom Toten Meer*, p. 631; Sokoloff, *A Dictionary of Jewish Palestinian Aramaic*, p. 332. Note that the Targum takes the 'body' in the Hebrew as מתיקה, 'from its sheath', i.e., the 'body' is the sword's casing; Jastrow, *A Dictionary of the Targumim*, p. 1665.

6. Payne Smith, *A Compendious Syriac Dictionary*, p. 303.

with *in amaritudine sua*, 'in his gall/bitterness',[1] but adds the word *vadent* '(it shall) proceed'.[2] Does the use of these two translation equivalencies point to Jerome's attempt to preserve the pun?

Most of the medievals take ממררתו as 'gall', 'bitterness', etc., as do most of the moderns, such as Pope, Tur-Sinai, Guillaume, and Hartley, with the exception of Clines who reads it as 'liver'.[3] Interestingly, Saʿadiah Gaʾon renders both meanings: 'comes forth from his bile'. Only Gordis is aware of the expression's other meaning as he translates: 'and its glitter as it passes, casts terror upon him'. As Gordis notes, the reading rests 'on the basis of the Arabic root *marra*, "pass", which also occurs in Job 13.26'.[4]

The use of מרר in its various meanings is ubiquitous in Job. That מרר was heard in 20.14 meaning 'gall, venom', establishes for the lexeme an expected semantic range upon which the allusive and referential polyseme plays. The interconnectedness of מרר in 20.25, like that of בלחומו in 20.23, with Zophar's previous discourse on the words of evildoers as the agents of God's wrath can be demonstrated by appealing to the context of the Janus usage. The terms which are used to frame the polyseme, ברק, גוה, and שלף, all refer back to the weapon of God's wrath in the previous verse. Yet the appearance of מרר demands from the hearer a decision as to which context it belongs. Does it belong to the previous description of words as asps' venom or to the mention of brazen weapons? The ambiguity sets up a comparison between evil words, which pass from the body through vomiting (20.15), and the resultant wrath which passes through the body like a sharpened sword. The poet's plays achieve interconnections between 'wicked words', 'poison', and 'food', each of which relates to the mouth. The puns also drive home Zophar's contention that Job's words will be the cause of God's wrath. Confirmation of these connections comes in 21.20 when Job sharply responds by topping Zophar with a double polysemy: יראו עיניו כידו ומחמת שדי ישתה, 'Let his eyes see his ruin (cup), and let him drink

1. *OLD*, p. 112, s.v. *amāritūdō*.

2. *OLD*, pp. 2029-30, s.v. *venio*.

3. Driver, *Job*, I, p. 180; II, pp. 141-42; Dhorme, *Le Livre de Job*, p. 275; Pope, *Job*, pp. 150, 153; Tur-Sinai, *The Book of Job*, pp. 318-20; Guillaume, *Studies in the Book of Job*, p. 44; Hartley, *The Book of Job*, p. 303; Clines, *Job 1–20*, pp. 472, 478, 496.

4. Gordis, *The Book of Job*, pp. 212, 220.

the wrath (poison) of Shaddai'.[1] Moreover, 20.25 may refer to Job's allusions to rain in 16.13-15. The plays on 'rain' (i.e., מטר and רבב) in this pericope have been discussed above in relation to בלחומו in 20.23.[2] Of note here is the last line of the tristich in 16.13c which runs: ישפך לארץ מררתי, 'He spilled my gall onto the ground'. That מרר appears in 16.13 in connection with other plays on rain is no coincidence. It is precisely this allusive and referential quality which gives the Janus construction its impact.

Job 20.27-28

יגלו שמים עונו
וארץ מתקוממה לו
יגל יבול ביתו
נגרות ביום אפו

The heavens will reveal his iniquity and the earth will rise up against him.
יגל יבול his house. Poured out on the day of his wrath.

Job 20.27-28 has caused problems of interpretation for commentators. Most difficult is the phrase יגל יבול ביתו. The verb יגל is parsed as if derived from the root גלה; thus a meaning 'driven out, exiled' would seem fitting.[3] But the consonants also permit a derivation from גלל; thus 'roll away' would seem appropriate.[4] Note that the latter finds support in Jer. 51.25 in which the root גלל appears in conjunction with ארץ. A similar situation obtains in the case of יבול. The word can be read in two ways: 'produce',[5] in which case it parallels 'earth' in the previous stich, or as 'a violent rain'[6] (on the basis of Arabic *wabalu*), in which case it parallels 'poured out' in the next stich. Both meanings are attested in the Bible. The first is common enough not to warrant citation here, the second occurs in Jer. 17.5 (where it is written יובל), and in Isa. 30.25; 44.4. Accordingly, with all these meanings in mind, the stich is to be understood as 'the produce of his house is driven away', and as 'a

1. On this verse as a Janus parallel see below. Also, for a similar play on חמתם see Job 6.4.
2. For further discussion on מרר in connection with rain, see my comments on תטף in 29.22.
3. So BDB, p. 162; KB, pp. 182-83.
4. So *HALAT*, I, p. 186.
5. So BDB, p. 385; KB, p. 359.
6. With KB, p. 359; *HALAT*, II, p. 366.

violent rain rolls away his house'. The possibility of reading the expression in two ways demonstrates once again the presence of a Janus-type polysemous usage: the use of יגל belonging to the strictly visual and symmetrical groups, and that of יבול belonging to the oral, visual, and symmetrical classes.

The LXX clearly treats the stich as referring to a cataclysm of sorts by ignoring the reading 'produce' and opting for ἑλκύσαι τὸν οἶκον αὐτοῦ ἀπώλεια εἰς τέλος, 'Let destruction bring his house to an end'.[1] The Targum renders with the equally ambiguous phrase יטלטל עבור: 'the produce/passing (of his house) will be exiled/shaken'.[2] That both meanings were noticed by the Targumist is demonstrated by the fact that rendering עבור according to its more common meaning 'produce' still leaves us with two Targumic additions, משחיה וחמריה, 'its destruction and its ruins', which, like the LXX's reading, clearly point to a catastrophe. Similarly, the Peshitta translates יבול with נתגלין שתאסא דביתה, 'they will uncover the foundations of his house'.[3] In line with the Targum, which reflects an awareness of the pun, is the Vulgate's *apertum erit germen domus*, 'the offspring (lit. shoot) of that house will be exposed (to natural forces)'. Note here that while the use of *germen*, 'shoot', reflects only the meaning 'produce' for יבול, its etymological base, *gero*, suggests that both meanings were intended: 'bear, carry (produce)' and 'reveal, show', that is, the other meaning of גלה.[4] Similarly, the Latin *aperio* means both 'expose to natural forces' and 'reveal'.[5] Thus, there is reason to believe that Jerome understood the polysemy here.

Some of the medievals also seem to have espied the dual meaning. While all read יגל as an expression of exile,[6] a difference of opinion exists on how to read יבול. Rashi takes it as 'destruction', whereas Moshe Qimḥi and the commentary *Metsudat Zion* read it as 'produce'. Ibn Ezra and Y. Altschuler's other commentary, *Metsudat David*, correctly see in it both meanings. Of the modern commentators, only Driver and

1. LSJ, pp. 207, 534, s.v. ἀπολυμμι, ἑλκύσαι.
2. From טלטל; *DISO*, p. 202; Jastrow, *A Dictionary of the Targumim*, pp. 536, 1066-67; Beyer, *Die aramäischen Texte vom Toten Meer*, p. 651; Sokoloff, *A Dictionary of Jewish Palestinian Aramaic*, p. 393.
3. Payne Smith, *A Compendious Syriac Dictionary*, pp. 69, 600, s.v. גל, שתס.
4. *OLD*, p. 762.
5. *OLD*, p. 146, s.v. *apertum*.
6. With the exception of Moshe Qimḥi who renders as יראה, 'reveal'.

Guillaume take יבול as 'produce'.[1] Dhorme, Pope, Gordis, and Tur-Sinai favor 'flood'.[2] Hartley and, to some extent, Clines admit both readings.[3]

Zophar has referred several times in this chapter to 'wealth, produce' (for example, חיל 20.15, 18, חמוד 20.20, טוב 20.20). That it should become the subject of a twist on its meaning therefore should not surprise us, for Zophar already has demonstrated his ability to prepare the reader with false expectations. Zophar also has made it clear that the wealth of the wicked will come to ruin (cf. for example 20.17-22). Therefore, in order to entrench the connection between the evildoer's 'wealth' and his 'ruin' Zophar uses יבול. Similarly referential is יגלו which reminds us of 20.27: יגלו שמים עונו, 'the heavens will reveal his iniquity'. By playing on the polysemous nature of both יגלו and יבול, Zophar equates the loss of Job's wealth with the exposing of his sin. Zophar's brilliant conciseness also responds to Job's insult in 14.19 in which the main protagonist accuses his friends of wearing down his hope like a flood wearing away stones. In sum, like Bildad in 18.4, Zophar plays upon Job's words in 14.18-19, subverting their context by transforming the floods which wear down Job (i.e., the friends) into the wrath of God.

Job 21.12-13

יכאו שתף וכנור
וישמחו לקול עוגב
יבלו בטוב ימידהם
וברגע שאול יחתו

They carry a drum and lyre rejoice to the sound of a pipe.
Their days יבלו in goodness. In a moment they descend to Sheol.

Job 21.12-13 presents us with a *qere*/*kethib* variation: the *kethib* is יבלו and the *qere* is יכלו. As both have similar semantic ranges and as the orthographic difference between the *kaph* and the *beth* is not great, it is easy to understand the confusion. Nevertheless, if we accept the *kethib*,[4] the word יבלו could derive from two roots, both of which are apposite

1. Driver, *Job*, I, p. 181; II, p. 143; Guillaume, *Studies in the Book of Job*, p. 44.
2. Dhorme, *Le Livre de Job*, p. 277; Pope, *Job*, pp. 150, 153; Gordis, *The Book of Job*, pp. 212, 221; Tur-Sinai, *The Book of Job*, pp. 320-21.
3. Hartley, *The Book of Job*, p. 304 n. 30; Clines, *Job 1–20*, pp. 472, 479.
4. For a venerable defense of the *kethib* here, see Minḥat Shai.

here: בלה, 'waste away, consume',[1] and יבל, 'carry, bear along'. As the former, the stich reads 'their days are worn out in goodness', and as the latter, 'their days are borne along in goodness'. Again, we have here a Janus-type construction in which the idea of 'wasting away' parallels the mention of the great waster Sheol in the following stich (cf. Ps. 49.14; Job 10.19; 21.32), and as 'bearing along', the use of ישאו (i.e., as 'bear fruit') in the previous stich. The latter connection also can be found in God's words in Job 40.20: כי בול הרים ישאו לו, 'the mountains bear him produce'. It seems that the *qere* has removed the ambiguity by insisting on the meaning 'waste away'. The different etymologies proposed for the Janus construction require differences in pronunciation. Thus, Job 20.27-28 falls into the strictly visual and symmetrical groups.

The LXX must have relied on the *qere*, as it translates συνετέλεσαν, 'spend'.[2] While the Targum is also based on the *qere*, it reflects an awareness of the polysemy here by its use of יגמרון, 'they complete, spend', or 'they destroy'.[3] Such is also the case with the Peshitta which renders the verb with מגמרין.[4] The Vulgate too apparently attempted to bridge the two meanings with *ducunt*, from the root *duco*, 'carry away, take away', but also 'spend (time)'.[5]

Of the rabbinical commentaries, Rashi's is most interesting: הזיקו ימיהם בטובה וכאשר בא עתם ירדו לקבר ברגע מבלי אריכת המכאוב: 'Their days will grow old in goodness and when their time comes, they will descend to the grave in a moment without prolonged pain'. Is Rashi demonstrating his awareness of the two meanings of יבלו, that is, 'growing old' and 'the spending of time'?[6] The moderns disagree on how to read the stich. Pope reads 'they pass their days'.[7] Gordis feels that both the *kethib* and *qere* are acceptable readings, but opts for 'they spend their days', basing his reading on the root בלה.[8] Driver, Dhorme, Guillaume, and Hartley

1. So BDB, p. 115; KB, p. 128; *HALAT*, I, p. 127; *HAHAT*[18], p. 151.

2. LSJ, p. 1800. See also H.M. Orlinsky, 'Studies in the Septuagint of the Book of Job: Chapter V', *HUCA* 35 (1964), p. 44.

3. *DISO*, p. 51; Jastrow, *A Dictionary of the Targumim*, p. 255; Beyer, *Die aramäischen Texte vom Toten Meer*, p. 544; Sokoloff, *A Dictionary of Jewish Palestinian Aramaic*, p. 132. For the root גמר as 'destroy' see also *Pes. R.* 87b.

4. Payne Smith, *A Compendious Syriac Dictionary*, pp. 72-73, s.v. גמר.

5. *OLD*, pp. 576-77.

6. Rashi, as well as Altschuler's *Metsudat David*, probably obtains the interpretation 'grow old' from Gen. 18.12.

7. Pope, *Job*, p. 155.

8. Gordis, *The Book of Job*, pp. 224, 229.

prefer to read along with the LXX and the *qere*.[1] Ironically, Tur-Sinai notes: 'there is no room for a form of בלה, whose sense in the Bible is always the negative one of destruction'.[2] In my opinion, Tur-Sinai misses the point here, for it is upon the negative use of בלה which the poet plays! Job subtly intertwines the notion of a happy prosperity with his gloomy outlook.

The Janus in 21.13 is an artful presentation of both sides of the argument concerning whether sinners receive punishment in this world. The camps have been formed with Zophar and his friends on one side asserting that 'the heavens will expose his [the wicked person's] iniquity' (20.27) and Job on the other, wondering why 'the wicked live on, prosper, and grow wealthy' (21.7). In one keen remark Job puts forth the ambiguity of the real-life situation. He causes his friends to question whether he believes that they 'spend their days in peace' or 'wear out their days until death'. The ambiguity both illustrates Job's point and draws his friends into the discourse by spelling out the ambiguity of the problem of sin and retribution.

Moreover, as with the previous examples, this Janus parallel serves a referential function. In this case, it prepares the reader for two statements by Job, the first in 21.30: 'On the day of wrath he will be borne along (יובלו) to his doom', and the second in 21.32: 'He will be borne along (יובל) to the grave'. In addition, the impact on Job's friends of his word-play in 21.12-13 is evident in 36.11, in which Elihu quotes Job's statement in part: יבלו ימיהם בטוב, 'they spend their days in goodness'.[3]

Job 21.19-20

אלוה יצפן לבניו אונו
ישלם אליו וידע
יראו עינו כידו
ומחמת שדי ישתה

[You say] 'God is reserving punishment for his sons', let it be paid back to him that he may know it.
Let his eyes see כידו. And let him drink the wrath of Shaddai.

1. Driver, *Job*, I, p. 184; II, p. 146; Dhorme, *Le Livre de Job*, pp. 284-85; Guillaume, *Studies in the Book of Job*, pp. 44, 104; Hartley, *The Book of Job*, p. 312 n. 4.

2. Tur-Sinai, *The Book of Job*, p. 326.

3. Interestingly, 36.11 also bears the *qere* יכלו.

The *hapax* כידו has caused some difficulty for translators, both ancient and modern. If we base our understanding of the word on its Arabic cognate *kayd*, we translate 'downfall'.[1] If we see in it a dialectical variant of *kad*, we read 'pitcher, jar'.[2] If 'destruction' is read, then it parallels the notion of receiving punishment in the previous stich. If we see in it a 'pitcher', then it stands in parallelism with 'drink' in the following stich. As the examples above and below point out, such ambiguity was intentional. It is only later, and especially in modern scholarly circles, that such ambiguity has become the subject of an 'either/or' debate (see Chapter 1). Job 21.19-20, therefore, is a visual and symmetrical polysemous parallel.[3]

The LXX reads ἑαυτοῦ σφαγὴν, 'his own destruction'.[4] So also the Targum, Peshitta, and Vulgate render the *hapax* with תבירֵיה, אבדנה, and *interfectionem*,[5] respectively. The ancients as well as most modern commentators, such as Driver, Dhorme, Pope, Gordis, Guillaume, and Hartley,[6] follow the versions. Only Grabbe and Tur-Sinai read the stich 'let his own eyes see the cup', the latter basing his reading on the plural construct form כדוי in Job 6.7 and on an assumed play on 'let him drink of the poison (wrath) of Shaddai' in that passage.[7]

As we have seen above in connection with ממררתו in Job 20.25, Tur-Sinai's reference is on target. Job's use of כידו, 'cup, calamity', and מחמת, 'poison, wrath', constitutes both a double polysemy and a Janus construction.[8] The impact of the polysemy must be seen in the light of Zophar's rantings in ch. 20, in which he binds together notions of

1. Wehr, *A Dictionary of Modern Written Arabic*, p. 849; KB, p. 433.

2. For Punic, Imperial Aramaic, and Samaritan Hebrew cognates, see Grabbe, *Comparative Philology and the Text of Job*, pp. 78-79.

3. Cognate evidence does not help to ascertain whether this Janus is accomplished on an oral level as well.

4. LSJ, p. 1737, s.v. σφαγῖον.

5. From תבר; *DISO*, p. 290; Jastrow, *A Dictionary of the Targumim*, pp. 1645-46; Beyer, *Die aramäischen Texte vom Toten Meer*, p. 721; Sokoloff, *A Dictionary of Jewish Palestinian Aramaic*, p. 575; Payne Smith, *A Compendious Syriac Dictionary*, p. 2, s.v. אבד; *OLD*, p. 943, s.v. *interficiō*.

6. Driver, *Job*, I, p. 187; II, p. 148; Dhorme, *Le Livre de Job*, p. 288; Pope, *Job*, pp. 156, 160; Gordis, *The Book of Job*, pp. 224, 231; Guillaume, *Studies in the Book of Job*, pp. 45, 104; Hartley, *The Book of Job*, p. 316.

7. Grabbe, *Comparative Philology and the Text of Job*, pp. 78-79; Tur-Sinai, *The Book of Job*, pp. 328-29.

8. See the Conclusion for a discussion on the relationship between the two.

poison and wrath as well as evil talk and sin. In 21.20 Job has inverted Zophar's taste for insinuation: Zophar's venom, by which he meant the evil words of wicked people, is now the venom (wrath) of Shaddai.[1]

Subtle allusions to כידו also occur in God's retort in 39.23: להב חנית וכידון, 'and the flashing spear and javelin', and again antanaclastically in 41.11: כידודי אש יתמלטו, 'fiery sparks escape', and in 41.12: כדוד נפוח ואגמן, 'as from a steaming, boiling pot'.

Job 21.23-24

זה ימות בעצם תמו
כלו שלאנן ושליו
עטיניו מלאו חלב
ומח עצמותיו ישקה

Yet one man dies in the fullness of his strength, wholly at ease and secure.
His עטיניו are filled with milk, and the marrows of his bones are moist.

The word עטיניו in line 24 gives the poet an opportunity to play once again on two separate meanings. If we read our word with the Hebrew *ʿaṭinaw*, 'resting place around a watering hole',[2] we may join it according to the fashion of Janus parallels with כלו שלאנן ושליו, 'wholly at ease and secure', in line 23. If, however, we read it with its meaning 'dripping olives', a common Mishnaic Hebrew euphemism for 'testicles',[3] we join עטיניו with ומה עצמותיו ישקה, 'the marrows of his bones are moist', in the following line. As the latter is a common expression for good health in the Bible,[4] we find support for both the secondary euphemistic rendering of עטיניו and for the existence of a Janus construction. Thus, Job 21.23-24 is an oral, visual, and symmetrical Janus parallel.

Again, some of the versions seem to be aware of the polysemy. The LXX translates ἔγκατα, 'entrails'.[5] While ἔγκατα cannot mean 'watering hole' here, it is clear that some body part is meant, possibly to parallel in an *ad sensum* fashion the occurrence of 'marrow' in the next stich. For reasons which are at best unclear, the Targumist, as does Ralbag,

1. See also the discussion above on this passage's relationship with Job 20.25.
2. Grabbe, *Comparative Philology and the Text of Job*, pp. 79-81.
3. Gordis, *The Book of Job*, pp. 232-33.
4. See Deut. 34.7 and Prov. 3.8.
5. LSJ, p. 470. Might this be a euphemism for 'testicles'? See a similar usage in the Vulgate below.

translates 'breasts'.[1] They are a source of (mother's) milk, and are a body part (which seems required by context); and so perhaps goes the logic behind the reading, but there is no reason to see in the Targum the meaning 'watering hole'. Jerome's rendering *viscus*, while serving as a perfect translation for 'testicles',[2] also means 'the most essential part of something for its survival, i.e., of a country or state'.[3] The Syriac represents our word, oddly enough, with וגבוהי, 'his camel hump', or 'his side'. Is this an attempt to render what Ibn Ezra describes as its meaning: 'a place where camels kneel for the sake of water'? The 11QTgJob fragment is mutilated but suggests the reading 'buttocks'.[4] Saʿadiah Gaʾon translates as 'his veins' and Moshe Qimḥi as 'his (sexual) vessel'(?), whereas Rashi and Y. Altschuler's *Metsudat David* and *Metsudat Zion* render עטיניו as 'olives, the fat of olives'.[5]

The moderns provide as many translations as there are versions. Driver reads 'His pails are full of milk'.[6] Dhorme and Pope, though aware of the multiple possibilities for this *hapax*, read 'His haunches are full and plump'.[7] Gordis, perhaps basing his reading on the LXX and Vulgate, translates 'his vital organs full of milk'.[8] Only Hartley reads as 'his testes full of milk'.[9] Tur-Sinai rejects the versions and renders 'He is full of oil and milk'.[10] Finally, Guillaume, preferring the Targum, reads 'His breasts are full of fat'.[11]

The one-upmanship which often characterizes bitter arguments is quite prevalent in this most heated debate. Job and his friends constantly quote and misquote each other with special attention paid to the turn of a phrase. Such is the case in 21.24, where Job's words 'Yet one man dies in the fullness of his strength, wholly at ease and secure. His watering

1. From שד; Jastrow, *A Dictionary of the Targumim*, p. 1523; Sokoloff, *A Dictionary of Jewish Palestinian Aramaic*, p. 538 (but as 'side').

2. This seems to have escaped the modern commentators.

3. It seems a stretch to posit such a reference as meaning a 'water source'; *OLD*, p. 2077, s.v. *viscus*.

4. With Grabbe, *Comparative Philology and the Text of Job*, p. 80.

5. On the basis of the Mishnah, *Men.* 8.4.

6. Driver, *Job*, I, p. 188; II, p. 149.

7. Dhorme, *Le Livre de Job*, p. 290; Pope, *Job*, pp. 156, 161. The latter bases his reading on Akkadian *eṣmu* and Arabic *ʿiṭmāʾ*, both 'haunches'.

8. Gordis, *The Book of Job*, pp. 224, 233.

9. Hartley, *The Book of Job*, p. 317.

10. Tur-Sinai, *The Book of Job*, pp. 330-31.

11. Guillaume, *Studies in the Book of Job*, pp. 45, 105.

holes (testes) are filled with milk, and the marrows of his bones are moist', respond to Zophar's statement in 20.17: 'let him not enjoy the streams, the rivers of honey, the brooks of cream'. The scenario Job describes in 21.24 joins the prosperity which Job sees the wicked enjoying with sexual potency. Job made this connection earlier in 21.10-12: 'their bull breeds and does not fail; their cow calves and never miscarries; they let their infants run loose like sheep, and their children skip about', but now chooses to play upon it.[1] Job's cunning speech also responds to Zophar's opinion on the punishment of the wicked sinner in 20.10-11: בניו ירצו דלים וידיו תשבנה אונו עצמותיו מלאו עלומו ועמו על עפר תשכב, 'his sons will try to appease the poor, and his offspring will return his ill-gotten gains. His bones still full of vigor, lie down in the dust with him.' Note the use in both 20.10-11 and 21.24 of מלא and עצם to strengthen the reference. Moreover, in 21.26 Job adds: יחד על עפר ישכבו, 'Alike (the wicked and the good) lie down in the dust'.[2] The reason why Job inverts his friend's words is given at the end of his discourse in 21.34: 'How then do you comfort me with empty words (הבל), while of your answers only treachery remains?'

Job 22.5-6

הלא רעתך רבה
ואין קץ לעונתיך
כי תחבל אחיך חנם
ובגדי ערומים תפשיט

Is not your wickedness great? There is no end to your inquities.
You תחבל your brothers without reason, and leave them naked, stripped of their clothes.

The Janus here hinges on the word תחבל, whose orthography may represent two roots; either *ḥbl*, 'bind, pledge', or *ḫbl*, 'act injuriously'.[3] Each provides a very different translation, but both are justified by context and parallelism. If read as the former, 'You exact a pledge of your brother without reason', it parallels the following stich which mentions 'the stripping of the naked', a parallel found elsewhere in the Bible and in Akkadian documents (see, for example, Exod. 22.26; Job 24.9;

1. A similar correlation between the two also obtains in the noun און.
2. Other referential plays on Zophar's speech include מתק (20.12; 21.33) and יבול (20.28; 21.30, 32).
3. BDB, pp. 286-87.

Ezek. 18.12; Amos 2.8).[1] If read as the latter, 'You act injuriously against your brother without reason', it parallels the preceding stich which makes use of the word עונת, 'iniquities'. Note that חבל and עונות occur in parallelism also in Prov. 5.22. We have here, then, a strictly visual and symmetrical polysemous parallel.

Only the meaning 'take as a pledge' is represented by the LXX's ἠνεχύραζες, 'you have taken security'.[2] The renderings of the Targum, Vulgate, and Peshitta, on the other hand, are as ambiguous as the MT. The Targum uses תמשכן, whose root משך means both 'take a pledge' and 'seize (in a violent fashion)'.[3] The Vulgate renders with *abstulisti*, which is derived from *tullo/tollo*, either 'take away' or 'remove by killing'.[4] The Syriac's דנסבת, 'you have received', also means 'you have taken by force (as in war)', which reflects the second root concealed by the orthography of יחבלו.

Of the medievals and the moderns,[5] only Y. Altschuler in his *Metsudat Zion* derives the word from *ḥbl*, 'act injuriously', noting that it occurs in Deut. 22.6 in the context of treating a mother bird injuriously by seizing its young.

Eliphaz's utterance in 22.6 is a paraphrase of Zophar's comment in 20.19: כי רצץ עזב דלים בית גזל ולא יבנה, 'because he crushed and forsook the poor, he will not build up his house by force'. Yet Eliphaz rephrases the doctrine of his friends in such a way as to play on Job's prior response in 21.17-19:

> כמה נר רשעים ידעך ויבא עלימו אידם חבלים יחלק באפו: יהיו כתבן
> לפני רוח וכמץ גנבתו סופה. אלוה יצפן לבניו אונו ישלם אליו וידע.

1. The law required that a garment taken in pledge be returned before sundown; Exod. 22.26; Deut. 24.10-13. For Akkadian sources and their relationship to the biblical law see R. Westbrook, *Studies in Biblical and Cuneiform Law* (Cahiers de la *Revue biblique*, 26; Paris: Gabalda, 1988), pp. 28-30.

2. LSJ, p. 565, s.v. ἠνεχυράζω.

3. The Hebrew חבל is used with גזל 'seize', in Ezek. 18.12, 16 and Job 24.9; *DISO*, pp. 170-71; Jastrow, *A Dictionary of the Targumim*, pp. 853-54; Beyer, *Die aramäischen Texte vom Toten Meer*, p. 709; Sokoloff, *A Dictionary of Jewish Palestinian Aramaic*, p. 334.

4. *OLD*, pp. 13, 1947.

5. Driver, *Job*, I, p. 193; Dhorme, *Le Livre de Job*, p. 297; Pope, *Job*, pp. 163, 165; Gordis, *The Book of Job*, pp. 240, 245; Tur-Sinai, *The Book of Job*, pp. 338-39; Guillaume, *Studies in the Book of Job*, p. 46, 106; Hartley, *The Book of Job*, p. 324, each without comment.

How (seldom) does the lamp of the wicked fail, does the calamity they deserve befall them; does he apportion (their) lot in anger! Let them become like straw in the wind, like chaff stolen by a storm. (You say) 'God is reserving punishment for his sons'. Let it be paid back to him that he may feel it.

Note how each of the characters makes reference to 'theft': Eliphaz with חבל (22.6), Job with גנב (21.18), and Zophar with גזל (20.19). In addition, the polyseme חבל which Eliphaz uses in 22.6 also reminds us of Job's remark in 21.17: 'Does he apportion (their) lot (חבלים) in anger!' It is no wonder that Eliphaz plays on this word, for Job's allegation also plays on the alternate meanings of חבל, 'lot' and 'destruction' (cf. for example Mic. 2.10).[1] Therefore, it is fitting for Eliphaz to employ the polyseme.

Job 24.9-10

יגזלו משד יתום
ועל עני יחבלו
ערום הלכו בלי לבוש
ורעבים נשאו עמר

They snatch the fatherless from the breast, and the child of the poor they יחבלו.
They go about naked for lack of clothing, and the hungry carry sheaves.

As in Job 22.5-6 above, יחבלו in Job 24.9-10 can be derived from two different roots, *ḥbl*, 'bind, pledge',[2] or *ẖbl*, 'act (ruinously) corruptly',[3] both of which are at work here. As the former, the stich parallels the reference to 'the naked', and as the latter, the 'snatch(ing) of the fatherless' in the previous stich. The former parallel can be demonstrated also in Job 22.5-6 and Amos 2.8. The latter parallel finds support in the conjunction of חבל and גזל in Ezek. 18.12, 16. Again, as in Job 22.5-6 above, we have a strictly visual and symmetrical Janus parallel.

Unlike Job 22.5-6, however, the versions here reflect the second root *ẖbl*, 'to act injuriously'. The LXX uses ἐταπείνωσαν, 'afflicted'.[4] The Targum again renders with the root משך, 'take as a pledge, seize by

1. Job's remark may be an asymmetrical Janus parallel as well, for as 'lot' חבל parallels חלק just afterwards and as 'destruction' it parallels איד in the previous stich.
2. So BDB, p. 286; KB, p. 271; *HALAT*, I, p. 274.
3. BDB, pp. 286-87.
4. LSJ, p. 1757, s.v. ταπεινόω.

force',[1] which lends support to the idea that the root be used to translate either of the two Hebrew roots. The Vulgate translates *fecerunt*, 'they have stripped, inflicted',[2] and the Peshitta as חובלא ארמיו, 'they hurl destruction'.[3]

The medievals who comment on this verse disagree. Saʿadiah Gaʾon, Rashi, and Ralbag[4] read it as 'take as a pledge', whereas the commentary *Metsudat David* connects the word with the root עלל, 'act arbitrarily, injuriously'.[5] Moshe Qimḥi gives both possibilities.[6] With the sole exception of Pope, who translates 'the suckling of the poor they seize',[7] the polysemy has escaped the moderns, who invariably derive our word from the root *ḥbl*.[8]

Job's response in 24.9 follows upon a litany of word-plays on the two roots concealed in the consonants חבל. We already have seen how Job's statement in 21.17 and Eliphaz's accusation in 22.6 employ the polyseme. Now in 24.9 Job feels compelled to twist its use: יגזלו משד יתום ועל עני יחבלו. Several allusions are at work in this remark. First, the use of גזל recalls Zophar's related attack in 20.19: 'because he crushed and forsook the poor, he will not build up the house he took by force (גזל)'. This connection is made even more apparent by the mention of 'the poor' in both. Job inverts not only his friend's words in 24.9, but also his own. Compare, for example, the exclamation he makes just prior in 24.2-3: גבלות ישיגו עדר גזלו וירעו...יחבלו שור אלמנה, 'people remove boundary stones; they rob flocks and pasture them...and seize the

1. *DISO*, pp. 170-71; Jastrow, *A Dictionary of the Targumim*, p. 854; Beyer, *Die aramäischen Texte vom Toten Meer*, p. 709; Sokoloff, *A Dictionary of Jewish Palestinian Aramaic*, p. 334.

2. *OLD*, p. 668, s.v. *faciō*.

3. Payne Smith, *A Compendious Syriac Dictionary*, pp. 129, 542-43, s.v. חבלא, רמא.

4. As Ralbag uses the root משך, probably under the influence of the Targum, it is uncertain if he read it as 'take as a pledge' or 'act injuriously'.

5. The others do not comment.

6. ובעבור העני יחבלו ישימו משכון או יחבלו ישימו חבל ללכדו.

7. Yet Pope (*Job*, pp. 174-75), seeing our verse as 'out of place', inserts it between vv. 3 and 4, thus destroying the Janus effect here.

8. Driver, *Job*, I, p. 207; II, p. 167; Dhorme, *Le Livre de Job*, p. 324; Gordis, *The Book of Job*, p. 256; Tur-Sinai, *The Book of Job*, p. 362; Guillaume, *Studies in the Book of Job*, p. 49. Except for Driver, none comments on the word. Note that although Hartley (*The Book of Job*, p. 344) translates by way of a compromise, i.e., 'they seize the infant of the poor as a pledge', he follows Dhorme, Driver, and Pope in moving the verse between vv. 3 and 4.

widow's bull as a pledge'. Not only is חבל used here, but also גזל. Moreover, binding the connection between 24.2-3 and the Janus construction in 24.9 is another play on words immediately following in 24.11: בין שורתם יצהירו, 'between the rows (of olive trees) they make oil'. Observe how the poet has connected the two passages by using שורתם, 'rows', which reminds us of שור, 'bull', in 24.3.

Equally referential is Elihu's use of חבל, 'act injuriously', in Job 34.31. That he is attempting to outwit Job can be seen by Elihu's penchant for antanaclasis. For example, he uses חבל as 'friend, league' (34.8), 'cords (of affliction)' (36.8), and 'direction, counsel' (37.12). That Elihu intends his use of חבל to act referentially to Job's remark in 24.9 is best seen by 36.8, where חבלי עני, 'cords of affliction', plays upon Job's use of ועל עני יחבלו, 'the child of the poor they take as a pledge/destroy'. Undoubtedly, this adds yet further twists on the expectations built around the use of the root חבל. Moreover, the root occurs antanaclastically twice in God's whirlwind speech: as 'birth pangs' (39.3) and 'cord' (40.25).

Job 24.20-21

ישכחהו רחם
מתקו רמה
עוד לא יזכר
ותשבר כעץ עולה
רעה עקרה לא תלד
ואלמנה לא ייטיב

May the womb forget him, may he be sweet to the worms. May he be no longer remembered. May wrongdoers be broken like a tree.
May he רעה a barren woman who bears no child, leave his widow deprived of good.

Job 24.20-21 presents us with another Janus construction, this time based on the pivot רעה, which can be derived from two roots: רעע I, 'be evil, bad',[1] or רעע II (*rḍḍ* = Heb. רצץ), 'crush, destroy'.[2] If translated as 'he is evil to the barren woman', the stich anticipates 'leaves his widow deprived of good' in the following stich, and if read as 'he crushes the

1. See BDB, pp. 947-48; KB, pp. 901-902; *HALAT*, IV, pp. 1184-85.
2. BDB, pp. 949-50; KB, p. 902; *HALAT*, IV, p. 1185. Conceivably, another root, *rḍy*, 'to consort, befriend' (= standard Hebrew רצה, but dialectally רעה), is possible, but unlikely here because of the context. This contra *NJPSV*, p. 1374; KB, p. 899; *HALAT*, IV, p. 1177.

barren woman', the line parallels the previous 'may wrongdoers be broken like a tree'. The parallelism between רעע I, 'be evil, bad', and טוב, 'good', obtains also in Gen. 44.4; Num. 13.19; 1 Sam. 16.16; Jer. 15.11; Amos 9.4; Mic. 3.2; 2 Chron. 18.7; Ps. 35.12; Prov. 11.27 and Qoh. 7.14, for example. The latter association between רעע II, 'crush', and שבר, 'break', is strengthened by the two roots in parallelism in Jer. 4.6; 6.1; 17.18; and Nah. 3.19. The two roots also appear in conjunction with one another (though not in parallelism) in Ezek. 6.9; 34.16; and Zech. 11.16. By making use of the two sets of word-pairs the poet accomplished a strictly visual and symmetrical Janus parallelism.

Support for both readings again comes from the versions. οὐκ εὖ ἐποίησε, 'he has not treated well',[1] is how the LXX renders the stich, reflecting a derivation from רעע I. The Targum is extremely periphrastic and cryptic, and preserves the pun by translating with מרע, 'feeds on, be injurious, evil', and 'shatter, break'.[2] The Vulgate prefers to read רעה as if derived from רעע II, translating with *pavit*, 'crush'.[3] Interestingly, the Vulgate also adds *et quae non parit et viduae bene non fecit*, 'and who did not attend to and did not do good to the widow', of which the first half is superfluous, unless understood as preserving the meaning of רעע I. The Peshitta opts to derive רעה from רעע I, translating with בישתא, 'treat wickedly'.[4]

Ibn Ezra, Y. Altschuler's *Metsudat David* and *Metsudat Zion*, Ralbag, Driver, and Dhorme all derive the word from רעע I, 'do evil'. Saʿadiah Gaʾon takes the word as if from רעה II, 'associate with'.[5] Rashi translates as if derived from רעה I, 'pasture, feed', and he is followed by Pope and Guillaume.[6] Of the medievals, only Moshe Qimḥi translates the lexeme as 'crush', using as his prooftext a line from Ps. 2.9: שובר העקקה שאין לה בנים והאלמנה שאין לה בעל, 'smashing the barren woman who has no children, and the widow who has no husband'. Gordis, in the tracks of the Targum and Vulgate, translates 'because he crushes the

1. LSJ, pp. 1427-29, s.v. ποιέω.

2. From רעע; *DISO*, p. 781; Jastrow, *A Dictionary of the Targumim*, p. 1488; Beyer, *Die aramäischen Texte vom Toten Meer*, p. 697; Sokoloff, *A Dictionary of Jewish Palestinian Aramaic*, p. 528.

3. *OLD*, p. 1313, s.v. *paviō*.

4. Payne Smith, *A Compendious Syriac Dictionary*, p. 43.

5. Similarly, F.I. Andersen, *Job: An Introduction and Commentary* (Downers Grove, IL: Inter-Varsity Press, 1976), p. 214: 'a female companion'. He is followed by Hartley, *The Book of Job*, p. 351 n. 5.

6. Pope, *Job*, p. 174; Guillaume, *Studies in the Book of Job*, p. 49.

barren woman'.[1] On the basis of זונות in Prov. 29.3, Tur-Sinai renders our stich 'when he mateth, she is barren and beareth not'.[2]

Job plays here upon Zophar's subtle reprimand in 20.12: אם תמתיק בפיו רעה יכחידנה תחת לשונו, 'though evil is sweet in his mouth, he conceals it under his tongue'. We examined this verse above in the light of the context of Zophar's discourse which binds together notions of evil talk, poison, food, and wrath. That 20.12 refers to Job's talent to hide words (polysemously) offers an explanation for Job's turn of his phrase in 24.21. In both passages מתק and רעה occur. In addition, 20.12 follows immediately after the mention of death: ועמו על עפר תשכב, as does 24.20: שאול חטאו. These allusions serve to underscore their interrelatedness. Thus, by inverting Zophar's words, Job claims that it is not wickedness which is sweet to his mouth, but his death to worms. The twist on the meaning of רעה also contrasts the evil words which his friends accuse him of speaking (20.12) with the evil deeds of sinners who appear in Job's mind to escape God's wrath (24.21).

Job 24.19-21

ציה גם חם יגזלו מימי שלג שאול חטאו
ישכחהו רחם מתקו רמה עוד לא יזכר ותשבר כעץ עולה
רעה עקרה לא תלד ואלמנה לא "טיב

May drought and heat snatch away their snow waters, and Sheol, those who have sinned.

May the רחם forget him, may he be sweet to the worms. May he be no longer remembered. May wrongdoers be broken like a tree.

May he crush a barren woman who bears no child, leave his widow deprived of good.

Job 24.20-21 contains yet another Janus construction, the two together comprising some of the most sophisticated poetic polysemy to be found in the Bible. In v. 21a we read: 'May the רחם forget him, may he be sweet to the worms.' The root רחם has many meanings, two of which are appropriate here: 'womb'[3] and 'rain'.[4] The first is so widely attested

1. Gordis, *The Book of Job*, pp. 256, 270.
2. Tur-Sinai, *The Book of Job*, p. 370.
3. So BDB, p. 933; KB, p. 886; *HALAT*, IV, p. 1136.
4. See G. Rendsburg, 'Hebrew RḤM = "Rain"', *VT* 33.3 (1983), pp. 357-62. I would add to this article not only Job 24.20 but also a third level of play (i.e., besides that on 'rain') in Hos. 1.6; namely a pun on 'womb'. Note that in Hos. 1.6 רחמה follows upon ותלד, 'and she conceived'.

as not to require citation here. The second is rarer, but can be found in Hos. 1.6 and in postbiblical Hebrew. As 'may the womb forget him', the stich parallels the 'barren woman' and 'widow' in the next line (cf. Gen. 29.31 where רחמה, 'womb', and עקרה, 'barren', appear together and Isa. 9.16 where the root רחם and the noun אלמנה appear together [though not in parallelism]). As 'may the rain forget him', the stich parallels nicely the 'drought' and 'snow waters' in the previous verse. This latter association also may exist in Prov. 30.16 and Isa. 49.10 where רחם, 'womb/rain(?)', and מים, 'water', stand in tandem. Therefore, Job 24.19-21 constitutes an oral, visual, and (possibly)[1] semantic asymmetrical polysemous parallel.

The LXX is paraphrastic and verbose, adding what seem to be several stichs: ἀγκαλίδα γὰρ ὀρφανῶν ἥρπασαν. εἶτ' ἀνεμνήσθη αὐτοῦ ἡ ἁμαρτία. ὥσπερ δὲ ὁμίχλη δρόσου ἀφανὴς ἐγένετο. ἀποδοθείη δὲ αὐτῷ ἃ ἔπραξε, 'for they have plundered the bundles of the fatherless. Then is his sin brought to remembrance, and he vanishes like a vapor of dew: but let what he has done be recompensed to him.' Despite the variance, it is clear that the LXX renders רחם as ὁμίχλη δρόσου, 'misty dew',[2] that is, as some form of water.[3] The Targum is equally paraphrastic, first translating the word with the cognate רחם, 'mercy',[4] and then adding, like the LXX, mention of 'rain': 'they withheld the מימי מטרא and the תלגא', that is, because of their sin in withholding the summer tithe. While the Vulgate is aware only of the meaning 'compassion' (*misericordia*),[5] another meaning of the root רחם, the Peshitta translates with מרבעא, 'womb',[6] which may play on רביעא and רבעי, 'early rain, spring rain'.[7] That the Peshitta attempted to

1. I presume a semantic development like that of the Ugaritic words *ddym*, 'mandrakes', and *šlm*, 'peace'. See *UT*, ʿAnat IV: 67-68: [*barṣ*] *.mlḥmt* [*aš*]*t.b*ʿ*prm ddy*[*ym*] *ask* [*šlm*] *lkb arṣ ar*[*bdd*] *lkb*[*dš*]*dm.yšt*, 'Shall I put bread (war) in [the earth]? Shall I set mandrakes in the dust? I shall pour [peace] in the midst of the earth, a plethora [of lovely things] in the mids[t of the fi]elds.'

2. LSJ, pp. 450, 1222, s.v. δρόσος, ὁμιχλαίω.

3. Could it be that the expression ἀγκαλίδα γὰρ ὀρφανῶν, 'bundles of the fatherless', refers to the mother's womb as well? LSJ, p. 9, s.v. ἀγκάλη.

4. *DISO*, pp. 277-78; Jastrow, *A Dictionary of the Targumim*, p. 1467; Beyer, *Die aramäischen Texte vom Toten Meer*, pp. 693-94; Sokoloff, *A Dictionary of Jewish Palestinian Aramaic*, pp. 521-22.

5. *OLD*, p. 1118, s.v. *misericordia*.

6. Payne Smith, *A Compendious Syriac Dictionary*, p. 298.

7. Payne Smith, *A Compendious Syriac Dictionary*, p. 526.

render the pun is brought out more clearly by the fact that Syriac could have translated with the cognate רחם, 'womb',[1] but did not.

Rashi, Ibn Ezra, Moshe Qimḥi, the commentary *Metsudat David*, Ralbag, as well as Driver, Dhorme, Pope, Gordis, Guillaume, and Hartley take our word to mean 'womb'.[2] Tur-Sinai views the passage as so corrupt and 'unintelligible' as to warrant omitting רחם.[3]

The connection between 24.21 and 20.12 has been dealt with above. In addition, we may note that the word רחם occurs only in the mouth of Job (3.11; 10.18; 24.20; 31.15) and God (38.8). Only in 24.20, however, does Job use it polysemously. Elsewhere he uses it only to lament his own birth, that is, as 'womb'. Thus, its appearance here illustrates the referential aspect of the Janus phenomenon. The poet has prepared a false expectation for the word by using it consistently as 'womb' so that when the reader encounters it in 24.20 the play on 'rain' is surprising. Yet it is interesting to note that the author portrays God as aware of the polysemous nature of רחם in 38.8, where he rhetorically asks: ויסך בדלתים ים בגיחו מרחם יצא, 'who closed Yam behind doors when it gushed forth out of the womb?'[4] Note the allusion to water with ים and גיח. Of further interest is that God groups together two of the polysemes used elsewhere, סוך and רחם. The use of the phrase יגזלו מימי שלג in 24.19 also recalls the מימי שלג of 9.30, a verse which also contains a Janus-type play on בר (see Chapter 2). Such references charge the verse with the anticipation of polysemy.

Job 27.18-19

בנה כעש ביתו
וכסכה עשה נצר
עשיר ישכב ולא יאסף
עיניו פקח ואיננו

1. Payne Smith, *A Compendious Syriac Dictionary*, p. 537.

2. Doubtless, this also underlies Saʿadiah Gaʾon's reading 'kinswomen'. Others do not comment; Driver, *Job*, I, p. 212; II, p. 172; Dhorme, *Le Livre de Job*, p. 355; Pope, *Job*, pp. 188, 195; Gordis, *The Book of Job*, p. 256; Guillaume, *Studies in the Book of Job*, p. 49; Hartley, *The Book of Job*, p. 351.

3. Tur-Sinai, *The Book of Job*, pp. 368-69.

4. For the semantic connection between 'flooding' and the 'womb', within a discussion of the Mesopotamian background of the book of Job, see J.B. Burns, 'Namtara and Nergal—Down but Not Out: A Reply to Nicolas Wyatt', *VT* 43 (1993), pp. 1-9.

> He builds his home like a moth, and as a booth a watchman עשה.
> He lies down a rich man, wealth intact. When he opens his eyes it is gone.

The polysemy in Job 27.18-19 involves עשה, normally read as the verb 'do, make',[1] in which case it parallels the Hebrew בנה, 'builds'. If derived from the Arabic *ǵašawa*, 'hide, conceal, cover',[2] as in Job 9.9-11 above, the verse, then read as 'and as a booth which a watchman covers', parallels the following line 'when he opens up his eyes, he/it is gone'. As mentioned in connection with Job 9.9-11, the root עשה as 'hide, cover' can be found in Gen. 25.26 (in the etymology of the name עשו); Obad. 6; Job 23.9; Prov. 12.23; 13.16; Isa. 32.6. Its association with the root כסה in Gen. 18.17; Exod. 28.42; Deut. 22.12; Mal. 2.13; and Job 15.27 strengthens the parallelism posited here.[3] Further, that עשה frequently appears with the root אסף, 'gather', for example in Gen. 29.22; Exod. 3.16; Deut. 16.13; Judg. 2.10; 1 Sam. 5.8; 11.27; 13.11; 15.6; Ezek. 38.12; 2 Chron. 24.11; 28.24; 30.13 demonstrates the aptness of the association in Job 27.18-19. Thus, this polysemous parallel is of the strictly visual and symmetrical types.

The versions, aside from exhibiting a confusion as to whether the builder in v. 18 is a 'moth', 'spider', or 'worm', also read the verb עשה primarily as 'he makes'. Only the LXX, which omits a translation for בנה, clearly treats our verb as if it refers to 'hiding' or 'covering'. It renders the first two stichs: ἀπέβη δὲ ὁ οἶκος αὐτοῦ ὥσπερ σῆτες, καὶ ὥσπερ ἀράχνη, 'And his house is gone like moths, and like a spider's web'. In any event, the LXX does not treat the verb as if it means 'do, make'.[4] Both the Targum and the Peshitta use forms of the root עבד, 'do, make',[5] and the Vulgate similarly uses *fecit*, 'he has made'.[6]

Saʿadiah Gaʾon, Rashi, and Y. Altschuler's *Metsudat David* and

1. So BDB, pp. 793-95; KB, pp. 739-41; *HALAT*, III, pp. 842-45.
2. Wehr, *A Dictionary of Modern Written Arabic*, p. 615.
3. In fact, the root עשה may mean 'conceal' in these passages as well.
4. Cf. Job 9.9-11 where ποιῶν is used.
5. *DISO*, pp. 198-202; Jastrow, *A Dictionary of the Targumim*, p. 1035; Beyer, *Die aramäischen Texte vom Toten Meer*, pp. 649-51; Sokoloff, *A Dictionary of Jewish Palestinian Aramaic*, pp. 391-92; Payne Smith, *A Compendious Syriac Dictionary*, pp. 396-97. Note, however, that the Targum's use of מטללתא for the Hebrew וכסכה may also be read 'shade, shadow'. See Jastrow, *A Dictionary of the Targumim*, p. 537.
6. *OLD*, pp. 668-70, s.v. *faciō*.

Metsudat Zion treat עתה as 'he makes', but Ibn Ezra notes that the guard (נצר), referred to in v. 18b, 'guards his house as a wall which he guards *at night*'. This also suggests that the watchman's booth was concealed, at least by the night. Driver, Dhorme, Pope, Gordis, Tur-Sinai, and Guillaume all take the verb to mean 'make'.[1]

The flexible meaning of עשה has been discussed above in connection with a Janus construction in 9.9-10. There Job used it to underscore the paradox of an invisible God who creates a visible world. Here Job employs it again[2] to point out how, despite all earthly attempts to guard one's wealth, it vanishes upon death. Further warranting an equation between the passages is the use in both of עש, though again with different meanings. In 9.9 it refers to the constellation Ursa Major, in 27.18 it means 'moth'. Also confirming this association is the use of בנה, כסכה, and ביתו in 27.18, all of which refer to structures, and חדרי תמן, 'the chambers of Teman', in 9.9. Compare for example the similar use of 'chamber' to represent death, חדרי מות, in Prov. 7.27 which parallels דרכי שאול. Once again Job has inverted a previous statement by exploring the fullest associative range of words. What formerly glorified the cosmic wonders of God has now become the means by which he laments the impermanent structure of life.

Job 28.3-4

קץ שם לחשך
ולכל תכלית הוא חוקר
אבן אפל וצלמות
פרץ נחל מעם גר
הנשכחים מני רגל
דלו מאנוש נעו

He sets a boundary for darkness, to every limit he probes; to rocks in deepest darkness.
They open up a shaft, far from where there are גר. In places forgotten by wayfarers.

The word גר in Job 28.3-4 gives the poet another occasion to display his sophistication. At first blush גר appears to be the common word for

1. Driver, *Job*, I, pp. 230-31; Dhorme, *Le Livre de Job*, p. 361; Pope, *Job*, pp. 188, 193; Gordis, *The Book of Job*, p. 292; Tur-Sinai, *The Book of Job*, p. 392; Guillaume, *Studies in the Book of Job*, p. 52.
2. Gordis sees this as part of Zophar's speech; *The Book of Job*, p. 283.

'stranger, foreigner';[1] however, as Yellin and Gordis note,[2] there is reason to see in these two consonants the word 'deep hole, crater'. This is based on the Arabic cognate *jawrat^un^* of the same meaning, and the related Hebrew word גִיר, 'limestone'.[3] The meaning 'crater' is quite appropriate for both the metallurgical context of the whole section and the parallelism with אבן אפל וצלמות (cf. אבני מזבח כאבני גר in Isa. 27.9). As 'foreigner' it parallels 'the wayfarers' in the next stich. The latter connection is brought out by the parallelism between the root דלל, 'hang, be low, languish', and גר as 'foreigner'. Though the two are not parallel elsewhere, they do have several word-pairs in common, for example, אביון with גר in Ps. 94.6 and with דלל in Isa. 2.8; Job 5.16; Ps. 72.13; 82.4; 113.7; Prov. 22.9 and Jer. 39.10; עני with גר in Ps. 94.6 and with דלל in Job 34.28 and Ps. 82.3; and יתום with גר in Deut. 24.17; 27.19; Jer. 7.6; 22.3 and Zech. 7.10; and with דלל in Ps. 82.3. Notice also the close connection between גר and the verb שכח in Deut. 24.19 and 26.13. Hence, we have in Job 28.3-4 a strictly visual and symmetrical Janus construction.

The LXX is rather unclear in its treatment of the passage, rendering the expression מעם גר as διακοπὴ χειμάῤῥου ἀπὸ κονίας, 'There is a cutting off of the torrent by reason of chalk'. Of note is κονίας, usually 'dust', but here 'chalk', which often stands metaphorically for 'a multitude'.[4] Is this meant to echo the meaning 'foreigners', that is, as 'people'? Regardless of whether the LXX caught the polysemy at work here, it is clear that it is a geomorphic feature which the translators sought to render. The Targum translates: אתרא די מזדלח מרזביא, 'a place which gurgles (and forms) gutters'.[5] Clearly, a limepit or crater is intended here.[6] The Peshitta and Vulgate treat גר similarly, translating עמא גיורא, 'a foreign people', and *a populo peregrinate*, 'away from a foreign people'.[7]

1. So BDB, pp. 157-58; KB, p. 176; *HALAT*, I, p. 177; *HAHAT*[18], p. 228.
2. Yellin, איוב-חקרי מקרא, p. 153; Gordis, *The Book of Job*, p. 305.
3. BDB, p. 162; KB, p. 192; *HALAT*, I, 193; *HAHAT*[18], p. 227.
4. LSJ, p. 977. See for example *Iliad* 9.385, 13.393.
5. From דלח, מרזב; *DISO*, p. 56; Jastrow, *A Dictionary of the Targumim*, pp. 309, 840; Sokoloff, *A Dictionary of Jewish Palestinian Aramaic*, p. 150.
6. *Contra* Mangan, *The Targum of Job*, p. 65 n. 3, who assumes a derivation for the Hebrew גר from נגר, 'flow'.
7. Payne Smith, *A Compendious Syriac Dictionary*, pp. 68, 416, s.v. גורא, עמא; *OLD*, pp. 822, 1404-1405, 1342, s.v. *ignarus*, *populus*, *perignārus*.

Saʿadiah Gaʾon, Rashi, Ibn Ezra, Moshe Qimḥi, Y. Altschuler's *Metsudat David* and *Metsudat Zion*, and Ralbag, under the influence of the Targum and a similar expression in Mic. 1.4, translate as 'a place where water flows'; again a geomorphic item and not 'a foreigner', as the Vulgate and Syriac rendered it. Dhorme, Pope, Tur-Sinai, and Hartley follow the Vulgate and Syriac here,[1] whereas Yellin and Gordis, as mentioned above, and Guillaume render as 'crater' and 'chalk', respectively.[2] Driver, seeing reason to emend the text, reads 'from them that sojourn in the light'.[3]

The Janus construction in 28.4, like that in 27.18 discussed above, must be seen as a clever development of Job's thoughts in 9.9-11, especially of his statement in 9.10: עשה גדלות עד אין חקר ונפלאות עד אין מספר. The contrast set up in 28.3 characterizes humans as they who 'search the limits of things', ולכל תכלית הוא חוקר. The polysemous גר מעם, therefore, contrasts those things like craters which human beings are able to search out with the things of God which are beyond mortal ken. Additional support for the close relationship between 28.4 and 9.10-11 comes from the use of חוקר as the last word heard before human beings are contrasted with God concerning their inability to find wisdom. The polysemous parallel in 28.4 also serves an anticipatory function to 28.12 where the subject moves from human wisdom to God's: 'but wisdom, where may it be found, and where is the place of understanding?' That wisdom is not to be found in 'the land of the living' (בארץ החיים, 28.13) confirms the connection with humankind's search into the heart of the earth (ארץ) in 28.5. Moreover, the contrast between divine and mortal deeds is developed further in 28.9 where we hear that הפך משרש הרים, 'He [God] overturns the mountains by their roots', which reminds us of another overturning in 28.5b: ותחתיה נהפך כמו אש, '(the earth) is changed below as if into fire', and also of Job's similar words in 9.5: המעתיק הרים ולא ידעו אשר הפכם באפו, 'Him who moves mountains without their knowing it, who overturns them in his anger'.

Note that Job 28 usually is considered an individual poem which has crept into the book at a later time. Yet the above evidence suggests that

1. Dhorme, *Le Livre de Job*, pp. 366-67; Pope, *Job*, p. 97; Tur-Sinai, *The Book of Job*, pp. 396-98; Hartley, *The Book of Job*, p. 374 n. 10.

2. Gordis, *The Book of Job*, p. 300, 305; Guillaume, *Studies in the Book of Job*, pp. 52, 110.

3. Driver, *Job*, I, p. 238; II, pp. 192-93.

it is an integral part of the larger poem and that it contains a complex set of references to earlier and later statements.[1]

Job 28.9-10

בחלמיש שלח ידו
הפך משרש הרים
בצורות יארים בקע
וכל יקר ראתה עינו

To flint he sets his hand. He overturns the mountains by the roots.
בצורות he carves out channels. Every precious thing his eyes behold.

The Jobian poet continues to prove himself adept with words in Job 28.9-10, in which he utilizes the construction בצורות to mean both 'from the rock'[2] and 'precious ore' (from the root בצר).[3] The first echoes the previous mention of 'flint' and 'mountains', and the second anticipates 'every precious thing' in the next stich. Though such a shift requires revocalization, it is important to remember that we are dealing here with a pre-Masoretic consonantal system in which either reading would have been possible. Moreover, support for the parallels comes from elsewhere in the Bible. הר and צור are parallel also in Job 14.18 and occur together in Job 24.8 and Isa. 30.29. As 'precious ore', בצר parallels יקר in Job 28.10. Though the two roots are not parallel elsewhere in the Bible, the close association between them can be demonstrated on the basis of a parallelism between יקר and פנינים and זהב in Prov. 3.15; 20.15, between בצר and אופיר in Job 22.24, and between בצר and כסף in Job 22.25. Interestingly, just a few verses later, in Job 28.16, we find אופיר parallel with שהם יקר וספיר. Finally, I also should note that the root בצר bears the meaning of a 'secret, hidden thing' (cf. Jer. 33.3 and Ezek. 21.5). As such, we may see here a parallel between בצר in Job 28.10 and תעלמה, 'secrets', in 28.11. Thus, Job 28.9-10 is a strictly visual and symmetrical polysemous parallel.

Interestingly, the LXX translates בצורות with δίνας δὲ ποταμῶν, 'whirlpools of rivers'.[4] While this might suggest that the translators understood the Hebrew as referring to a channel in the rock, it may also represent a play on δεινός, 'wondrous, marvelous',[5] that is, 'precious'.

1. See Chapter 4.
2. From צור. So BDB, p. 849; KB, p. 799; *HALAT*, III, pp. 952-53.
3. See BDB, p. 131; KB, p. 142; *HALAT*, I, p. 142; *HAHAT*[18], p. 167.
4. LSJ, pp. 431-32, s.v. δίνευμα.
5. LSJ, p. 374, s.v. δεινός.

Note also the use of δῖνος for a precious item, namely, 'a jewelled goblet made of silver'.[1] It also is possible that the LXX translation understood the Hebrew as 'fortresses, enclosures'. δῖνος can be anything that is enclosed and rounded, and this is the root meaning of בצר.[2] As for the Targum, there is no doubt that its writers understood the Hebrew as 'rock', since they translate with בטינרין, 'in the rock, flint'.[3] The Vulgate also saw בצרות as 'in the rock', as it rendered *in petris*.[4] That the LXX alludes to the root בצר as 'fortress'[5] is supported by at least one tradition, namely that which is preserved in the Peshitta's use of בחוסנה, 'in a fortress'.[6] This suggests that at least one source understood the *beth* in בצר (translated as 'fortress') as part of the root.

Though the medieval commentators I examined translated בצרות as 'in the rock', it is important to all of them that each found it necessary to clarify the reading, suggesting the presence of an element of ambiguity. With the exception of Tur-Sinai, who included the second meaning here by translating the stich 'He broke through to the *treasure* of the rivers',[7] modern translators opt for the reading 'in the rock'.[8]

The Hymn to Wisdom again shows an interest in references, this time responding to Eliphaz in 22.24-26a, where we read: 'If you regard precious ore (בצר) as dirt, Ophir-gold as stones (בצור) from the wadi; (let) Shaddai be your precious ore (בצריך) and precious silver for you when you seek the favor of Shaddai.'[9] Job's response in the hymn compares Eliphaz's view that God is humankind's precious ore (בצר) with

1. Note that δῖνος is 'frequently... found in puns with δεινός'; LSJ, p. 432, s.v. δῖνος. For other uses of δῖνος in connection with precious metals, see *Iliad* 3.391, 13.407 and *Odyssey* 19.56.

2. BDB, pp. 130-31.

3. Jastrow, *A Dictionary of the Targumim*, p. 533; Sokoloff, *A Dictionary of Jewish Palestinian Aramaic*, p. 224.

4. *OLD*, p. 1370, s.v. *petris*.

5. See BDB, pp. 130-31; KB, p. 142; *HALAT*, I, p. 142; *HAHAT*[18], p. 167.

6. Payne Smith, *A Compendious Syriac Dictionary*, p. 152, s.v. חוסנה.

7. Italics my own; Tur-Sinai, *The Book of Job*, pp. 400-401. Cf. Job 22.24. In this he followed Yellin.

8. Driver, *Job*, I, p. 239; Dhorme, *Le Livre de Job*, p. 370; Yellin, איוב־חקרי מקרא, pp. 154-55; Pope, *Job*, pp. 197, 202; Gordis, *The Book of Job*, pp. 300, 307; Guillaume, *Studies in the Book of Job*, pp. 53, 111; Hartley, *The Book of Job*, p. 375.

9. 22.24-25 may also be a polysemous parallelism. See, for example, the use of בציר in v. 24b, which as 'in the rock' parallels עפר previous to it, and as 'precious ore' parallels אפיר in the same stich.

humankind's attempt to mine gold from the rock (בצור). Here it is humankind, not God, who 'bring[s] hidden things to light' (28.11). That Eliphaz's use of בצריך, 'your precious ore', in 22.24-26a also plays on the word צר, 'enemy', can be seen in 22.20 where Eliphaz remarks: 'Indeed, our enemies will be annihilated (נכחד).' The last time the root כחד was heard was in 20.12 where Zophar accuses Job of 'concealing' (כחד) wickedness under his tongue. This sets up Eliphaz for his additional pun on צר, 'enemy', in 22.24, which 'conceals' the 'enemy' (צר) under his tongue by use of בצריך, 'your precious ore'. This also might explain why קימנו, 'our enemies', parallels יתרם, 'their wealth', in 22.24. Finally, Elihu joins the word-play fray by using בצר antanaclastically in 36.19 as 'profit', undoubtedly in an attempt to outwit its previous users.

Job 29.18-19

ואמר עם קני אגוע
וכחול ארבה ימים
שרשי פתוח אלי מים
וטל ילין בקצירי

I thought I would end my days with my nest. And be as long lived as חול.
My roots reaching water, and dew lying on my branches.

These lines are a famous *crux interpretum*. Part of the difficulty lies in the ambiguous use of חול, normally 'sand, coast',[1] but here also the mythological bird 'Phoenix'.[2] Also ambiguous is קני, either literally 'my nest' or metaphorically 'my family' (cf. Hab. 2.9 where it parallels בית, 'dynasty', and Isa. 16.2 where it is used figuratively for בנות מואב).[3] The ambiguous context and parallelism have led scholars to debate the priority of one or the other renderings. Yet it is precisely with this ambiguity that the poet charges his lines.[4] As the Janus examples above

1. So BDB, pp. 296-97.

2. So KB, p. 282; *HALAT*, I, 285. See also M. Dahood, 'HÔL "Phoenix" in Job 29.18 and in Ugaritic', *CBQ* 36 (1974), pp. 85-88. For an excellent bibliography on the word חול, see A.R. Ceresko, *Job 29–31 in the Light of Northwest Semitic: A Translation and Philological Commentary* (Rome: Biblical Institute Press, 1980), p. 22 n. 89.

3. BDB, p. 890; KB, p. 842; *HALAT*, III, p. 1036. So also the Targum; Yellin, איוב-חקרי מקרא, p. 156; Hartley, *The Book of Job*, p. 392 n. 1.

4. Note also that this pericope is called a משל in 29.1. As D. Stern has shown, word-play is quite common to the משל. See his *Parables in Midrash: Narrative and Exegesis in Rabbinic Literature* (Cambridge, MA: Harvard University Press, 1991),

demonstrate, such ambiguity is part of the telling, and so it is with Job 29.18-19.[1] As 'sand', the first stich in v. 18 parallels the mention of מים, 'water', and as 'Phoenix', it echoes קני in the previous stich as 'my nest'. The former parallel is buttressed by the common expression חול ימים, for example in Job 6.3; Ps. 78.27; and Jer. 15.8. The latter, though it cannot be demonstrated on the basis of a *hapax*, nonetheless seems obvious if the meaning 'Phoenix' is permitted. In addition, it is clear from extra-biblical sources that the Phoenix was a favorite subject for classical Greek and Latin punsters as well.[2] The words are etymologically similar (both derive from *ḥwl*), suggesting that the pun is both oral and visual as well as symmetrical.

The LXX conflates חול and קני by rendering with στέλεχος φοίνικος, 'the stem of a palm tree'.[3] While most who have commented on this rendering have noted the relationship between palm trees and the Phoenix and how the Vulgate adopted this reading (*palma*), only Pope[4] has seen it as an 'oblique' reference to φοῖνιξ, 'Phoenix'.[5] Does the fact that φοῖνιξ also means 'Phoenician(s)',[6] a 'coastal' people, suggest an attempt to catch the other meaning of 'sand, coast'? Note here also that ῥίζα translates well the Hebrew שרש[7] both as 'root' and as 'family'.[8] The Targum preserves the Janus on 'sand/phoenix' by rendering with חלא,[9] and perhaps also the pun on שרש with בית.[10] The Vulgate, as mentioned above, agrees with the LXX in rendering *palma*, 'palm tree',[11] and for קני and שרש it uses *nidulo*, 'nest', and *radix*, 'root'.[12] It is unclear whether the Syriac preserves the pun on the two meanings of חול, though it translates like the Targum, חלא.[13] For קני and שרש the

pp. 41, 44, 71, 73, 74, 59, 92, 111, 141, 146, 149, 155-56, 170-71, 181, 217.

1. What has not been noted in this passage is the presence of another polysemous word, namely שרש, 'root', but also 'kin'.
2. See Ahl, *Metaformations*, pp. 120-23.
3. LSJ, pp. 1637, 1947-48, s.v. στέλεχος, φοίνικος.
4. Pope, *Job*, pp. 214-16.
5. LSJ, p. 1948, s.v. φοῖνιξ.
6. LSJ, p. 1947, s.v. φονίκιας.
7. See BDB, p. 1057; KB, p. 1012; *HALAT*, IV, pp. 1530-32.
8. LSJ, p. 1570.
9. Jastrow, *A Dictionary of the Targumim*, pp. 433, 463.
10. Note that Moshe Qimhi regards קני as בני ובנותי.
11. *OLD*, p. 1286, s.v. *palma*.
12. *OLD*, pp. 1176, 1571, s.v. *nīdulus*, *rādix*.
13. Payne Smith, *A Compendious Syriac Dictionary*, p. 142, s.v. חלא.

Peshitta gives קנינא, 'reed item (i.e., nest)', and שרש, 'root'.[1]

The rabbis were aware that חול bore the meaning 'Phoenix' as well (it is attested in *Ber. R.* 19.9), and Rashi and Minḥat Shai translated Job 29.18 in this way.[2] Modern commentators typify the current attitude toward polysemy by choosing an 'either/or' policy when translating, that is, rendering with *either* 'sand' *or* 'Phoenix'. In the 'sand' camp are Driver, Dhorme, Pope, Tur-Sinai, and Hartley,[3] while in the 'Phoenix' camp are Gordis, Guillaume, Ceresko, and Grabbe.[4] By contrast, Yellin astutely remarks that 'in this word is a twofold meaning'.[5]

The last time we encountered the expression חול ימים was in 6.3 in the mouth of Job, who used it as a metaphor to describe the heaviness of his vexation (כעש). Job's use of it in 29.18 to express his hope for a long life, therefore, conjures the contrast between his hope and the vexation of his present situation. In addition, Job prefaces the contrast with ואמר עם קני אגוע, 'I had said, "I would end (my days) with my family".' The root גוע occurs previously only in the remarks of Job (3.11; 13.19; 14.10; and 27.5), suggesting a development of thought within the larger context of dialogue and debate. Closest to his statement in 29.18 is 14.7-11:

> There is hope for a tree; if it is cut down it will renew itself (יחליף); its shoots will not cease. If its roots (שרשו) are old in the earth, and its stump dies in the ground, at the scent of water (מים) it will bud and produce branches (קציר) like a sapling. But mortals languish and die; man expires (יגוע), where is he? The waters (מים) of the sea (ים) fail, and the river dries up and is parched.

Several lexical nexuses, noted in the parentheses above, bind the discourse in 14.7-11 with that in 29.18-20. Indeed, the contexts of the two passages are extremely similar, comparing humankind's time on earth to a plant. The difference between the two is one of time and specificity; that is, in 14.7-11 Job speaks generally of the fate which approaches all

1. Payne Smith, *A Compendious Syriac Dictionary*, p. 599. It is not certain whether חלא and שרש are polysemous in Syriac.

2. Ibn Ezra is strangely silent here.

3. Driver, *Job*, I, pp. 249-50; II, pp. 201-204; Dhorme, *Le Livre de Job*, pp. 389-90; Pope, *Job*, pp. 208, 213-16; Tur-Sinai, *The Book of Job*, pp. 415-16; Hartley, *The Book of Job*, pp. 392-93 n. 3.

4. Gordis, *The Book of Job*, pp. 314, 321-22; Guillaume, *Studies in the Book of Job*, pp. 54, 112; Ceresko, *Job 29–31 in the Light of Northwest Semitic*, pp. 6, 22-26; Grabbe, *Comparative Philology and the Text of Job*, pp. 98-101.

5. Yellin, איוב-חקרי מקרא, p. 268 (my translation).

humankind, whereas in 29.18-20 he speaks specifically of his former situation before the calamity befell him.

Job 29.20-23

כבודי חדש עמדי
וקשתי בידי תחליף
לי שמעו ויחלו
וידמו למו עצתי
אחרי דברי לא ישנו
ועלימו תטף מלתי
ויחלו כמטר לי
ופיהם פערו למלקוש

My vigor refreshed, my bow תחליף in my hand.
Men would listen to me and יחלו. At my counsel they would ידמו.
After I spoke they did not ישנו. My words תטף upon them.
They waited for me as for rain, for the late rain, their mouths open wide.

In Job 29.20-23 lie some of the most exquisite examples of polysemy in the entire Bible. No less than five polysemous words are present, forming what only can be described as a Janus cluster.[1] The polysemous roots involved are חלף, 'renew' (*ḥlp*) or 'pierce' (*ḥlp*)[2] (the root חלף means 'pierce' in Judg. 5.26; Job 20.24); יחל/חלל, 'pierce' or 'wait';[3] דמם/דמה, 'wait, cease' (from דמה)[4] or 'be silent' (from דמם);[5] שנן/שנה, 'reply' or 'sharpen (words)' (note that in Prov. 25.18 the root שנן occurs in connection with speaking 'sharp' words);[6] and נטף, 'argue against' or 'dew upon'.[7] The effect is one of unfolding and multiplying

1. For the phenomenon of literary clustering see J.C. Greenfield, 'The Cluster in Biblical Poetry', *maarav* 55–56 (1990), pp. 159-68.

2. BDB, p. 322; KB, p. 304; *HALAT*, I, p. 308.

3. It is posited here that in the consonantal text ויחלו can be read as if derived from either root. Note a similar play in Judg. 3.25 with ויחילו, which is pointed as if it were a *hiphil* from either חלל, 'pierce', or חול, 'writhe', though the context suggests a derivation from יחל, 'wait'. I thank Prof. G. Rendsburg for this observation.

4. BDB, p. 198; KB, pp. 213-14; *HALAT*, I, pp. 208, 216.

5. As with ויחלו, וידמו may be read as derived from either root; BDB, pp. 198-99; KB, pp. 213-14; *HALAT*, I, pp. 216-17. For a discussion on the relationship between these roots see J. Blau, 'Über Homonyme und Angeblich Homonyme Wurzeln', *VT* 6 (1956), pp. 242-48.

6. Another pair of roots with a similar semantic development is חדד/חדה.

7. For a similar use of water as a metaphor for speaking see the root דלף in Prov. 19.13.

interpretation, with each of the stichs both echoing one of the previous stich's meanings and anticipating one of the following stich's meanings. For example, a schematic translation of vv. 20-23 might read:

> My vigor refreshed, my bow (ever new)/(made to pierce by) in my hand,
> Men would listen to me, but (pierce)/(and wait), and they would (wait for)/(be silent at) my counsel.
> After I spoke, they would not (reply)/(sharpen [their words]), my words would (argue against them)/(dew upon them),
> They waited for me as for rain...

That this Janus string follows upon the heels of the previous example is a testament to the craft of the poet. As for the root חלף, the LXX's πορεύεται and Vulgate's *instaurabitur* reflect the meanings 'pass by, renew'.[1] The Targum's משתלחפא and Peshitta's אתלחף, however, may be attempts to preserve the pun by using cognates which contain both the accepted meanings.[2] Saʿadiah Gaʾon, Rashi, Y. Altschuler's *Metsudat David*, and Ralbag all see in חלף only the meaning 'renew'. Interestingly, Ibn Ezra, on the other hand, keenly remarks: יש אמרים בידי תחליף לא תכר' בכח ידי, 'some say...that by my hand you will be pierced, but not cut by the strength of my hand'. Moderns invariably miss the pun on 'pierce' here.[3] Similar are the remarks of Moshe Qimḥi: ותכרית אותם אם לא היו מכברים אותי, 'you will cut them if they do not make me mighty'.

As for ויחלו, the LXX renders with προσέσχον, 'gave heed';[4] the Targum with ואוריכו, 'waited';[5] the Vulgate with *expectebant*, 'waited';[6]

1. LSJ, p. 1449, s.v. πορευμα; *OLD*, p. 928, s.v. *instaurātiō*. So also BDB, p. 322; KB, p. 304; *HALAT*, I, p. 308.

2. From חלף; *DISO*, p. 89; Jastrow, *A Dictionary of the Targumim*, p. 471; Beyer, *Die aramäischen Texte vom Toten Meer*, p. 580; Sokoloff, *A Dictionary of Jewish Palestinian Aramaic*, pp. 203-204; Payne Smith, *A Compendious Syriac Dictionary*, p. 144.

3. Pope, *Job*, p. 208; Gordis, *The Book of Job*, pp. 315-16; Tur-Sinai, *The Book of Job*, p. 417; Guillaume, *Studies in the Book of Job*, pp. 54-55; Hartley, *The Book of Job*, p. 392.

4. LSJ, p. 1512, s.v. προσέχεια.

5. From ארך; *DISO*, pp. 24-25; Jastrow, *A Dictionary of the Targumim*, p. 119; Beyer, *Die aramäischen Texte vom Toten Meer*, pp. 522-23; Sokoloff, *A Dictionary of Jewish Palestinian Aramaic*, p. 75. So also BDB, p. 403; KB, pp. 377-78; *HALAT*, III, p. 389.

6. *OLD*, p. 656, s.v. *expecteō*.

and the Syriac with סברו, 'waited, hoped'.[1] The medievals who comment take ויחלו similarly as 'waited', as do the modern exegetes.[2] Despite the lack of support from the various versions, it is clear that if derived as a *qal* third-person masculine plural form of the geminate root חלל (to be vocalized יָחֹלּוּ), we also may read 'they pierced'. Note also that the *pual* and *polel* of this root are used of piercing the primordial serpent in Ezek. 32.26 and Job 26.13. A relationship between the roots יחל/חול/חלל can be seen best in Ps. 37.7, where התחולל, 'waiting', occurs in parallelism with דום, 'be silent'.

The majority of versions treat the expression וידמו, 'and they waited' or 'were silent', as if derived from דמם, 'be silent'.[3] The LXX renders with ἐσιώπησαν,[4] the Targum with ושתיקו, the Vulgate with *tacebant*, and the Peshitta with ושמעו, all of which basically mean 'be silent'.[5] The sages who comment on the word (Moshe Qimḥi, Y. Altschuler's *Metsudat David* and *Metsudat Zion*, and Ralbag), also see וידמו as 'be silent', as do the verse's modern interpreters.[6] Yet it seems likely that we may read the vocable as 'waited' in the light of the common use of דמם as 'be still', in Josh. 10.12 (said of the sun), in 1 Sam. 14.9 (said of soldiers), and in Jer. 47.6 (said of a sword [!]). The by-form דמה also carries connotations of stillness as it means 'cease, cause to cease, cut off'; see for example Jer. 14.17 and Lam. 3.49.

1. Payne Smith, *A Compendious Syriac Dictionary*, p. 359, s.v. סבר.

2. Driver, *Job*, I, p. 250; II, p. 205; Dhorme, *Le Livre de Job*, p. 384; Pope, *Job*, p. 207; Gordis, *The Book of Job*, pp. 315-16, 322; Tur-Sinai, *The Book of Job*, p. 417; Guillaume, *Studies in the Book of Job*, pp. 54-55; Ceresko, *Job 29–31 in the Light of Northwest Semitic*, pp. 6, 28; Hartley, *The Book of Job*, p. 393.

3. So also BDB, p. 198; KB, p. 214; *HALAT*, I, p. 217.

4. LSJ, p. 1603, s.v. σιωπάω.

5. From שתק; *DISO*, p. 322; Jastrow, *A Dictionary of the Targumim*, p. 1640; Sokoloff, *A Dictionary of Jewish Palestinian Aramaic*, p. 569; *OLD*, p. 1899, s.v. *taceō*; Payne Smith, *A Compendious Syriac Dictionary*, pp. 584-85, s.v. שמע. The Syriac may be settling for a compromise with ושמעו, which leans toward 'wait', but this is only conjecture. It is interesting to note that the Peshitta practices lexical leveling, translating חדל, שפט, שאנן, and שלה as 'be silent', but not ידמו here. See, for example, H.M. Szpek, *Translation Technique in the Peshitta to Job: A Model for Evaluating a Text with Documentation from the Peshitta to Job* (SBLDS, 137; Atlanta: Scholars Press, 1992), p. 299.

6. Driver, *Job*, I, p. 250; II, p. 205; Dhorme, *Le Livre de Job*, p. 384; Pope, *Job*, p. 207; Gordis, *The Book of Job*, pp. 315-16, 322; Tur-Sinai, *The Book of Job*, p. 417; Guillaume, *Studies in the Book of Job*, pp. 54-55; Ceresko, *Job 29–31 in the Light of Northwest Semitic*, pp. 6, 28; Hartley, *The Book of Job*, p. 393.

Most of the versions treat the polysemous phrase לא ישנו, 'did not reply' or 'did not sharpen (their words)', as if based on שנה.[1] However, we also may read it as if derived from שנן, 'sharpen'.[2] Note that the two roots are confused in the famous verse Deut. 6.7.[3] The LXX renders with οὐ προσέθεντο, 'did not speak again',[4] and the Vulgate with *addere nihil*, 'adding nothing'.[5] The Targum, however, may preserve the pun, again by using a cognate: לא יתנון.[6] One may only hazard a guess as to why the Syriac translates with לא טעו, 'they did not stray' or 'forget'.[7] Ibn Ezra, Y. Altschuler's *Metsudat David* and *Metsudat Zion*, and Ralbag all treat ישנו as a derivative of the root שנה,[8] as do most of the moderns.[9] Moshe Qimḥi, however, notes that such a reading is problematic, for 'it is not correct to derive ישנו from שנית because he who responds is not called שונה until he has spoken once afterwards'. Interestingly, Tur-Sinai suggests the possibility of revocalizing to יְשַׁנּוּ, '(they do not) alter',[10] also derived from שנה, without considering the possibility of the geminate here.

The verb נטף has been a source of unnecessary consternation to scholars. Its commonest meaning is to 'dew upon' (cf. Job 36.27),[11] and it is this meaning which underlies the translations of the Vulgate: *stillabat*, 'dropped (upon)', and the Peshitta: בסמת מלתי, 'my words were pleasant (lit. fragrant)'.[12] The LXX and Targum, on the other hand, perhaps attempt compromise translations, using περιχαρεῖς δὲ ἐγίνοντο ὁπόταν αὐτοῖς ἐλάλουν, 'and they were glad whenever I spoke to

1. So also BDB, p. 1040; KB, p. 996; *HALAT*, IV, p. 1477.
2. See BDB, pp. 1041-42; KB, p. 998; *HALAT*, IV, pp. 1483-84.
3. See KB, pp. 998-99; *HALAT*, IV, p. 1484.
4. LSJ, p. 1507, s.v. πρόσειμι.
5. *OLD*, pp. 36-37, s.v. *addō*.
6. From תנה; *DISO*, pp. 312-14, 331; Jastrow, *A Dictionary of the Targumim*, pp. 1681-82; Beyer, *Die aramäischen Texte vom Toten Meer*, p. 725; Sokoloff, *A Dictionary of Jewish Palestinian Aramaic*, pp. 585-86.
7. Payne Smith, *A Compendious Syriac Dictionary*, pp. 177-78, s.v. טעא.
8. Rashi is silent on ישנו.
9. Driver, *Job*, I, p. 250; Dhorme, *Le Livre de Job*, p. 384; Pope, *Job*, p. 207; Gordis, *The Book of Job*, pp. 315-16; Guillaume, *Studies in the Book of Job*, pp. 54-55; Ceresko, *Job 29–31 in the Light of Northwest Semitic*, p. 6; Hartley, *The Book of Job*, p. 394.
10. Tur-Sinai, *The Book of Job*, p. 417. Cf. Ps. 89.35.
11. So BDB, pp. 642-43; KB, p. 613; *HALAT*, III, p. 656.
12. *OLD*, p. 1820, s.v. *stillō*; Payne Smith, *A Compendious Syriac Dictionary*, p. 49, s.v. בסם.

them', and תשפר, 'were good, cleansed, conciliated'.[1] Most of the rabbis saw in תטף a metaphorical usage for speaking; however, Rashi, Moshe Qimḥi, and the commentary *Metsudat Zion* offer prooftexts (Deut. 32.2; Amos 7.16, also with על; Mic. 2.6) supporting נטף as 'prophesy, argue against'. This seems to have escaped the moderns, who translate 'dropped' or the like.[2]

In sum, the poet demonstrates a talent for polysemy in this pericope in the sequential twisting of semantic ranges. Moreover, it should be added here that while the poet exploits the lexemes דמה, שנה, חלל, חלף, and קשת for their suggestiveness of cutting or piercing, the roots נטף, חלף, חדש, and קשת also allude to rain.[3] This, coupled with the metaphoric use of some of the above for speech (for example, מלתי, תטף, שנה, דבר, עצתי, דמם, חלל, and יחל), bespeaks the sophistication with which the Jobian poet approached his composition. Regarding the categorization of the polysemes involved in this word-play cluster, דמם and נטף are oral, visual, symmetrical, and semantic, whereas חלף, יחל and שנה are strictly visual and symmetrical.

I can also demonstrate the referential aspect of polysemous parallelism for this passage. Note that the last time the root חלף appeared in conjunction with קשת was in Zophar's remark in Job 20.24, תחלפהו קשת נחושה, where חלף means 'pierce'.[4] Thus, the reader anticipates this meaning and is taken off guard by the ambiguity in 29.20. The connection of this pericope with that in 14.7-11 has been discussed above. We may add to these observations that the use of חלף in 14.7 is also somewhat ambiguous as it follows כרת, 'cut', and precedes חדל, 'cease'.[5] There also may be here a subtle allusion to 10.17: 'You renew (חדש) your witnesses against me, letting your vexation (כעש) with me

1. LSJ, pp. 1033-34, 1978-79, s.v. λέγω, χάρις; and Aramaic שפר. See *DISO*, p. 317; Jastrow, *A Dictionary of the Targumim*, p. 1619; Beyer, *Die aramäischen Texte vom Toten Meer*, pp. 717-18; Sokoloff, *A Dictionary of Jewish Palestinian Aramaic*, p. 564.

2. Driver, *Job*, I, p. 250; Dhorme, *Le Livre de Job*, p. 384; Pope, *Job*, p. 207; Gordis, *The Book of Job*, pp. 315-16, 322; Tur-Sinai, *The Book of Job*, p. 417; Guillaume, *Studies in the Book of Job*, p. 55; Ceresko, *Job 29–31 in the Light of Northwest Semitic*, p. 6; Hartley, *The Book of Job*, p. 394.

3. For the meaning of this expression see Sh. Paul, 'A Technical Expression from Archery in Zechariah IX 13a', *VT* 39 (1989), pp. 495-97.

4. This may be Zophar's way of punning on Job's use of חלף as 'pass away' in 14.7.

5. It occurs in an antanaclastic relationship with חלף, 'pass through', in 14.14.

grow. Passings (חליפות) and toil are with me.'

The roots יחל/חלל also are employed referentially. In 26.13 Job remarks about the chaotic serpent: חללה ידו נחש בריח, 'his hand pierced the evil serpent', itself an antanaclastic play on הרפאים יחוללו, 'the shades tremble', in 26.5. In 15.7 it means 'bear young' and in 27.5 it is used for 'forbidden'. יחלו in 29.21, therefore, is a flexible lexeme and conjures several associations, of which two are applicable by context.

As for וידמו, Job made a similar play in 16.17-18: 'let not the earth cover my blood' or 'wailing' (דמי). Here the semantic range of דמם/דמה serves to contrast Job's former condition when his friends 'listened and were silent at his counsel' (29.21) with his current state in which his friends wail on him with their accusations. Several times Job has recommended that his friends shut their mouths (for example, 16.5; 21.5), and at this point Job subtly reminds them again.[1] Compare, for instance, 16.10: פערו עלי בפיהם, 'men gape at me with open mouths', with what follows the Janus word וידמו in 29.23: ופיהם פערו למלקוש, 'and their mouths gape as if for the latter rains'.

That 29.20-23 refers to ch. 16 also can be demonstrated for the polyseme ישנו. Though its use in 29.22 in connection with words immediately suggests the idea of 'repeating', it is reminiscent of Job's bitter testimony in 16.9: אפו טרף וישטמני הרק עלי בשניו צרי ילטוש עיניו לי, 'In his anger he tears and persecutes me; he gnashes his teeth at me; my foe stabs me with his eyes'.[2] Here the root שנן in the form of 'gnashing teeth' parallels both ילטוש, 'stab', and טרף, 'tear'. The relationship between the two pericopes is confirmed by remembering that Eliphaz already equated 'sharpness' and 'speech' in 5.15: וישע מחרב מפיהם, 'and he saves (the just) from the sword of their mouths'.

Rain and dew have been the subject of several discourses already; for example, 20.23, 28.26, and 29.19. We also have dealt with the association of this section with ch. 16. Regarding תטף we may add that, as in the two polysemes discussed above (בלחומו 20.23, ממררתו 20.25) in relation to a concealed reference to rain in 16.12-13, 'sharpness' and 'rain' also intertwine here. Note that חרק עלי בשניו, 'he gnashes his teeth at me', and צרי ילטוש עיניו לי, 'my foe stabs me with his eyes', in 16.9 come just prior to Job's lament 'He has set me up as his target' or 'rain' (מטרה); 'his bowmen' or 'copious rains (רביו) surrounded me'

1. Might this be a reaction to Zophar's claims that God shuts the mouths of the wicked (5.16)?

2. There may be a play on צר, 'flint', as well.

(16.12-13). The common denominator semantically speaking is probably the tongue (לשון), which is used both for 'speaking' and for 'spears' (see for example Hos. 7.16).

These chapters (29–31) comprise Job's soliloquy, that is, his last full-length speech and last-ditch effort to save face; and this explains the abundance of polysemous clustering here. The frustration, uncertainty, and desperation which Job feels while speaking with his friends are underscored by the allusiveness of his language.

Job 30.3

בחסר ובכפן גלמוד
הערקים ציה
אמש שואה ומשאה

Wasted from want and starvation, they ערצים a parched land.
Wandering to a land dismal and desolate.

The poet again turns a phrase in Job 30.3 with his use of the verb ערק. The verb usually means 'gnaw'[1] (*ʿrq*), and is found as such in Arabic, and possibly in Job 30.17.[2] However, ערק can also mean 'flee' (*ʿrḍ*), as it does in Aramaic, Syriac, and at Deir ʿAlla.[3] Given the use of Aramaic and/or an Aramaic-like dialect in Job, one should not be surprised to find such a usage. I aver that both meanings are utilized here: as 'gnawing at dry ground', the stich parallels the previous stich's בחסר ובכפן גלמוד, 'wasted from want and starvation', and as 'fleeing to dry ground', the stich anticipates אמש שואה ומשאה, 'wandering[4] to a land dismal and desolate', which follows. Job 30.3, therefore, is a strictly visual and symmetrical polysemous parallel.

Support for both readings comes from the versions.[5] Though the LXX

1. So BDB, p. 792; KB, p. 739; *HALAT*, III, p. 841.

2. Wehr, *A Dictionary of Modern Written Arabic*, p. 607. See also M. Dietrich, O. Loretz, and J. Sanmartín, 'Zur Ugaritischen Lexikographie (VII)', *UF* 5 (1973), p. 107.

3. Jastrow, *A Dictionary of the Targumim*, p. 1123; Payne Smith, *A Compendious Syriac Dictionary*, p. 429. See also J.C. Greenfield, 'Philological Observations on the Deir ʿAlla Inscription', in J.J. Hoftijzer and G. van der Kooij (eds.), *The Balaam Text from Deir ʿAlla Re-Evaluated* (Leiden: Brill, 1991), p. 113; G. Rendsburg, 'The Dialect of the Deir ʿAlla Inscription', *Bibliotheca Orientalis* 3.4 (1993), pp. 309-30.

4. I derive אמש from the root מוש.

5. The Peshiṭta lacks this verse.

translates הערקים as οἱ φεύγοντες, 'they who fled',[1] after v. 4 it also adds οἳ καὶ ῥίζας ξύλων ἐμασσῶντο ὑπὸ λιμοῦ μεγάλου, 'who also ate roots of trees by reason of great hunger'.[2] Might this seemingly superfluous addition represent an attempt by the LXX translators to clue the reader in to the other meaning of the verb ערק? The Targum renders with a cognate (ערקין), but the meaning 'gnawing' is unattested in Aramaic.[3] The Vulgate, on the other hand, renders *rodebant*, 'they gnawed'.[4] Though fragmentary, the Qumran Targum also reflects a reading 'they gnawed'.[5] The division between the versions suggests that both meanings are entirely appropriate.

While medieval commentators saw הערקים as 'they flee', the modern opinion is as divided as the versions. Gordis, Tur-Sinai, and Hartley read 'flee',[6] whereas Driver, Dhorme, Pope, Guillaume, and Ceresko render 'gnaw'.[7]

Job's words in 30.3 recall his earlier statement in 24.5-12 in which he described the oppressed as wild asses in the desert who go out (יצאו) in search of food (לטרף) in the steppe. That both 'eating' and 'searching' (i.e., both meanings suggested by ערקים) are conveyed prepares the reader for both in 30.3 when waste, want, and starvation are mentioned. Moreover, Eliphaz recently used גלמוד to parallel ואש אכלה, 'a fire which devours', in 15.34, hence the expectation in 30.3 of mention of 'devouring'.[8]

1. LSJ, pp. 1924-25, s.v. φεύγω.
2. LSJ, p. 1051, s.v. λιμός.
3. *DISO*, pp. 222, 216; Jastrow, *A Dictionary of the Targumim*, p. 1123; Beyer, *Die aramäischen Texte vom Toten Meer*, p. 665; Sokoloff, *A Dictionary of Jewish Palestinian Aramaic*, pp. 420-21.
4. *OLD*, p. 1659, s.v. *rōdō*.
5. Noted by Pope, *Job*, p. 219. This is absent in Sokoloff, *The Targum to Job from Qumran Cave XI*.
6. Gordis, *The Book of Job*, pp. 326, 330; Tur-Sinai, *The Book of Job*, p. 420. Hartley (*The Book of Job*, p. 396 n. 2) incorrectly notes that if we were to read 'gnaw' we would be bereft of an object. Why not regard ציה as an object? In support of his claim he quotes Targum fragment from Qumran: 'In their hunger their desire was the vegetation of the desert.' It is important to remember that the Targum often fills gaps like this, i.e., to render *ad sensum*.
7. Driver, *Job*, I, p. 252; II, p. 208; Dhorme, *Le Livre de Job*, p. 93; Pope, *Job*, pp. 217, 219; Guillaume, *Studies in the Book of Job*, pp. 55, 113; Ceresko, *Job 29–31 in the Light of Northwest Semitic*, pp. 33, 47-48.
8. The poet again uses ערק antanaclastically as 'sinews' in 30.17b.

Job 30.5-6

מן גו יגרשו
יריעו עלימו כגנב
בערוץ נחלים לשכן
חרי עפר וכפים

Driven out from the midst, they are cried at like a thief.
They live בערוץ of the wadis, in holes of the ground, and in rocks.

The word בערוץ in Job 30.6, if taken from the root *ʿrḍ* (known to Arabic), means 'in the gully';[1] if derived from *ʿrṣ*, it means 'in terror'.[2] Both meanings are present here; the former as a parallel to חרי עפר וכפים, 'in holes in the ground, and in rocks', and the latter as a parallel to the expression יריעו עלימו כגנב, 'they shout out at him like a thief'. Confirming the former parallel is a similar connection between *ʿrṣ*, 'terror', and the noun עפר in Isa. 2.19 which may conceal a similar pun.[3] Support for the latter parallel comes from Isa. 15.4 in which we find the form ירעו meaning 'tremble'. This Isaiah passage points to a similarity in semantic ranges between the roots ירע and ערץ as 'terror'. The difference in pronunciation between the two lexemes involved in the polysemy groups Job 30.5-6 with the strictly visual and symmetrical Janus parallels.

The LXX presents something of a problem as it appears to diverge greatly from the MT: it makes no mention of 'terror' or of 'shouting'. There may be conflation here between v. 6a and v. 6b. Whatever the explanation, it is clear that the LXX does not read 'terror' for בערוץ, but rather 'caves of the rocks' (τρῶγλαι πετρῶν).[4] It is a curiosity that the LXX renders יריעו עלימו כגנב in v. 5b as ἐπανέστησάν μοι κλέπται, 'thieves have risen up against me'. The Greek (ἐπαν-στασις) can mean both 'uprising', i.e., 'a terror', and 'a rise in rhetorical tone', i.e., 'shouting'(?).[5] Did the LXX use a different word in the previous stich to convey both meanings implied in בערוץ? The Targum's בתקוף פצידי נחליא, 'in the protection (stronghold) of the gullies' or 'under the attack of the strongmen of the wadi' (i.e., a terror),[6] is as ambiguous as the Hebrew

1. So KB, p. 735; *HALAT*, III, p. 836.
2. So BDB, p. 792.
3. Note that the verse also contains מערות צרים, 'caves of the rocks'.
4. LSJ, pp. 1397, 1831, s.v. πειρα, τρώγλη.
5. LSJ, p. 608, s.v. ἐπανίστημι.
6. From פצד, תקף; *DISO*, p. 333; Jastrow, *A Dictionary of the Targumim*,

original, perhaps suggesting an attempt to preserve the pun. Similarly ambiguous is the Peshitta's use of בעושנא דרגלתא, either 'a foot soldier in a surging torrent' or 'with the strength (fierceness, i.e., terror) of a foot soldier'.[1] Of the versions, only the Vulgate renders explicitly: *torrentium*, 'channels',[2] though perhaps with an eye toward a play on *territum*, 'terror'.

Rashi, Y. Altschuler's *Metsudat David*, and Ralbag translate as 'gullies', while Ibn Ezra, Moshe Qimḥi, and Y. Altschuler's other commentary, *Metsudat Zion*, give both interpretations. In the succinct words of Ibn Ezra the word may be defined as meaning 'in *a place* to which man *feared* to descend'.[3] Of the modern commentators,[4] only Driver, Dhorme, and Ceresko render בערוץ as if derived from *ʿrḍ*: 'in the most dreaded of ravines to dwell'.[5]

Up to this point the poet of Job has employed the consonants ערץ only as 'terror' (see for example 13.25; 15.20; 27.13). Therefore, the expected meaning which Job plays upon here is 'terror, oppression'. That all the references occur within the context of the fate of the evildoer strengthens their interrelatedness. Of the passages listed above, Job's previous harangue in 27.13 appears to be the source of his complaint: זה חלק אדם רשע עם אל ונחלת עריצים משדי יקחו, 'This is the evil man's portion from God; the lot that the oppressors receive from Shaddai'. Note how נחלת, 'portion', also echoes in 30.6 in נחלים, 'wadis'.

pp. 1204-1205, 1690; Beyer, *Die aramäischen Texte vom Toten Meer*, pp. 726-27; Sokoloff, *A Dictionary of Jewish Palestinian Aramaic*, p. 590.

1. Payne Smith, *A Compendious Syriac Dictionary*, pp. 408, 528, s.v. רגלתא, עושנא. Note that the Peshitta's use of the verb נבע, 'spring up, flow, burst forth', in the first stich also may suggest the notion of a gully. See Payne Smith, *A Compendious Syriac Dictionary*, p. 326, s.v. נבע.

2. *OLD*, p. 1951, s.v. *torrens*.

3. Italics my own. Similar is Saʿadiah Gaʾon's translation: 'in most fearsome hollows'.

4. Pope, *Job*, pp. 217, 220; Gordis, *The Book of Job*, pp. 326, 331; Tur-Sinai, *The Book of Job*, p. 422; Guillaume, *Studies in the Book of Job*, pp. 55, 113; Hartley, *The Book of Job*, p. 397 n. 7. Note that Hartley does recognize both readings.

5. Driver, *Job*, I, p. 253; II, p. 210; Dhorme, *Le Livre de Job*, p. 395; Ceresko, *Job 29–31 in the Light of Northwest Semitic*, pp. 33, 53.

Job 30.7-8

בין שיחים ינהקו
תחת חרול יספחו
בני נבל גם בני בלי שם
נכאו מן הארץ

Braying among the bushes, among the nettles they יספחו.
Scoundrels, nobodies, stricken from the earth.

Job 30.7-8 is yet another example of a Janus construction; this time the poet utilizes the polysemy of יספחו, either 'they huddle, gather',[1] or 'they shed, pour out (blood)'.[2] If read as the former, יספחו parallels בין שיחים ינהקו, 'braying among the bushes', and as the latter, it parallels נכאו מן הארץ, 'stricken from the earth': an oral, visual, and symmetrical polysemous parallel.

Curiously, the Greek does not appear to render our stich. Instead, it jumps from v. 7a to v. 8a. Could it be because the LXX's translation of the root דכא in v. 8b, ἐσβεσμένον, acts both as 'they were stricken' and as 'they were quenched?'[3] One must similarly question the Targumist's use of מתחברין, whose root חבר, normally 'associate with (i.e., to gather)', in the *hithpael* also means 'wound'.[4] Note also that the Targum's use of the root שוף is also polysemous, meaning both 'smear over, plaster' and 'crush'.[5] Even the Vulgate, though it translates as *delicias conputabant*, 'they counted it delightful (to be under the

1. So BDB, p. 705; KB, p. 664; *HALAT*, III, p. 721.

2. The second meaning is attested in Job 14.9 (BDB, p. 705; KB, p. 664; *HALAT*, III, p. 721) and is cognate with the Arabic *safaḥa*. Cf. *Qur'an* 6.146. For a similar correspondence between the Hebrew *śin* and the Arabic *sod*, see Isa. 3.17; 5.7; J. Blau, '"Weak" Phonetic Change and the Hebrew Śîn', *HAR* 1 (1977), pp. 67-119; 'On Polyphony in Biblical Hebrew', *Proceedings of the Israel Academy of Sciences and Humanities* 6 (1983), p. 3; *On Pseudo-Corrections in Some Semitic Languages* (Jerusalem: Israel Academy of Sciences and Humanities, 1970), pp. 116, 120-21.

3. LSJ, p. 1587, s.v. σβέσνυμι.

4. *DISO*, pp. 81-82; Jastrow, *A Dictionary of the Targumim*, p. 421; Beyer, *Die aramäischen Texte vom Toten Meer*, pp. 571-72; Sokoloff, *A Dictionary of Jewish Palestinian Aramaic*, pp. 185-86.

5. Jastrow, *A Dictionary of the Targumim*, p. 1539; Beyer, *Die aramäischen Texte vom Toten Meer*, p. 704; Sokoloff, *A Dictionary of Jewish Palestinian Aramaic*, p. 541.

nettles)',[1] uses to translate 'braying among the nettles' the ambiguous *esse sub sentibus*; either 'to bray under the thornbush', or 'to (be) killed under the thornbush'.[2] The Peshitta, on the other hand, clearly reads נסתחפון, 'thrust down, ruined'.[3] Thus, while the translators of the various versions, with the exception of the Peshitta, were unable to render the pun into their target language in the same stich as the Hebrew original, they were able to do so in the prior or next stich, as a compromise of sorts.

Rashi, Ibn Ezra, Moshe Qimḥi, the commentaries *Metsudat David* and *Metsudat Zion* translate as 'gather, huddle'; only Ralbag[4] presents both possibilities, citing as prooftexts Lev. 13.2, where ספחת means 'wounds, scabies', and 1 Sam. 2.36, where ספחני, 'gather, attach', occurs. Whether translating as if the animals are doing the huddling, or as if they are braying under gathered (i.e., 'wild') bushes, the modern translators prefer the root ספח here to mean 'huddle, gather'.[5]

The root ספח also appears in Job's harsh insult in 14.19: אבנים שחקו מים תשטף ספיחיה עפר ארץ ותקות אנוש האבדת, 'water wears away stone; torrents wash away earth; so you destroy man's hope'. This insult has given Job's friends occasion to refer polysemously to it several times, as we have seen above. Now in his last full-length speech Job reminds them again of his disappointment in them. The reference to this rare lexeme allows Job to deepen his insult by correlating his friends with asses 'braying among the bushes, huddling among the nettles' (30.7).[6] Perhaps in an attempt to rehearse the pun, the author of Job further plays on the word יספחו a few lines later in 30.16: ועתה עלי תשתפך נפשי, 'now my life is poured out upon me'. Note the paronomasia between the roots שפך in 30.16 and ספח in 30.7.[7]

1. *OLD*, pp. 383, 509, s.v. *dēlicia*, *computō*.
2. *OLD*, p. 586, s.v. *edo*[1] and *edo*[2].
3. Payne Smith, *A Compendious Syriac Dictionary*, p. 372, s.v. סחף.
4. Possibly also Saʿadiah Gaʾon, who renders: 'exposed beneath the nettles'.
5. Driver, *Job*, I, p. 253; II, p. 210; Dhorme, *Le Livre de Job*, p. 396; Pope, *Job*, pp. 217, 220; Gordis, *The Book of Job*, pp. 326, 332; Tur-Sinai, *The Book of Job*, pp. 422-23; Guillaume, *Studies in the Book of Job*, pp. 55, 114; Ceresko, *Job 29–31 in the Light of Northwest Semitic*, p. 33; Hartley, *The Book of Job*, p. 397. Yellin, however, posits that we read נקאו for נכאו; איוב-חקרי מקרא, p. 157.
6. Cf. Job 6.5 where the rare root נהק, 'bray', occurs with פרא, 'wild ass'.
7. Cf. the famous play on words in Isa. 5.7: 'He waited for justice (משפט), and behold, bloodshed (משפח).'

Job 31.2-3

ומה חלק אלוה ממעל
ונחלת שדי ממרמים
הלא איד לעול
ונכר לפעלי און

What fate is decreed by God above? What lot, by Shaddai ממרמים.
Calamity is surely for the iniquitous, misfortune for the workers of mischief.

The consonants ממרמים in Job 31.2-3 may be read both as 'from the heights'[1] and as 'on account of the deceivers'.[2] The former derives from the root רום and the latter from רמה.[3] As 'from the heights', the stich mirrors ומה חלק אלוה ממעל, 'and what fate is decreed by God above' (cf. the association of רמה and מעל in Ezra 9.6; Isa. 14.3 and Dan. 12.7), and as 'on account of the deceivers', it parallels nicely הלא איד לעול, 'is not calamity for the iniquitous?', in the next stich. The former word-pair (רום/ממעל) is contextually obvious. The second (רמה/ עול) occurs in Ps. 43.1. Also, עול parallels עון in Ezek. 28.18, and עון parallels און in Hos. 12.9. This helps solidify the connection between רמה and both עול and און in Job 31.2-3. Most of the versions read 'from the heights'.[4] The Syriac, however, uses מרומא, both 'from the heights' and 'falsehood, liar'.[5] Job 31.2-3, therefore, is a strictly visual and symmetrical Janus parallel.

The medievals and moderns follow the Targum, translating 'on high', 'above' and the like.[6] Despite the lack of support from the versions and

1. From רום. So BDB, pp. 926-27; KB, pp. 879-81; *HALAT*, IV, pp. 1121-25.

2. The use of the preposition מ here for 'on account of' is common in biblical Hebrew. See for example Job 22.4; 38.19; Prov. 20.4.

3. For interplay of the roots רום and רמה see Mic. 2.3. Cf. BDB, p. 928; KB, p. 881; *HALAT*, IV, p. 1156.

4. LSJ, p. 600, s.v. ἐξυψόω; *OLD*, p. 633, s.v. *excelsus*.

5. Payne Smith, *A Compendious Syriac Dictionary*, pp. 300, 535. Actually, the Targum's מרומא also could be a pun (only aural) on רמא, 'deceiver', but the preceding שמי shows that the 'heavenly heights' are primarily intended.

6. Driver, *Job*, I, p. 263; II, p. 222; Dhorme, *Le Livre de Job*, p. 410; Pope, *Job*, pp. 225, 229; Gordis, *The Book of Job*, pp. 340, 345; Tur-Sinai, *The Book of Job*, p. 436; Guillaume, *Studies in the Book of Job*, pp. 57, 116; Ceresko, *Job 29–31 in the Light of Northwest Semitic*, pp. 100, 108-109; Hartley, *The Book of Job*, p. 409.

commentators, the consonantal text speaks for itself, and both readings are possible. Interestingly, Ceresko questions whether this verse plays on Job 27.13. in which occurs 'the wicked': זה חלק אדם רשע עם אל ונחלת עריצים משדי יקחו, 'This is the evil man's portion from God, and the lot that the ruthless receive from Shaddai'.[1] This may be the reason why polysemy comes into play here.

The expression חלק אלוה ממעל has appeared twice before in the speeches of Zophar (20.29; 27.13). In 20.29 it is parallel to ונחלת אמרו מאל, 'the inheritance of his words from God'. In 27.13 it parallels ונחלת עריצים משדי יקחו, 'the inheritance that the oppressors receive from Shaddai'. Both passages illustrate that the stich which parallels חלק אלוה ממעל is expected to deal with retribution of evil deeds/words. Thus, when Job utters the same expression, חלק אלוה ממעל, in 31.2, the natural inclination is to expect similar mention of evil people, wicked words or the like (for instance, רשעים, עריצים, or אמרו); hence, ונחלת שדי ממרמים, 'the inheritance of Shaddai on account of deceit'. Job takes great pains to make certain that his friends heard 'deceit' imbedded in his words by following up his pun with הלא איד לעול ונכר לפעלי און, 'calamity is surely for the iniquitous; misfortune for the workers of mischief'. Just in case they still did not hear his point, he asks them in 31.5: 'has my foot ever hastened to deceit (מרמה)?'

Job 31.31-32

אם לא אמרו מתי אהלי
מי יתן מבשרו לא נשבע
בחוץ לא ילין גר
דלתי לארח אפתח

Indeed, the men of my clan never said, 'Can we consume his flesh insatiably?'
(Yet) no sojourner ever ילין outside; I opened my doors to the wayfarer.

The poet again explores the duality of meaning in Job 31.31-32 with the use of the root לין/לון, 'lodge'[2] and 'murmur, complain'.[3] The pertinent stich may be translated as 'no sojourner ever lodged/complained outside'. As 'lodged' ילין parallels the use of דלתי לארח אפתח in the next stich. According to Gordis, the previous line 'the men of my clan never

1. Ceresko, *Job 29–31 in the Light of Northwest Semitic*, pp. 108-109.
2. So BDB, p. 533; KB, p. 481; *HALAT*, II, p. 503.
3. See BDB, p. 534; KB, p. 477; *HALAT*, II, pp. 498-99.

said, "Can we consume his flesh insatiably"' means that 'his servants never *complained* of lack of food'.[1] The notion of 'complaining' in v. 31 parallels perfectly the second meaning of ילין, 'murmur, complain'. Note that the roots לון as 'complain' and אמר, 'speak', are word-pairs in Exod. 15.24; 17.3; Num. 14.2; 17.6, and that in some biblical passages there is a correlation between the complaint (i.e., the root לון) and the lack of foodstuffs or satiation. For example, see Exod. 16.8 (used with אכל and שבע); Exod. 15.24 (used with שתה); and Exod. 17.3 (used with צמא). Perhaps the best prooftext to support the pairing of לון, 'complain', and שבע, 'satiate', is Ps. 59.16: המה ינועון לאכל אם לא ישבעו וילינו, 'they wander in search of food; and complain if they are not satisfied'.[2] Further reinforcement for the parallelism between לון as 'lodge' and the roots פתח and ארח in the following stich is brought out by a similar parallelism in Jer. 14.8, but also by Job 31.32: בחוץ לא ילין גר דלתי לארח אפתח 'the foreigner has not lodged in the street; I have opened my doors to the traveller'. Again, this twist of a phrase constitutes an oral, visual, and symmetrical Janus parallelism.

The LXX takes our verb as ηὐλίζετο, 'lodge'.[3] The Targum's יבית, Vulgate's *mansit*, and Peshitta's אבית suggest the same,[4] as do the medievals and moderns.[5] Nevertheless, that ילין may be read in two ways is not negated by the lack of support from the versions or commentators. The root is attested widely and acceptable, and it is surprising that it has escaped the attention of a plethora of interpreters.

This witty play on words occurs after Job first asserts: ולא נתתי לחטא חכי לשאול באלה נפשו, 'never did I let my palate sin by asking for his [Job's enemy's] life with a curse' in 31.30. Therefore, one expects to hear in the following lines a reference to speaking. It appears in the polysemous ילין, 'lodge/murmur'. That Job selects this word for its dual meaning also is suggested by his rhetorical follow-up in 31.34: ואדם לא אצא פתח,

1. Italics my own; Gordis, *The Book of Job*, p. 352.

2. See also Prov 19.23.

3. LSJ, p. 276, s.v. αὐλίζομαι.

4. *DISO*, pp. 33, 35-36; Jastrow, *A Dictionary of the Targumim*, p. 167; Beyer, *Die aramäischen Texte vom Toten Meer*, pp. 530-31; Sokoloff, *A Dictionary of Jewish Palestinian Aramaic*, pp. 88-84; *OLD*, p. 1074, s.v. *mansitō*; Payne Smith, *A Compendious Syriac Dictionary*, p. 40, s.v. בית.

5. Driver, *Job*, I, p. 271; Dhorme, *Le Livre de Job*, p. 423; Pope, *Job*, p. 227, 237; Gordis, *The Book of Job*, pp. 342, 353; Tur-Sinai, *The Book of Job*, pp. 444-45; Guillaume, *Studies in the Book of Job*, p. 58; Ceresko, *Job 29–31 in the Light of Northwest Semitic*, p. 170; Hartley, *The Book of Job*, p. 419.

'Should I keep silent and not step outdoors?' Note that both אדם, 'keep silent', and פתח, 'outdoors', refer to our Janus usage, the former suggesting 'murmur' by its association with whispering (cf. for example Job 4.16), and the latter by direct reference to דלתי לארח אפתח. Moreover, that 'murmuring' should be equated with the sin of the mouth mentioned in 31.30 can be seen by the use of לון in the story of Moses, where the murmurings of the people are treated as a sin before God (cf. for example Exod. 16.8; Num. 14.2; 17.6).

The inspiration for Job's play on the roots לין/לון in 31.31-32 may be his earlier statement and similar play on these two roots in 19.3-4: 'These ten times you have insulted me, and are not ashamed to abuse me. If indeed I have erred, my error remains (תלין) with me.' What makes the reference to Job's words in ch. 19 especially strong is his rhetorical question in 19.22: ומבשרי לא תשבעו, 'And are you not sated with my flesh?!'

Job 31.35

מי יתן לי שמע לי
הן תוי שדי יענני
וספר כתב איש ריבי

O that I had someone to give me a hearing; O that Shaddai would answer תוי. Or my accuser write up a (true) bill!

The poet again turns to dazzling his readers in Job 31.35 with his use of תוי, 'my mark'[1] and/or 'my desire'. The latter is taken to be a defective spelling for תאותי.[2] According to Gordis, this tristich has troubled commentators who have sought to emend it.[3] Nothing could be farther from necessity. Not only do nouns appear in opposite genders (for example, שמש), but metaplastic forms are well documented in the Hebrew Bible and may serve a literary purpose.[4] As 'mark' the pivotal lexeme parallels וספר כתב איש ריב, 'that my accuser would write a (true) bill'. As 'desire', it parallels the expression מי יתן לי שמע לי, 'O that I had someone to give me a hearing'. Again, we have here an oral, visual, and symmetrical polysemous parallel.

1. So BDB, p. 1063; KB, p. 1020; *HALAT*, IV, p. 1561.
2. Cf. Job 32.11 below.
3. Gordis, *The Book of Job*, p. 354.
4. More on this below. For a convenient list of metaplastic forms in Job, see Gordis, *The Book of Job*, p. 368. This observation was anticipated by C.H. Gordon, 'New Light on the Hebrew Language', *Hebrew Abstracts* 15 (1974), pp. 29-31.

Support for both readings comes from the versions and commentators. The LXX and Peshitta use συγγραφὴν, 'written charge', and איתותי, 'my letter, sign',[1] which suggest a derivation of תוי from תוה I, 'mark, sign'.[2] The Targum and Vulgate, on the other hand, translate with רגוגי and *desiderium meum*, both 'my desire',[3] hence from אוה II, 'want, desire'.

Saʿadiah Gaʾon, Rashi, Ibn Ezra,[4] and Ralbag read תוי as 'my mark, sign', whereas Moshe Qimḥi and the commentary *Metsudat David* note that both meanings are possible. Finally, Y. Altschuler's *Metsudat Zion* follows the Targum in rendering 'my desire'. Among the modern commentators, those who read תוי as 'my mark, signature' include Driver, Dhorme, Pope, Tur-Sinai, Guillaume, Ceresko, and Hartley.[5] Gordis prefers 'my desire'[6] and only Yellin allowed for both readings.[7]

This polysemous parallel follows upon a list of grievances which Job raises against his friends and against God. He claims that he has erred neither with his mouth nor in the desire of his heart. As this is Job's last polysemous statement, it connects his own accusations and those of his friends with his desire to clear himself of wrongdoing. In essence, Job's only 'desire' is that God reply to his 'writ'.

Job 32.11

הן הוחלתי לדבריכם
אזין עד תבונתיכם
עד תחקרון מלין

Here I have waited out your speeches, I have אזין your insights, while you probed the issues.

1. LSJ, p. 1661, s.v. συγγραφεύς; Payne Smith, *A Compendious Syriac Dictionary*, p. 31, s.v. אתא.
2. As such it is attested in Ezek. 9.4, 8; 1 Sam. 21.14.
3. From רגג; *DISO*, p. 274; Jastrow, *A Dictionary of the Targumim*, p. 1447; Beyer, *Die aramäischen Texte vom Toten Meer*, p. 691; *OLD*, p. 525, s.v. *dēsīderium*. However, at least one Targum manuscript translates רישומי, 'my mark, record'.
4. Ibn Ezra, however, does note the variant reading.
5. Driver, *Job*, I, p. 274; II, p. 229; Dhorme, *Le Livre de Job*, pp. 427-28; Pope, *Job*, pp. 227, 238; Tur-Sinai, *The Book of Job*, pp. 446, 448; Guillaume, *Studies in the Book of Job*, pp. 58, 116; Ceresko, *Job 29–31 in the Light of Northwest Semitic*, pp. 102, 182-84; Hartley, *The Book of Job*, p. 423.
6. Gordis, *The Book of Job*, pp. 342, 355.
7. Yellin, איוב-חקרי מקרא, p. 159.

Another Janus construction utilizing defective spelling occurs in Job 32.11. Here we encounter a tristich in which the middle stich reads: אזין עד תבונתיכם, normally translated as 'I have given ear to your insights'. The word אזין, however, is polysemous, and may be read as reflecting two different etymologies: אזן (*ʾdn*), 'give ear, listen',[1] or וזן (*wzn*), 'weigh, test'. The former parallelism between אזין and דבריכם seems clear enough to need no further comment: 'giving ear (to words)'.[2] Cementing the latter parallel is Qoh. 12.9 in which the roots וזן and חקר are in parallelism, as they are here. The poet, therefore, has cleverly disguised two words in one. The difference in pronunciation required of the renderings classifies this example as a strictly visual and symmetrical Janus parallel.

The LXX, seemingly unaware of the polysemy here, translates ἀκουόντων, 'given ear'.[3] Similarly, the Targum and Peshitta render with אצית and וצתת respectively, 'I have listened, obeyed'.[4] The Vulgate likewise translates *audivi*, 'I have listened'.[5] The rabbis translate as if it were אאזין.[6] The moderns too, prefer to ignore the possibility of אזין meaning 'weighed'.[7]

Elihu's quip is a reference to Job's question in 12.11: 'Does not the ear (אזין) test (תבחן) words, as the palate tastes (יטעם) food?' In 32.11, Elihu has played upon Job's 'ear' (אזן) by using it polysemously and by employing the verb חקר, 'probe', as a substitute for בחן, 'test'. That the

1. So BDB, p. 24; KB, p. 25; *HALAT*, I, p. 27; *HAHAT*[18], p. 30.

2. See for example 1 Sam. 20.12, where חקר as 'searched' is used in conjunction with וגליתי את אזנך, 'disclose it to you'.

3. LSJ, pp. 53-54, s.v. ἀκούω.

4. *DISO*, p. 244; Jastrow, *A Dictionary of the Targumim*, p. 1272; Beyer, *Die aramäischen Texte vom Toten Meer*, pp. 675-76; Payne Smith, *A Compendious Syriac Dictionary*, p. 477. The Syriac also adds the phrase עדמא דטלקתון, 'until you were finished'. Does this in any way reflect the notion of 'weighing' (i.e., to completion)? See Payne Smith, *A Compendious Syriac Dictionary*, pp. 175-76, s.v. טלק.

5. *OLD*, pp. 208-209, s.v. *audiō*.

6. Though Y. Altschuler in *Metsudat David* remarks: 'I have duly observed the rules of etiquette by patiently waiting for you to finish your speech *and* by listening attentively to your reasons until you search out the matter. And it has a כפל ענין, "repeated meaning".' *Contra* J.L. Kugel, *The Idea of Biblical Poetry: Parallelism and its History* (New Haven: Yale University Press, 1981), pp. 176-77.

7. Driver, *Job*, I, p. 281; II, p. 236; Dhorme, *Le Livre de Job*, p. 435; Pope, *Job*, pp. 240, 249; Gordis, *The Book of Job*, pp. 360, 368; Tur-Sinai, *The Book of Job*, p. 460; Guillaume, *Studies in the Book of Job*, pp. 59, 117; Hartley, *The Book of Job*, p. 431 n. 7.

latter stands as a proxy for the former can be seen by Ps. 139.23, where the two verbs form a pair. Note also that Job's words in 12.11 refer to 'making sense of' (טעם) words, which may explain why Elihu chose his pun.[1]

Moreover, to appreciate the referential aspect of the polysemy in 32.11 one must look at the verses leading up to it in 32.9-10: 'The great are not (always) wise, nor the aged discerning of justice. Therefore, I will speak, and you listen to me; I will declare my knowledge, even I.' The words שמעה לי, 'listen to me', in 32.10 are a directional cue both for Job and for the reader to listen closely to what Elihu is about to say, that is, to catch his craft in the next line. They are also a verbal clue for understanding where to find the pun: שמעה לי, 'listen to me', focuses the reader's ear on the notion of 'listening', which comes in the very next line in the pun on אזין, 'give ear'. Elihu adds in 32.12: 'to you I gave consideration, but none of you have reproved Job, no one among you to answer his words'. That 31 chapters of argumentative dialogue have preceded this statement suggests that Elihu must imply something more than his friends' lack of reproof. What Job's friends have not done is respond to Job's penchant for polysemous wisdom, that is, top him word-play for word-play.[2] They have made their attempts, as seen throughout the book, but in Elihu's eyes they have been unsuccessful. That Elihu is concerned with the way Job speaks is clear from the next stich (32.13): '(beware) lest you say "we have discovered wisdom, let God chide him, not man"', and 32.14: 'He did not arrange (ערך) his words to me, and with your speeches I would not have responded.'

Job 32.17-18

אענה אף אני חלקי
אחוה דעי אף אני
כי מלתי מלים
הציקתני רוח בטני

I will answer, even I, my smooth words;
I will declare my knowledge, even I;
For I מלתי words; the wind in my belly presses me.

1. For a similar pun on this word in the book of Jonah see D. Marcus, *From Balaam to Jonah: Anti-Prophetic Satire in the Hebrew Bible* (BJS, 301; Atlanta, GA: Scholars Press, 1995), p. 141.

2. See the Conclusion for more complete discussion.

In Job 32.17-18, the pivot word is מלתי which may be derived from מלא, 'fill',[1] מלל, 'speak', or the Aramaic מלל, 'squeeze'.[2] The first, as in Job 32.11 above, would represent a defective spelling of the root מלא in the form of מלתי.[3] The second would parallel אחוה in the previous stich. The last would parallel הציקתני רוח בטני. Though the latter requires that we revocalize to מְלַּתִי, it should be remembered that the consonantal text could have been read in any of the three ways. As 'fill' מלא parallels דעי, 'my knowledge', in the previous stich. A similar parallel relationship for the two words can be found in Job 39.2. The words also appear together, albeit in a non-parallel manner, in Qoh. 11.5; Jer. 19.4; Ezek. 32.15; 36.38; and Hab. 2.14. For a connection between the noun רוח and מלל (but as 'speak') see Job 8.2 and possibly also Qoh. 11.5 (where the noun בטן also occurs). Job 32.17-18, therefore, is an oral, visual, and symmetrical Janus parallelism.

All the versions derive מלתי from מלא: LXX πλήρης γάρ εἰμι; Targum מליתי; Vulgate *plenus sum*; and the Peshitta מלית; all of which mean 'I am full'.[4] The rabbis and modern exegetes take the word in the same way.[5]

We have seen in 32.11 how concerned Elihu is with his friends' inability to top Job at his own punful game. That he now is on a quest to outdo him is clear from the Janus parallel in 32.18. In 32.17 also, Elihu arrogantly proclaims: אענה אף אני חלקי אחוה דעי אף אני, 'I will answer, even I, my smooth words; I will declare my knowledge, even I.' That חלקי refers to words is clear by comparing his nearly verbatim statement in 32.10: לכן אמרתי שמעה לי אחוה דעי אף אני. Such a usage for the root חלף also occurs in Ps. 5.10; Prov. 2.16; 5.3; 6.24; 7.5 and 28.23.[6] That

1. So BDB, p. 570; KB, p. 523; *HALAT*, II, p. 552.

2. *DISO*, pp. 154-55; Jastrow, *A Dictionary of the Targumim*, p. 792; Beyer, *Die aramäischen Texte vom Toten Meer*, p. 625; Sokoloff, *A Dictionary of Jewish Palestinian Aramaic*, p. 311.

3. GKC, p. 206, k.

4. LSJ, p. 1419, s.v. πλήρης; Jastrow, *A Dictionary of the Targumim*, p. 789, s.v. מלי; *OLD*, pp. 1390-91, s.v. *plēnus*; Payne Smith, *A Compendious Syriac Dictionary*, pp. 273-74, s.v. מלל.

5. Driver, *Job*, I, p. 282; II, p. 238; Dhorme, *Le Livre de Job*, p. 440; Pope, *Job*, pp. 241, 244; Gordis, *The Book of Job*, pp. 360, 370; Tur-Sinai, *The Book of Job*, pp. 460-61; Guillaume, *Studies in the Book of Job*, pp. 60, 117; Hartley, *The Book of Job*, p. 432.

6. For additional evidence on Elihu's slippery tongue see Curtis, 'Word Play in the Speeches of Elihu', pp. 23-30.

Elihu intends his hearers to catch the meaning 'speak' for מלתי is seen by his use of מלל in 33.3-4: ודעת שפתי ברור מללו רוח אל עשתני ונשמת שדי תחיני, 'the knowledge of my lips speak purely; the spirit of God formed me; the breath of Shaddai sustains me'. Note also his use of רוח as 'spirit', his use of נשמת שדי which echoes 32.8, and his often repeated accusation in 15.2: החכם יענה דעת רוח וימלא קדים בטנו, 'Does a wise man answer with windy opinions, and fill his belly with the east wind?'

Job 36.15-16

יחלץ עני בעניו
ויגל בלחץ אזנם
ואף הסיתך מפי צר
רחב לא מוצק תחתיה
ונחת שלחנך מלא דשן

He rescues the lowly from their affliction, and opens their understanding through distress.
Indeed, he draws you from the mouth of the צר. To a רחב where there is no מוצק; your table is laid out with rich food.

The poet's talents are again apparent in Job 36.15-16, where he exploits the polyvalent possibilities of two stichs. The first is מפי צר, which we may read as '(Indeed, he draws you away) from the mouth of distress' (based on the root צור/צרר: *ẓrr*), or as 'from the mouth of confinement' (based on the root צרר: *ṣrr*).[1] That this passage is a Janus construction is illustrated by the fact that as 'distress', the stich parallels ויגל בלחץ אזנם, 'he opens their understanding (lit. ears) through distress', in the previous line, and as 'confinement', it parallels רחב לא מוצק תחתיה, 'to a broad place without constraint', which follows. For support for the former parallel see the famous words of Isaiah in 30.20: לחם צר ומים לחץ. The latter parallel between the roots צרר and צוק is attested in Isa. 26.16.

The second punful stich is רחב לא מוצק תחתיה, 'to a broad place without constraint' or 'a flagon not poured out'. The first reading takes מוצק from צוק, 'squeeze, constrain';[2] the second, from צוק/יצק II, 'pour out'. The second reading also understands רחב like the Ugaritic *rḥbt*, 'flagon'.[3] In its second meaning, the stich acts as a fitting parallel to

1. So BDB, p. 865; KB, p. 818; *HALAT*, III, p. 984.
2. So BDB, pp. 847-48; KB, p. 505; *HALAT*, II, p. 530.
3. *UT*, p. 483. Though the gender of 'flagon' is different one should also note here that Gordis (*The Book of Job*, p. 416) takes the feminine suffix on תחתיה to refer to רחב. Note also the Ugaritic nouns *mrḥqt*, 'distance' (= Heb. מרחק); *drkt*,

ונחת שלחנך מלא דשן, 'your table is arrayed with rich food' in the next stich. We have here, therefore, a double Janus cluster, with the first polyseme צר belonging to the strictly visual and symmetrical classes, and the second, מוצק, belonging to the oral, visual, and symmetrical groups.[1]

Regarding the polysemous צר, the LXX translates with ἐχθροῦ, 'enemy',[2] which presumes a derivation from *ẓrr*. On the other hand, the Targum uses מעירא, 'oppressor' or 'confinement', which assumes a derivation from *ṣrr*.[3] Additionally, to translate הסיתך, 'he draws you', in the same stich, the Targum uses פצענך, whose root (פצע) means both 'squeeze' and 'wound'.[4] This may be the Targumist's way of capturing the pun in Aramaic, lest any reader miss the double meaning of מעיקא. The Vulgate's use of *ore angusto*, 'narrow mouth (lit. mouth of straits)', carries both our meanings.[5] Unlike the Targum, the Peshitta's מעיקנא means only 'distress'.[6]

The rabbis see the derivation of צר differently than the versions. Saᶜadiah Gaᵓon, Ibn Ezra, Moshe Qimḥi, Y. Altschuler's *Metsudat Zion*, and Ralbag read it as 'narrow, constrained'. The commentary *Metsudat David* gives both possibilities.[7] Driver and Dhorme treat as 'confinement' (*ṣrr*),[8] whereas Pope, Gordis, Tur-Sinai, and Hartley assume a derivation from *ẓrr* ('distress').[9] Guillaume reads as 'starving', which he takes as a participle of the Arabic root *ḍara*.[10]

'dominion' (= Heb. דרך, for instance in Hos. 10.13; Prov. 31.3); and *ḥrt*, 'grave, hole' (= Heb. חר), which exhibit the same opposition in gender.

1. There may be additional word-plays on body parts in this passage. Note the use of עניו, חלץ, אזנם, אף, פי, and possibly also תחת (?) with different meanings. For more on such clustering see Greenfield, 'The Cluster in Biblical Poetry', pp. 159-68.

2. LSJ, p. 748, s.v. ἔχθρα.

3. Jastrow, *A Dictionary of the Targumim*, p. 1056; Beyer, *Die aramäischen Texte vom Toten Meer*, p. 655; Sokoloff, *A Dictionary of Jewish Palestinian Aramaic*, p. 400.

4. Jastrow, *A Dictionary of the Targumim*, p. 1205; Sokoloff, *A Dictionary of Jewish Palestinian Aramaic*, p. 442.

5. The Latin may mean 'anguish' or 'narrow, crowded'. The English 'straits' renders the pun perfectly; *OLD*, p. 130, s.v. *angustē*.

6. Though they are based on the same root, i.e., עוק; Payne Smith, *A Compendious Syriac Dictionary*, p. 406.

7. Rashi is silent here.

8. Driver, *Job*, I, p. 312; Dhorme, *Le Livre de Job*, p. 497.

9. Pope, *Job*, pp. 267, 270; Gordis, *The Book of Job*, pp. 406, 416; Tur-Sinai, *The Book of Job*, pp. 498-99; Hartley, *The Book of Job*, p. 472.

10. Guillaume, *Studies in the Book of Job*, pp. 66, 124.

As for מוצק and רחב, the LXX regards the first as derived from יצק, 'pour out', and the second as 'wide', as it translates ἄβυσσος κατάχυσις ὑποκάτω αὐτῆς, '(there is) a deep gulf (and) a rushing stream beneath it'.[1] Note that κατάχυσις (καταχών-ευσις) literally means 'melting down', that is, the root meaning of יצק.[2] That ἄβυσσος may be used of liquids (perhaps to suggest that רחב is a container of liquid) may be seen by the LXX's use of the same word for תהום, 'the great deep waters', in Gen. 1.2. The Targum renders מוצק with the cognate יתעק, 'narrowness', and רחב with אפתי, 'expanse, chamber'.[3] Like the Targum, the Vulgate translates *latissime et non habentis fundamentum subter se*, '(to) a broad place and free of foundation beneath it'.[4] Interesting is the Vulgate's use of *fundamentum* to translate מוצק, which at first glance is clearly a 'foundation, base, structure'.[5] We may note, however, that its root (*fundo*) has another meaning quite apposite for מוצק if read as from יצק, 'pour (fluids from a vessel), cast found (metals), make by a cast'.[6] Are we witness once again to Jerome's cleverness? *Latissime*, for רחב, can only mean 'wide, broad'. Though it takes רחב as 'wide, broad', the Syriac may capture both nuances of מוצק with the cognate עקתא, 'where harm passes through'.[7]

Saʿadiah Gaʾon, Ibn Ezra, Moshe Qimḥi, and the exegetical work *Metsudat David* read מוצק and רחב as 'constraint' and 'wide place',[8] as do Driver, Dhorme, Pope, Gordis, and Hartley.[9] Only Tur-Sinai takes מוצק from יצק, as he notes:

> Here...מוצק does not mean 'straightness', but the sense is: I have saved you from the abundance of waters which threatened to engulf you as there was no מוצק, no firm dam underneath then to prevent them from falling upon you.[10]

1. LSJ, pp. 4, 922, s.v. ἄβυσσος, καταχών-ευσις.
2. BDB, p. 427.
3. Jastrow, *A Dictionary of the Targumim*, p. 1056; Sokoloff, *A Dictionary of Jewish Palestinian Aramaic*, pp. 71-72 (but as 'eventide').
4. *OLD*, p. 1007, s.v. *lātitūdō*.
5. *OLD*, p. 746, s.v. *fundo*¹.
6. *OLD*, pp. 746-47, s.v. *fundo*¹, *fundō*².
7. Payne Smith, *A Compendious Syriac Dictionary*, p. 424, s.v. עקתא.
8. The other medievals do not comment.
9. Driver, *Job*, I, p. 312; Dhorme, *Le Livre de Job*, p. 497; Pope, *Job*, pp. 267, 270; Gordis, *The Book of Job*, pp. 406, 416; Hartley, *The Book of Job*, p. 472.
10. Tur-Sinai, *The Book of Job*, p. 499.

Guillaume omits the line altogether.[1] In 36.16 Elihu's desire to outstrip Job and his friends in double-talk shines through. That the roots צרר I, צרר II, and צור have been manipulated before by Bildad (18.4-5), Job (19.11-12), and Eliphaz (22.24-25) gives the young Elihu an opportunity to prove his verbal acumen. By artfully including subtle references to their previous statements, Elihu layers his words with allusion. That both Bildad's and Job's speeches occur in contexts which concern God's anger (אף) provokes Elihu to employ אף in 36.16 as 'indeed' and previously (36.13) for an antanaclastic set-up as 'anger'. Elihu also refers to Eliphaz's remarks with צר in 36.16 and again by antanaclasis in 36.19 with בצר, '(without) limit'. In this way, Elihu is able to respond to his friends' quips and simultaneously answer his own call to do Job one better. Elihu also handles מוצק antanaclastically by using it again in 37.10: ורחב מים במוצק, 'and the expanse of water becomes solid'.

Interestingly, though it is Job who first uses the lexeme צר to express his anguish, it is God who last uses the lexemes צר and מוצק, as 'tight' (41.17) and 'cast, firm' (38.38; 41.15, 16), respectively.

Job 36.24-25

זכר כי תשגיא פעלו
אשר שררו אנשים
כל אדם חזו בו
אנוש יביט מרחוק

Remember, then, to magnify his work, of which all men have שררו.
Which all men have beheld. Men have seen from a distance.

One of the most pithy Januses in the book of Job occurs in 36.24-25. Here שררו is used to convey two ideas: 'singing' (by-form of שיר)[2] and 'looking' (from שור). The former can be found in Zech. 2.14; 1 Chron. 6.18; 29.28; Ezra 2.65; and Neh. 7.67. The latter occurs in the *polel*, as one must read it here, in Ps. 5.9; 27.11; 54.7; 56.3; 59.11 and 92.12. As 'which men have sung' the stich parallels זכר כי תשגיא פעלו, 'remember to magnify his works', in the previous stich. As 'which men have seen', the stich parallels כל אדם חזו בו, 'which all men have beheld', and also 'men have seen from a distance', in the next stich (cf. Job 35.5 and Ps. 92.12 where the roots שור, 'see', and נבט, 'see', are word-pairs).

1. Guillaume, *Studies in the Book of Job*, pp. 66, 124.
2. So BDB, p. 1010; KB, p. 966; *HALAT*, IV, p. 1372.

Again, this is an excellent example of an oral, visual, and symmetrical Janus parallelism.

Support for both readings comes from the versions. Though the Targum's שבחו, the Vulgate's *cecinerunt*, and Syriac's ושבחוהי suggest the reading 'sing, praise',[1] the LXX's ὧν ἦρξαν ἄνδρες, 'which men have overseen (i.e., ruled)',[2] and the Qumran Targum fragment's ...די חזו המון suggest the reading 'seen, beheld'.

Rashi, Ibn Ezra, Moshe Qimḥi, and the commentary *Metsudat Zion* also take שררו as 'they beheld', Saᶜadiah Gaʾon as 'they described them', and Ralbag cites both meanings.[3] Of the modern exegetes, Driver, Dhorme, Pope and Hartley read 'of which men have sung'.[4] Pope rejects the meaning 'beheld' because, if taken as such, the verb would then occur three times, which he believes to be 'a bit too much'.[5] In the light of the duality of the word, it is clear that it is precisely this 'excess' which the poet exploits. Gordis, Tur-Sinai, and Guillaume all read as if derived from שור.[6]

Elihu played upon the roots שור and שיר previously. In 33.3 he proclaimed: ישר לבי אמרי ודעת שפתי ברור מללו, 'my words bespeak the uprightness of my heart'. This verse was mentioned above in connection with the antanaclastic use of the root מלל, 'speak'. Notable here is the use of ישר, 'uprightness', which we may read, along with Gordis, as 'sing' from the root שיר.[7] In 33.27 Elihu asserts that God speaks to mortals: ישר על אנשים ויאמר חטאתי וישר העויתי ולא שוה לי, 'he sings to men, "I have perverted what was right"'. Note here the play between שיר, 'sing', in v. 27a and ישר, 'right', in v. 27b connecting this verse to 33.2-3 above.[8] That Elihu refers to 33.27 in his Janus construction in 36.24-25 can be seen in the similarity between the opening stichs, both

1. Jastrow, *A Dictionary of the Targumim*, p. 1512; Beyer, *Die aramäischen Texte vom Toten Meer*, pp. 699-700; Sokoloff, *A Dictionary of Jewish Palestinian Aramaic*, p. 534; *OLD*, p. 266, s.v. *canō*; Payne Smith, *A Compendious Syriac Dictionary*, pp. 555-56, s.v. שבח.

2. LSJ, p. 254, s.v. ἄρχω.

3. Others are silent.

4. Driver, *Job*, I, p. 314; II, pp. 281-82; Dhorme, *Le Livre de Job*, p. 503; Pope, *Job*, pp. 267, 272; Hartley, *The Book of Job*, p. 473.

5. Pope, *Job*, p. 272.

6. Gordis, *The Book of Job*, pp. 408, 419; Tur-Sinai, *The Book of Job*, pp. 502-503; Guillaume, *Studies in the Book of Job*, pp. 66, 126.

7. Gordis, *The Book of Job*, pp. 371-72.

8. Elihu also plays on the root in 33.23.

of which contain אנשים, 'men'. Elihu's previous plays between the roots שיר, 'singing', and ישר, 'right', bind the two meanings in such a way that when the reader encounters שיר again, in 36.24 (שררו), it implies by association and expectation the notion of 'right'. The expectation to hear in the lexeme an allusion to ישר, 'right', is precisely what Elihu subverts by connecting it with שור, 'see'. That Elihu desires his hearers to anticipate and be duped by this set-up is apparent by the preface to his polysemy in 36.23b: ומי אמר פעלת עולה, 'who ever said, "You have done iniquity?"'. This recalls 33.27, in which he says of Job 'he sings (ישר) to humankind, "I have perverted what was right"...'

Job 36.27-28

כי יגרע נטפי מים
יזקו מטר לאדו
אשר יזלו שחקים
ירעפו עלי אדם רב

He forms the droplets of water, which יזקו rain, from a mist.
The skies rain; they pour down on all humankind.

In Job 36.27-28, the poet utilizes the polysemous root זקק, 'purify, distil'[1] and 'refrain, withhold'.[2] The relevant stich runs: יזקו מטר לאדו, 'they distil into rain from a mist' or 'the rain is withheld from a mist'. The former parallels אשר יזלו שחקים, 'which the clouds pour down', and the latter parallels כי יגרע נטפי מים, 'he withholds the droplets of water'.[3] The polyseme in 36.27-28, therefore, is of the oral, visual, and symmetrical types.

The LXX, especially in v. 28,[4] is very paraphrastic and appears as an interpolation, or as if it is based on an altogether different text from the MT. However, v. 27b is probably a direct translation of our pivot line. ἐπιχυθήσονται, 'pour out',[5] renders יזקו. The Targum is less paraphrastic, translating as יזלפון, 'drip'.[6] However, the Targumist captured

1. So BDB, p. 279; KB, p. 264; *HALAT*, I, p. 267.

2. See, for instance, s.v. זק, 'manacles', from זקק: BDB, p. 279; KB, p. 264; *HALAT*, I, p. 267.

3. That the root זקק occurs in *qal* only here may serve to signal the pun's presence.

4. But also in v. 27 where the Hebrew יגרע is rendered ἀριθμηταὶ, 'numbered'; LSJ, p. 239, s.v. ἀριθμέω.

5. LSJ, p. 673, s.v. ἐπιχέω.

6. Jastrow, *A Dictionary of the Targumim*, p. 402; Sokoloff, *A Dictionary of Jewish Palestinian Aramaic*, p. 178.

both meanings of זקק by translating the Hebrew of v. 29, אף אם יבין מפרשי עב תשאות סכתו, 'Can one, indeed, understand the expanse of clouds, the thunderings from his pavilion?', with the Aramaic polyseme טלל, 'drop' and 'cover',[1] and by using it in conjunction with the root רכף, 'bind':[2] לחוד אין אתבין פרישות דעיבא רכפת ענניה טלליה, 'Can one understand the expanse of the cloud which binds up his clouds, his pavilion (droppings)?' The Vulgate uses *effundit*, 'pours out, rains',[3] but one cannot help but wonder if the phrase *ad instar gurgitum* was chosen to capture the pun of זקק, for it may be rendered 'like a flood', or 'like a greedy man'.[4] The latter might convey the sense of 'withholding, refraining', that is, as one who withholds wealth. The Peshitta translates paraphrastically, yet differently than the LXX.[5] Not only does it take the first line as referring to עמודי שמיא, 'the pillars of heaven', but it also adds two stichs: ונצור נוטפי מטרא בלחודוהי דמחתין שמיא בזבנא, 'and fashions the drops of rain by himself, which the heavens diffuse in (due) season'. One can only guess which of the lines translates our Janus stich, if any; a plausible suggestion is that it is rendered by דמחתין שמיא בזבנא, with the root מחי, 'diffuse, wash away', standing for זקק.[6] The Targum from Qumran renders with וזיקי, 'distil'.

The medievals[7] and moderns[8] who comment on יזקו agree that it must mean 'distil, refine', or something similar. Yet that some ambiguity is present is suggested by the rendering of Saʿadiah Gaʾon, who resolved

1. *DISO*, p. 101; Jastrow, *A Dictionary of the Targumim*, p. 537; Beyer, *Die aramäischen Texte vom Toten Meer*, p. 590; Sokoloff, *A Dictionary of Jewish Palestinian Aramaic*, p. 225.

2. Jastrow, *A Dictionary of the Targumim*, p. 1480.

3. *OLD*, p. 593, s.v. *effundō*.

4. *OLD*, p. 778, s.v. *gurges*.

5. Yet the Syriac's נמנא, 'numbers', reflects an original which is closer to the LXX. See note above.

6. Payne Smith, *A Compendious Syriac Dictionary*, p. 263. Is the Peshitta attemting to create its own Janus here, with the root מחי, as 'diffuse', paralleling רסן, 'sprinkle', in the following stich, and as 'smite, beat out', paralleling נצור, 'fashion, form', in the previous stich?

7. Ibn Ezra, *Metsudat Zion*, and Ralbag.

8. Driver, *Job*, I, p. 315; II, p. 282; Dhorme, *Le Livre de Job*, p. 505; Pope, *Job*, pp. 267, 273; Gordis, *The Book of Job*, pp. 408, 420; Tur-Sinai, *The Book of Job*, pp. 502-504; Guillaume, *Studies in the Book of Job*, pp. 66, 126; Hartley, *The Book of Job*, p. 475.

the problem by paraphrasing: 'the drops of water which he *sops up* as vapor *and distils* as rain'.

Puns involving 'rain' have occurred before (20.23-24; 24.19-21; 29.20-23). In 36.27 Elihu takes his turn by using יזקו. That polysemous parallelism relies on referential allusion can be seen again from Elihu's play. Elihu used the root זקק to mean 'fetters' just prior in 36.8: ואם אסורים בזקים ילכדו בחבלי עני, 'if they are bound in fetters and caught in trammels of affliction...' Its use for 'fetters' associates the root זקק with notions of 'withholding, refraining' which are then played upon in 36.27. Notice that the polyseme יזקו in 36.27 follows the root גרע, 'withhold, refrain', and tricks the ear by conjuring images which correlate to זקק as 'fetters'. That Elihu wants his hearers to make this false connection is made even clearer by the use of גרע to preface 36.7.

Job 38.24-25

אי זה הדרך יחלק אור
יפץ קדים עלי ארץ
מי פלג לשטף תעלה
ודרך לחזיז קלות

By what path is the west wind dispersed, the east wind יפץ over the earth?
Who cut a channel for the torrents, and a path for the thunderstorms?

יפץ קדים עלי ארץ is exploited for its double meaning in Job 38.24-25. How one interprets it depends on how one deciphers יפץ; whether, for example, one derives it from the more common פוץ I (cf. Arabic *faẓẓ*), 'scatter, disperse',[1] or from the rarer פוץ II (cf. Arabic *f̕aẓ*), 'flow, overflow'. This last root appears in Job 40.11; Prov. 5.16; and Zech. 1.17. If we use the former derivation, we translate 'the east wind scattered over the earth' and see it in parallelism with אי זה הדרך יחלק אור, 'by what path is the west wind dispersed?' If we use the latter derivation, 'the east wind flowed over the earth' parallels the question מי פלג לשטף תעלה, who cut a channel for the torrent?', in the next stich. Support for the former parallelism comes from Ezek. 36.19 and Nah. 2.2, where פוץ I occurs in conjunction with the noun דרך, and Gen. 49.7, where it appears with the root חלף. That Prov. 5.16 also uses פוץ II in reference to a פלג bolsters the latter parallelism proposed here. It also should be noted that aside from the polysemous verb, the phrase עלי ארץ is

1. So BDB, p. 807; KB, p. 755; *HALAT*, III, pp. 868-69.

exploited as a perfect segue to introduce v. 25. What we have here is a strictly visual and symmetrical polysemous parallel.

The LXX translates: διασκεδάννυται Νότος, 'the south wind is dispersed'.[1] Perhaps the LXX's translation 'south wind' for a Hebrew word which obviously means 'east' (i.e., קדים) should be seen as an attempt to bring out the pun on 'flow' implied in פוץ II, as the basic meaning of Νότος is 'wet wind'.[2] Note also that the LXX takes אור as πάχην, 'frost', which the Greeks understood as 'frozen rain'.[3] The Targum is extremely paraphrastic, citing three traditions. The first renders יפץ with יבדר, 'dispersed',[4] which is used only in connection with wind, not water. The two other traditions discuss only v. 25, but make it clear that the 'channels' (פלג) referred to there were believed to exist both below and above the earth.[5] The Vulgate also treats יפץ as 'dispersed, divided' (*dedit*), as does the Qumran fragment (יפק), and the Syriac, which employs the somewhat compromising 'proceed' (ונפקא).[6]

Though Saʿadiah Gaʾon, Rashi, and Ibn Ezra do not comment on יפץ, the commentary *Metsudat David* and Ralbag take it to refer to both 'hot wind' and 'hail', i.e. (frozen) water.[7] Y. Altschuler in *Metsudat Zion* renders the word with יפזר, 'scatters', and the modern commentators translate similarly.[8]

The poet's talent for antanaclasis is apparent again in God's pun in 38.24. Elihu used the root פוץ just prior in 37.11: אף ברי יטריח עב יפיץ ענן אורו, 'He also loads the clouds with moisture and scatters his

1. LSJ, p. 411, s.v. διασκεδάζω.

2. From νοτεῶ, νοτία, 'damp, wet, moist'; LSJ, p. 1182, s.v. νότος. Perhaps the LXX translators in Egypt were affected by the Egyptian orientation to the south, instead of to the east like the Canaanites. The etymological association between Egyptian *ỉmn*, 'west', and ימן, 'south', would support this.

3. *Odyssey* 14.476; LSJ, p. 1350.

4. *DISO*, p. 32; Jastrow, *A Dictionary of the Targumim*, p. 141; Beyer, *Die aramäischen Texte vom Toten Meer*, p. 529; Sokoloff, *A Dictionary of Jewish Palestinian Aramaic*, p. 86.

5. Compare the Targum's use of קובה, 'arched room from which rain proceeds'; Jastrow, *A Dictionary of the Targumim*, p. 1323.

6. *OLD*, p. 496, s.v. *dēdō*; Payne Smith, *A Compendious Syriac Dictionary*, pp. 345-46, s.v. נפק.

7. Cf. LXX.

8. Driver, *Job*, I, p. 332; II, p. 304; Dhorme, *Le Livre de Job*, p. 534; Pope, *Job*, pp. 289, 297; Gordis, *The Book of Job*, pp. 436, 439; Tur-Sinai, *The Book of Job*, pp. 528, 529; Guillaume, *Studies in the Book of Job*, pp. 69. 131, Hartley, *The Book of Job*, p. 498.

lightning clouds'. In 38.24 God uses יפץ as 'scatter' (of wind) and 'flow' (of water). Such a combination is quite fitting for it binds together Elihu's references to 'clouds' and 'moisture'. That the reader is to make this connection is strengthened by God's rehearsal in 38.25: מי פלג לשטף תעלה ודרך לחזיז קלות, 'who has cleft a channel for the torrents of rain [i.e., water], and a path for the thunderbolt [i.e., light]'. Finally, it is God who uses the word unequivocally in 40.11: הפץ עברות אפך, 'scatter your raging anger'.

Job 39.10-11

התקשר רים בתלם עבתו
אם ישדד עמקים אחריך
התבטח בו כי רב כחו
ותעזב אליו יגיעך

Can you hold the water buffalo by ropes to the furrow? Would he plough up עמקים behind you?
Would you rely on his great strength and leave your toil to him?

In Job 39.10-11 God asks Job the rhetorical question: 'Would he plough up עמקים behind you?' The common meaning of the root עמק is 'deep, valley',[1] as found in Jer. 49.4 and Job 39.21. However, the lexeme, as its Ugaritic cognate *ʿmq* demonstrates,[2] can mean 'strong' as well.[3] Here, the poet plays on both of its meanings, using the idea of 'valleys' to parallel התקשר רים בתלם עבתו, 'Can you hold the water buffalo by ropes to the furrows', in the previous stich, and the notion of 'strong' to parallel התבטח בו כי רב כחו, 'would you rely on his great strength?' The parallel between עמקים and תלם seems obvious despite the lack of biblical prooftexts (note that תלם is a rare word). As for the latter parallel between עמקים and כח, witness God's comment on the horse in Job 39.21: יחפרו בעמק וישיש בכח יצא לקראת נשק, 'he paws and rejoices, runs with vigor; charging into battle', wherein a similar word-play may be present. The use of עמק in Job 39.10-11, therefore, belongs to the oral, visual, and symmetrical groups.

1. So BDB, p. 771; KB, p. 716; *HALAT*, III, p. 802.
2. *UT*, p. 457.
3. See for example *HALAT*, III, p. 802. Cf. Job 39.21; Ps. 92.6; Ezek. 3.5, 6; Isa. 28.21; 1 Chron. 12.16; and Jer. 49.4. See A. Wieder, 'Ugaritic-Hebrew Lexicographical Notes', *JBL* 84 (1965), p. 162; W.G.E. Watson, 'Archaic Elements in the Language of Chronicles', *Bib* 53 (1972), p. 196.

The LXX's αὔλακας ἐν πεδίῳ, 'furrows in the plain', reflects only the reading 'valley'.[1] The Targum and Vulgate also treat our Janus word as 'valley', using גלמתא and *vallium*,[2] though the latter might have been chosen because of its similarity to *vallo*, 'strengthen, fortify'.[3] The Peshitta renders עמקים with עסקא, 'difficulty, obstinate',[4] which suggests that its translators understood עמקים as 'strong'. The Targum fragment from Qumran also renders with בקעה, 'valley'. Most of the sages are mute regarding our Janus word and the moderns translate as 'valley'.[5]

Yahweh's statement is somewhat of a paraphrase of Job's proclamation in 31.38: 'If my land cried out against me, its furrows (תלם) weep together...' The lexeme תלם is heard only twice in Job (31.38; 39.10), thus illustrating the effectiveness of God's reference. Adding to the impact of the reference is כח which immediately follows both passages and acts to connect them antanaclastically. In 31.39 it is used as 'produce': אם כחה אכלתי בלי כסף, 'if I have eaten its produce without payment...', and in 39.11 as 'strength' in the question: התבטח בו כי רב כחו, 'would you trust in him because of the greatness of his strength?' Supporting the associative connection between עמקים and כח is 39.21, in which God rehearses the ambiguity of his rhetorical question in 39.10: יחפרו בעמק וישיש בכח יצא לקראת נשק, 'they paw with strength (in the valley) and rejoice; in strength they go out to meet the battle'. Note how עמק can mean either 'valley' or 'strength' and that it is parallel to כח, 'strength'.[6] In addition, the poet's use of paronomasia in 39.8-10 may have acted to alert the reader to the pun on עמק. Note the repetition of the word רים, 'water buffalo', in 39.9 and 39.10, and the previous allusion to it in v. 8: יתור הרים, 'he roams the hills...', itself a possible Aramaic play on תור, 'bull'. Also alliterative is עבדך, 'serve you', in 39.9 which resounds in 39.10 with עבתו, 'his ropes'. Such paronomasia

1. LSJ, p. 1352, s.v. πεδίον.

2. *DISO*, pp. 50, 213-14; Jastrow, *A Dictionary of the Targumim*, p. 249; Sokoloff, *A Dictionary of Jewish Palestinian Aramaic*, p. 130; *OLD*, p. 2009, s.v. *vallēs*. One also wonders if גלמתא was intended to play on עלם, 'strong'.

3. *OLD*, p. 2009, s.v. *vallō*.

4. Payne Smith, *A Compendious Syriac Dictionary*, p. 421.

5. Driver, *Job*, I, p. 341; Dhorme, *Le Livre de Job*, p. 549; Pope, *Job*, pp. 304, 308; Gordis, *The Book of Job*, pp. 440, 457; Tur-Sinai, *The Book of Job*, p. 542; Guillaume, *Studies in the Book of Job*, pp. 70, 133; Hartley, *The Book of Job*, p. 507; Grabbe, *Comparative Philology and the Text of Job*, p. 126.

6. Note that the root חפר, an equally ambiguous lexeme, also occurs here. Cf. 6.20-21 discussed above.

forces the reader to concentrate more closely on the relationship of the verse to the stichs which surround it. In turn, this increases the likelihood that the reader will catch any polysemy imbedded in the text.

Job 39.19-20

התתן לסוס גבורה
התלביש צוארו רעמה
התרעישנו כארבה
הוד נחרו אימה

Do you give the horse its strength? Do you clothe his neck with רעמה?
Do you make him quiver like locusts, his majestic snorting (spreading) terror.

רעמה has long stood as a crux to scholars, both ancient and modern.[1] Its root suggests the meaning 'thunder', or by extension 'terror'.[2] As such, it serves as an excellent parallel for התרעישנו כארבה הוד נחרו אימה, 'Do you make him quiver like locusts, his majestic snorting (spreading) terror?' in the next line. This parallel finds support in Ps. 77.19, where the roots רעם and רעש are parallel, and also Isa. 29.6, where רעם and רעש occur as a hendiadys. However, as Pope and Gordis note, the word may be akin to the Arabic expression *umm riʿm*, 'mother of the mane'.[3] If we take רעמה as 'mane', the stich parallels התתן לסוס גבורה, 'do you give the horse its strength?' Again, the poet expresses two ideas with one word: this constitutes an oral, visual, and symmetrical polysemous parallel.

The LXX's use of φόβον, 'terror',[4] to render רעמה suggests an attempt to capture the pun by way of a play on φοβήν, 'mane'.[5] That the LXX translators chose to render the root רעם with φόβον only here,

1. See for example I.W. Slotki, 'A Study of רעם', *AJSLL* 37 (1920–21), pp. 149-55.

2. So BDB, p. 947.

3. So KB, p. 901; *HALAT*, IV, p. 1182; Pope, *Job*, p. 311; Gordis, *The Book of Job*, p. 461.

4. LSJ, p. 1947, s.v. φοβέω.

5. LSJ, p. 1946, s.v. φόβη. Pope derives the two Greek words one from the other, and Gordis and Tur-Sinai call attention to the similarity without further comment; Pope, *Job*, p. 311; Gordis, *The Book of Job*, p. 461; Tur-Sinai, *The Book of Job*, pp. 547-48. For the related etymologies of the two Greek words see B. Snell, *The Discovery of the Mind: The Greek Origin of European Thought* (New York: Harper, 1960), p. 230 n. 6.

though typically they chose to render the root with a variety of different Greek words, for instance ἅλμα, βοᾶν, βοβεῖν, δακρύειν, σαλεύειν, ἀθυμεῖν, κραυγή, and especially βροντᾶν (for example, in Ps. 77.19 and Isa. 29.6), argues in favor of this.[1] The Targum and Qumran fragment translate with תוקפא and בתקף respectively, both 'strength, anger[2] (terror?)'. The Vulgate's *hinnitum*, 'neighing',[3] seems an *ad sensum* attempt. The Peshitta, on the other hand, takes a compromise position between the two meanings by rendering with a word which means 'terrifying clothing', i.e., 'armour' (זינא).[4]

The word has evoked numerous comments from exegetes, both ancient and modern. Saᶜadiah Gaᵓon, Rashi, and Ibn Ezra read it as 'terror', and Moshe Qimḥi, Y. Altschuler's *Metsudat David*, and Ralbag suggest, along with the Vulgate, that the 'thundering' refers to the horse's neighing. Driver understood it as 'might'.[5] Yellin read it as 'quivering'.[6] Dhorme, Pope, Gordis, and Hartley all see in רעמה 'a mane'.[7] Tur-Sinai hedgingly translates 'with [power]'.[8] Guillaume, attempting to bridge the two translations, gives 'quivering mane' without comment.[9]

God's pun in 39.19 must be seen as a partial reference to Job's rhetorical question in 26.14: ורעם גבורתו מי יתבונן, 'and the thunder of his power, who can understand?' The art of lingual subversion can be seen again by comparing the two quotations. God has taken the words which Job used to describe him and incorporated them into his

1. See E. Hatch and H.A. Redpath (eds.), *A Concordance to the Septuagint and Other Greek Versions of the Old Testament*, I–II (Graz: Akademische Druck–Universitäts-Verlagsanstalt, 1954).

2. *DISO*, p. 333; Jastrow, *A Dictionary of the Targumim*, pp. 1655-66; Beyer, *Die aramäischen Texte vom Toten Meer*, pp. 726-27; Sokoloff, *A Dictionary of Jewish Palestinian Aramaic*, p. 590. The word is used to translate the root רגז in Job 35.15.

3. *OLD*, p. 797, s.v. *hinnītus*.

4. Payne Smith, *A Compendious Syriac Dictionary*, p. 115, s.v. זינא.

5. Driver, *Job*, I, p. 345; II, pp. 320-21.

6. On the basis of Isa. 29.6 where it appears with the root רעש; Yellin, איוב-חקרי מקרא, p. 163.

7. Dhorme, *Le Livre de Job*, p. 554; Pope, *Job*, pp. 305, 311; Gordis, *The Book of Job*, pp. 440, 461. Interestingly, Hartley notes that 'there may be a play on the homonyms "quiver" and "mane"'; *The Book of Job*, p. 510 n. 1.

8. Tur-Sinai, *The Book of Job*, pp. 546-48.

9. Guillaume, *Studies in the Book of Job*, pp. 71, 134.

description of a horse's power. The gist of the turn of phrase forces the comparison and implies that if a horse has strength which one cannot understand, how much more does God possess unfathomable power.[1] As with 39.10-11 above, God rehearses his play on רעם antanaclastically in 39.25: רעם שׂרים ותרועה, 'the roaring and the shouting of the officers', and in 40.9: ובקול כמהו תרעם, 'do you thunder with a voice like his?'[2] The latter reference is strengthened by the use of הוד (39.20; 40.10) and the root לבש (39.19; 40.10).

1. Is this type of referencing related to the rabbinic hermeneutical principle קל וחמר, 'if x, then how much more so y'?

2. That rehearsals often appear in the third line of a tristich suggests the need for a comprehensive examination of the rhetorical technique of cross-referencing.

Chapter 4

CONCLUSION

In the light of the foregoing chapters it should be clear that Janus parallelism was a literary device familiar to the the author of the book of Job. Indeed, it is so commonplace in Job that it is difficult not to see the device as fundamental to the book's message. It will be beneficial, therefore, to synthesize the observations made in the previous chapters and to present them below in the hope that others will undertake further research on this and similar topics.

1. *Janus Parallelism and its Referential Function*

References as Integral to Job

As I mentioned in the Introduction, when seen within the larger context of dialogue and debate, the polysemous quips and retorts become a demonstration of one-upmanship among the contestants. When one also takes into consideration the ancient belief in the power of words, the antanaclastic tossing about of polyvalent referents by Job and his friends are tantamount to a show of force. The use of תקוה in Job 7.6-7 will serve to illustrate. The lexeme first is heard in the mouth of Job in 3.9 meaning 'hope'. In 4.6 Eliphaz uses it again to mean 'hope', but in 5.16, Eliphaz alludes to its meaning 'thread' by using it in conjunction with the word דל, 'poor', which suggests the meaning 'thread'. Herein lies the source for Job's play in 7.6-7 in which he tops Eliphaz's allusion in 5.16 by using Eliphaz's own play against him: 'My days are more trifling than a weaver's shuttle (ארג). They go without תקוה (hope/thread).' That Job's pun in 7.6-7 is intended to subvert the expectation of his friends can be seen by his use of the root קוה again as 'hope' in 7.2 just prior to his Janus usage. As mentioned in Chapter 3, this connection is strengthened by a similar phraseology in both verses.

Bildad, not content to let Eliphaz be outstripped by Job, whom he believes to be a sinner with an unbridled tongue, enters the debate with his own play on קוה in 8.14-15, in which he likens the 'hope' (תקוה) of the godless, by which he means Job, to the web of a spider (עכביש).

Yet Job's friends do not best him with their words, for in the end (38.5), from a whirlwind, and as if to get in the last say on Job's 'hope', God reprimands his friends unequivocally, thundering: 'Who has laid its [the earth's] pillars, do you know?! Or who has measured it with a plumbline (קו)?'

God: The Final Referee

Such a networking of referential nexuses[1] is at work for each of the polysemes used by Job and his friends,[2] and it is interesting to note that for many of them, it is God who uses the pivot word last, usually without ambiguity. We have seen this already in Job 38.5 with God's use of the root קוה. To cite additional examples we may utilize the polyseme יסד, 'hedge in/pour out' (3.23), which appears again in God's rhetorical question in 38.8: ויסך בדלתים ים, 'who closed Yam behind doors?'; and גוד, 'fear/stir up' (3.25) and 'stranger/crater' (28.4), which appears in 41.17: משתו יגורו אלים, 'divine beings are in fear as he rises'.

We may add to these many others: compare חפר, 'be ashamed/search' (6.20), with 31.29 and 39.21 where the same lexeme is used unambiguously as 'search' and 'digs', respectively; עשה, 'make/conceal' (9.10, 18), with its use as 'make' in 40.15, 19, 25; 41.25; ברח, 'flee/evil' (9.25), with the same root as 'bars' and 'flee' in 38.10 and 41.20, respectively; בר, 'pit/lye' (9.30), with בר, 'field' (39.4); the oft-used צור/צרר as 'rock/enemy' (18.4), 'enemy/besiege' (19.11), 'rock/precious ore (= בצר)' (28.10), and 'distress/confine' (36.16) with 38.23: 'which I have put aside for a time of distress' (צר) and 41.7: 'locked with a binding (צר) seal'.

Moreover, God's use of the root לחם as 'war' in 39.25 and 40.32 is reminiscent of the polyseme בלחומו (20.23); his use of the root גלל as 'wave' (38.11) and 'dew drop' (38.28) and the root יגל, 'reveal' (38.17; 41.5), reminds us of the previous play between these roots in the expression יגל יבול (20.28). Equally reminiscent of this play is God's

1. Note a similar use of linguistic references in some acrostics. See, for example, J. Renkema, 'The Meaning of the Parallel Acrostics in Lamentations', *VT* 45 (1995), pp. 379-82.

2. Studies utilizing advances in rhetorical criticism have noted similar referencing elsewhere in Job. See, for example Holbert, 'The Function and Significance of the "Klage" in the Book of Job'; Habel, *The Book of Job*; Course, *Speech and Response*.

unambiguous use of בול as 'produce' in 40.20. The polysemous root חבל, 'act injuriously/take as a pledge' (22.6; 24.9), appears from the whirlwind as 'birth pangs' (39.3) and 'cord' (40.25).

In 39.8 God also refers to the play on the roots רעע/רעה, 'do evil/crush/feed' (24.21), by commenting on the wild onager: 'He roams the hills for his pasture (מרעהו).' Similarly referential is God's use of רחם as 'womb' in 38.8 which reminds us of its polysemous usage as 'womb/rain' in 24.20. Note also how a recognition of the polysemous use of רחם in 24.20 sheds light on God's rhetorical questions in 38.28-29 in which רחם never occurs either as 'womb' or as 'rain': 'Does the rain (מטר) have a father? Who begot the dew drops (אגלי טל)? From whose belly (בטן) came forth the ice? Who gave birth (ילדו) to the frost of heaven?'

The list of final references continues. Compare, for example, the polysemes יחל/חלל, 'pierce/wait' (29.21), with חלל as 'give birth' (39.1) and as 'slain' (39.30), and with יחל as 'hope' (41.1); דמם/דמה, 'cease/be silent' (29.21), with דם, 'blood' (39.30); שנן/שנה, 'reply/sharpen' (29.22), with שניו, 'teeth' (41.6); רמם/רום, 'be high/deceive' (31.2), with רמה, 'upraised/deceitful'[1] (38.15), במרום, 'on high' (39.18), and ירים, '(soar) on high' (39.27); ליץ/לון, 'murmur/lodge' in 31.32, with 'lodge' in 39.9, 28; 41.14; מלא/מלל, 'talk/squeeze/fill' in 32.18, with the *plene* spelling of מלא, 'fill', in 38.39; 39.2; צוק/יצק, 'pour out/cast/confine' (36.16), with 'melted mass' (38.38) and 'cast' (41.15, 16, 17). Note also that רחב, 'broad/flagon' (36.17), appears as 'broad' in 38.18.

Even for his own polysemous parallels, God gives the final reference. Compare, for example, פוץ, 'disperse/flow' (38.24), with הפץ, 'scatter' (40.11); עמק, 'valley/strength' (39.10), with its somewhat ambiguous use as 'valley'[2] in (39.21); and רעמה, 'thunder/quiver/mane' (39.19), with the root רעם as 'thunderous noise' in 39.25 and 40.9.

In a few instances, God appears to make oblique references to earlier polysemous usages without employing the identical polyseme. I already have mentioned one such reference in connection with רחם, 'womb/rain' (24.20), which God implies in 38.28-29. Witness also his question in 38.41: 'Who provides food for the raven (ערב), when his young cry out to God and wander about without food (אכל)?' Note how his remark both plays on the root רעב, 'hungry' (i.e., the polyseme of 18.12), and entrenches the connection by way of אכל, 'food'.[3] Similarly, one hears

1. The consonantal text can be read either way.
2. Possibly also 'strength'.
3. Perhaps also נכון (18.12) and יכין (38.41).

the polysemous כיד, 'ruin/cup' (21.20), echoed in כידון, 'javelin' (39.23; 41.21), כידודי, 'firebrands' (41.11),[1] and כדוד, 'pot' (41.12). Compare also the use of קני, 'nest' (39.27) and קנה, 'cane' (40.21), which hark back to the use of קני as 'nest/family' in conjunction with the polyseme חול, 'sand/Phoenix' (29.18). Finally, there is God's question in 38.26b-27: '(Who makes it rain) on the wilderness where no man is, to saturate the desolate wasteland (שאה ומשאה), and make the crop of grass sprout forth?', which reminds us of the play on ערק, 'flee/gnaw', in 30.3, which also employs the terms שאה ומשאה.

The Best at Besting

Though God often appears to have the last say when it comes to the polysemes tossed about in the debate, it is Zophar who speaks most often with a double-edged tongue. By calculating the number of Janus constructions used by each character and dividing that number by the number of verses spoken by each we get a statistical estimate of polysemous proclivity. Zophar speaks polysemously for 8.5% (4/47) of his discourse; Job comes in second with 6.3% (32/507); Bildad in third with 4.3% (2/46); Elihu, the youngest opponent, with 3.8% (6/157); Eliphaz, the eldest, with 2.7% (3/110); and interestingly, God trails with 2.3% (3/129).

While I have based these results on the total of polysemous parallels discovered in Job, an obviously subjective enterprise when one considers that additional examples may still lie hidden, and that other types of word-play (paronomasia, antanaclasis, etc.) are not included, they nonetheless establish a trend.

Though Zophar speaks less than all the other characters, he uses the highest number of polysemes. His penchant for word-play fits well with his views on crafty verbosity. As he remarks: 'Is a multitude of words unanswerable? Must a loquacious person be right?' (11.2), and in 11.5-6: 'But would that God might speak, and talk to you himself. He would then tell you the secrets of wisdom, for there are two sides to sagacity.' That Zophar packs his brief discourses with polysemy may explain why he lacks a retort in the third cycle of the debate; he already has outstripped Job and thus he feels no need to respond a third time. On the other hand, that God employs polysemy least often lends to the directness of his rhetoric from the whirlwind. Though his three Janus constructions (38.24-25; 39.10-11, 19-20) demonstrate his ability to

1. Note how 'firebrands', parallels לפידים, 'torches', itself a play on פיד, 'ruin'.

respond quip for quip, he is content with his role as the final arbiter and referee for polysemes.

Also provocative is the fact that the youngest member of the debate, Elihu, uses polysemy more often than the eldest, Eliphaz. This statistic finds support in the expressed intentions of Elihu in 32.6-10:

> I have but few years, while you are old; therefore I was too awestruck and fearful to hold forth among you. I thought, 'let age speak; let advanced years declare wise things'. But truly it is the spirit in men, the breath of Shaddai, that gives them understanding. It is not the aged who are wise, the elders who understand how to judge. Therefore, I say, 'Listen to me; I too would hold forth.'

That he should provide a polysemous parallel immediately after this (32.11) is therefore completely apposite.[1]

Finally, a word needs to be said about Job, who, as it appears, did not win the word contest with regard to polysemy. Though Job speaks the greatest number of verses in the book, it is Zophar, who speaks the least number of verses, who bests him. Nevertheless, as God makes clear from the onset of his whirlwind speech (38.2), it is not the manner in which one speaks which makes one wise, but rather the oration's content and intent: 'Who it is who darkens counsel, speaking without knowledge?'

Janus Parallels as Referential Devices in Other Near Eastern Literatures

The examples of polysemous parallelism in Akkadian, Sumerian, Hittite, Ugaritic, Arabic, hieroglyphic Egyptian, and medieval Hebrew (see Appendix 2) demonstrate a widespread awareness of the device despite the obvious differences between the specific cultures which produced the respective literatures.

Cuneiform lends itself well to polysemy due to its complex system of polyvalent signs with multiple meanings. That the Mesopotamian scribes intended these word-plays is evident in the hermeneutic methods preserved for posterity in the commentaries of the ancient scribes. For example, the ancient commentaries on *Enuma Eliš* V.53-56 and the *Commentary to the Assyrian Cultic Calendar* demonstrate a tendency to explain a passage or name by breaking it up into its constituent signs

1. Perhaps we should see here a connection between word-play and the genre known as 'dispute poems'. See, for example, G.J. Reinink and H.L.J. Vanstiphout (eds.), *Dispute Poems and Dialogues in the Ancient and Mediaeval Near East: Forms and Types of Literary Debates in Semitic and Related Literatures* (ALBO, 42; Leuven: Peeters, 1991).

and reading them as separate words in a manner which is reminiscent of the later midrashic form of hermeneutics.[1]

Though I have not checked exhaustively for the referential use of polysemes in the ancient Near Eastern texts discussed in Appendix II, some referencing does appear evident in a few of the texts. For example, we find the play on the two meanings of *ubla* ('wash away' and 'determine') in XI.14 echoed later in the homecoming statement of Utu-napištim's wife: 'let him wash, throw away his pelts, let the sea carry (them) away (*libil tamtû*)' (XI.241). Similar is the highly polysemous line XI.19, which when read as 'You [Utu-napištim] sat with prince ^{d}Ea', answers Gilgameš's question in XI.7: 'How is it that you have stood in the assembly of the gods and have found life?'

The Chester Beatty papyrus also exhibits a referential quality. Note how the poet has bolstered his play on *wḏ3t*, 'eye of Horus/seeing', by saturating the text with references to 'seeing' (I.1, 2, 6; II.1, 3, 4, 7; III.1, 7; IV.2, 6), 'medicine' (I.8; III.3; IV.7, 8, 10), 'doctors' (IV.7, 8), 'diagnoses' (IV.8), and 'revival' (IV.9, 10). That the polyseme should connect 'seeing' and 'medicine', therefore, is quite appropriate.

2. *Polysemy and Wisdom Literature*

Virtually every commentator who has worked on the text of Job classifies it as a 'wisdom text' or as belonging to the 'wisdom genre'.[2]

1. For an excellent assessment of ancient hermeneutics see A. Livingstone, *Mystical and Mythological Explanatory Works of Assyrian and Babylonian Scholars* (Oxford: Clarendon Press, 1986); S.J. Lieberman, 'A Mesopotamian Background for the So-Called *Aggadic* "Measures" of Biblical Hermeneutics?', *HUCA* 58 (1987), pp. 157-225; A. Cavigneaux, 'Aux sources du Midrash: l'herméneutique babylonienne', *AcOr* 5.2 (1987), pp. 243-55; J. Bottéro, 'La creation de l'homme et sa nature dans le poème d'Atraḫasîs', in M.A. Dandamayev *et al.* (eds.), *Societies and Languages of the Ancient Near East: Studies in Honor of I.M. Diakonoff* (Warminster: Aris & Phillips, 1982), pp. 24-32; *idem*, *Mesopotamia: Writing, Reasoning, and the Gods* (Chicago: University of Chicago Press, 1992), pp. 87-102.

2. See, for example, J. Fichtner, *Die altorientalische Weisheit in ihrer israelitisch-jüdischen Ausprägung* (BZAW, 62; Giessen: Töpelmann, 1933); M. Noth and D.W. Thomas (eds.), *Wisdom in Israel and in the Ancient Near East* (VTSup, 3; Leiden: Brill, 1960); J. Patterson, *The Wisdom of Israel* (London: Lutterworth; Nashville: Abingdon Press, 1961); J. Wood, *Wisdom Literature* (London: Gerald Duckworth, 1967); G. von Rad, *Wisdom in Israel* (Nashville and New York: Abingdon Press, 1972); J.L. Crenshaw, 'Wisdom', in J.H. Hayes (ed.), *Old Testament Form Criticism* (San Antonio: Trinity University Press, 1974); *idem*,

To gain a clearer understanding of what constitutes a wisdom text, we appeal to the words of Robert Gordis:

> In its literature, Wisdom seeks to transmit its ideas about man's duty and destiny to readers and pupils. To achieve this objective, one of its principal methods is to call attention to the similarity existing between two objects, activities, situations, or types of character, thus revealing a relationship which the reader had not previously suspected.[1]

We may obtain some insight into how the ancient Israelites acquired wisdom by reading the book of Proverbs (1.2, 3, 6):

> To know wisdom and instruction, to comprehend the words of understanding, to receive the discipline of wisdom, justice, right, and equity... to understand a proverb (משל), and a figure (מליצה), the words of the wise, and their riddles (חידתם).

Clearly, to receive the wisdom of the ancients one must be capable of discerning meaning by analogy (משל)[2] and allusion through word-play (מליצה, חידתם).[3]

Interestingly, we also find the exhortation to listen carefully in order to perceive the imbedded riddles or mysteries of the wise in many of the texts which exhibit polysemous parallelism.[4] The numerous exhortations in the book of Job to listen closely, especially by Elihu, have been discussed above in conjunction with the poet's belief in words as reflected in the text. It is not necessary to repeat them here. Suffice it to add that

Studies in Ancient Israelite Wisdom (New York: Ktav, 1976); *idem*, *The Old Testament Wisdom: An Introduction* (Atlanta: John Knox, 1981); J. Gammie, *et al.* (eds.), *Israelite Wisdom: Theological and Literary Essays in Honor of Samuel Terrien* (Missoula: Scholars Press, 1978); M. Gilbert (ed.), *La Sagesse de l'Ancien Testament* (Gembloux: Duculot; Leuven: Leuven University Press, 1979); P. Skehan, *Studies in Israelite Poetry and Wisdom* (Washington, DC: Catholic Biblical Association of America, 1980); C.M. Laymon (ed.), *Wisdom Literature and Poetry: A Commentary on Job, Psalms, Proverbs, Ecclesiastes, the Song of Solomon* (Nashville: Abingdon Press, 1983); M.V. Fox, 'Words for Wisdom', *ZAH* 6 (1993), pp. 149-69.

1. Gordis, *The Book of God and Man*, p. 199.

2. A close link between the genre known as משל and word-play has been noted by Stern; see his *Parables in Midrash*, pp. 41, 44, 71, 73, 74, 59, 92, 111, 141, 146, 149, 155-56, 170-71, 181, 217.

3. For a similar observation see Gordon, 'New Light on the Hebrew Language', p. 29.

4. Given the connection between polysemy and wisdom literature, one might do well to search for polysemy in the proverbs of Aḥiqar.

in 39.17 God's comment equates smooth speech with wisdom: כי השה אלוה חכמה ולא חלק לה בבינה, 'for God deprived her [the ostrich] of wisdom, gave her no portion/smooth speech (חלק) for understanding'. This statement has all the more impact when one remembers that in the end, it is Job's manner of speaking which God justifies: 'I am incensed at you (Eliphaz) and your two friends, for you have not spoken to me correctly as did my servant Job' (42.7).

So too in the book of Hosea, a book which exhibits numerous polysemous parallels (see Appendix I), we find the statement: 'He who is wise will consider these words, he who is prudent will take note of them' (14.10). Perhaps it is in this light that we also should understand God's famous words to the punster of Deutero-Isaiah in 51.4, 'Each morning he awakens my ear to hear as disciples do', and to the first Isaiah in 6.9:

> You indeed shall hear, but not understand; see, but not perceive. This people's intellect is dull; heavy of ear, and eyes sealed. Lest, seeing with their eyes and hearing with their ears, its intellect understand, repent, and be healed.

What has been said above regarding the urge to listen carefully and its connection to wisdom can be said of other ancient Near Eastern literatures. In Mesopotamia, wisdom has always been connected with writing. The Assyrian monarch Aššurbanipal, for instance, praised Nabû, the god of the scribes, for giving him the wisdom to acquire the arts of reading and writing. We saw this connection in our texts in Utu-napištim's words to Gilgameš in XI.9-10: '"I will reveal to you, Gilgameš, a thing that is hidden, a secret of the gods I will tell you!"' Utu-napištim's declaration refers both to the contents of the secret (i.e., that the flood is coming) and the manner in which the secret will be delivered (i.e., through polysemy). Further support for the connection between what one hears and wisdom can be found in the noun *ḫasis* which means 'wisdom' and 'ears'.[1]

Similarly, we find at the close of the *Rights of Egašankalamma*: '[Secret lore of the great gods. An initiate may] show it [to another initiate]; the uninitiate may not see it.'[2] The same interest in preserving the secret polysemous knowledge of the gods also occurs in line 91 of the

1. See, for example, the four ears (*ḫasis*) of Marduk in *Enuma Eliš* I.97.

2. For excellent discussions on the lingual dimension of secret lore see H. Limet, 'Le secret et les écrits: aspects de l'ésotérisme en Mésopotamie ancienne', *Homo Religiosus* 13 (1986), pp. 248-49; P.A. Beaulieu, 'New Light on Secret Knowledge in Late Babylonian Culture', *ZA* 82 (1992), pp. 98-111.

Descent of Ištar in which the creation of a *zikru*, a polyseme meaning 'man/idea/penis', takes place through the 'wisdom (*emqi*) of Ea's mind'.[1]

An example of Ugaritic polysemy in the *Baal and ʿAnat* story (51.IV.14-18) also demonstrates the connection between wisdom and polysemy. The use of *šbʿr*, 'shine/load a caravan', in line 16 of that text follows shortly after Lady Asherah's command: '[Hear, Qadish-and-Amrar!]' (51.IV.1). Moreover, the decrees of the Ugaritic gods, in particular El, are treated as if imbued with magical power. For example, later in the text we find Lady Asherah equating Ea's wisdom with his word: 'Your word, El, is wise, your wisdom eternal; a lucky life is your word' (51.IV.41-42). Elsewhere, in *Baal and ʿAnat* III.12-16, El sends a message to the craft god Kothar-and-Ḫasis (lit. 'Skilled-and-Wise') in which he connects his secret speech with the mysteries of nature:

> For [I have] a w[ord that I shall tell you],
> a matter that I shall declare to you;
> [It is the word of a tree and the whisper of the stone],
> the murmur of the heavens to [the earth] of the [deep to the stars];
> A word that me[n] do not know,
> [nor the multitudes of the earth understand].
> Come and I shall rev[eal it].

Interestingly, the Qur'anic use of the polysemous *najmu*, 'stars/herbs', in *Surah* 55.6 follows immediately after a marked concern with the origin of mortal speech reminiscent of Elihu's remarks to Job: 'the beneficent has made known the Qur'an; he has created men, (and) he has taught him utterance' (55.1-4).

All of these texts are discussed again and in greater detail in Appendix 2, devoted to examples of Janus parallelism in extra-biblical literature.

In short, polysemy in particular and perhaps word-play in general is conventional to wisdom literature;[2] to the ancients, recognition of the device was tantamount to the acquisition of wisdom.[3]

1. This may also explain the fronting of the adjective *emqi* which one expects to find after the noun. For Ea's role as a double-speaker see Kramer and Maier, *Myths of Enki, the Crafty God*, pp. 99-126.

2. *Contra* J. Lindblom, 'Wisdom in the Old Testament Prophets', in Noth and Thomas (eds.), *Wisdom in Israel and in the Ancient Near East*, p. 203 n. 1, who remarks: 'Paronomasia, alliteration and such matters are to be found in the prophetic books as well as in the Wisdom writings... but I think the prophets use them simply as poetical forms, not specially in dependence on Wisdom.'

3. Note also the apocryphal work Bar. 3, in which the 'wise ones' are tellers of stories, allegories, and legends.

3. *The Continued Importance of Preserving Polysemy in the Ancient Translations*

The ancient belief in the importance of preserving words' multiple meanings extends into the periods which saw the production of the LXX, Targum, Peshitta, and Vulgate. In several instances, the various ancient translators attempted to render the pun with a pun.

The LXX shows clear evidence for this in 10.8 where it renders עצבוני, 'formed me/hurt me', with ἔπλασάν, 'formed' (from πλάσσω). Given the similarity and documented confusion[1] between πλάσσω and πλήσσω, 'smite, strike', the Greek may be seen as an attempt to bridge the two meanings of the Hebrew polyseme. The LXX also seems to have espied the Hebrew pun in 29.18. The polyseme at work here is חול, 'sand/Phoenix', which the LXX treats as στέλεχος φοίνικος, 'the stem of a palm tree'. The translation has been seen as an *ad sensum* attempt based solely on the context of 'roots reaching to water and dew lodging on my branches' (v. 19). What few have noticed,[2] however, is the closeness between φοίνικος and φοῖνιξ, 'Phoenix'. That this Greek word also means 'Phoenicians', that is, a coastal people, may represent an effort to render 'sand' as well. To offer just one more demonstration of the LXX's awareness of Hebrew polysemy I turn to 39.19. As I argued above, the LXX translated רעמה, 'quiver/mane', with φόβον, 'terror', in order to play upon φοβήν, 'mane'. Other passages discussed above which show an awareness of polysemy on the part of the LXX include 3.23-24, 25-26; 5.24; 9.9-11; 13.22-23; 18.11-13; 20.23-24; 24.19-21; 27.18-19; 28.3-4, 9-10; 29.20-23; 30.3; 36.15-16, 24-25, and 38.24-25.

The Targum also attempts to preserve polysemy either by rendering with a pun or by adding to the text. Clear examples for the former again can be found in 29.18 with the polyseme חול, 'sand/Phoenix', for which the Targum uses the cognate חלא, 'sand/Phoenix'. Similarly, for עצבוני, 'fashion me/hurt me', in 10.8 the Targum uses צירוני, both 'fashion me' and 'hurt me'. The Targum does not always rely on cognates to render puns. For example, to render בלחומי, 'with his food/in his battle fury', in 20.23 the Targum uses בשלדיה, 'into his burnt (decayed) carcass' or 'flake of flesh'. Sometimes, in order to preserve the polysemy, the Targum resorts to additions. For instance, in order to bring out both

1. *Iliad* 21.269 and *Odyssey* 5.389.

2. With the possible exception of Pope, *Job*, pp. 214-16, who suggests that it may be an 'oblique' reference to the Phoenix.

meanings of רחם, 'womb/rain', in 24.20, the Targum first renders the line with the cognate רחם (but as 'mercy') and then adds: '(the sky) withheld the rain water (מימי מטרה) and the snow (תלגא)' because of the people's sin in withholding the summer tithe. For additional examples of the Targumist's ability to capture the Hebrew polysemy see *Targ. Job* 3.23-24, 25-26; 5.24; 6.30–7.1; 7.6-7; 9.9-11; 13.22-23; 18.4-5; 19.11-12; 20.25, 27-28; 21.12-13; 22.5-6; 24.9-10, 20-21; 29.20-23 (3×); 30.5-6, 7-8; 36.15-16 (2×), 24-25, and 38.24-25.

In a few places Jerome's Vulgate also renders Hebrew polysemy with a Latin pun. Witness, for example, the polysemous יגל יבול in 20.28, both 'he will wash away the produce of (his house)' and 'he will expose the offspring (of his house)'. In order to render the double polysemy the Vulgate uses the expression *apertum erit germen domus*. Not only does the Latin *germen*, 'shoot, offspring', capture both nuances of יבול, but the base of *germen*, *gero*, means 'bear, carry (produce)' and 'reveal, show', that is, the other meaning of יגל. Similarly, to translate the Hebrew ערוץ, 'gully/terror', in 30.6, Jerome chose the word *torrentium*, 'channels', probably for its similarity in sound to *territum*, 'terror'. Like the LXX and Targum, Jerome sometimes resorted to additions in order to bring out the inherent polysemy. This is seen clearly with תקוה, 'hope/thread', in 7.6-7. Though Jerome translated the Hebrew polyseme as *spe*, 'hope', at the end of the previous stich he appended the line *quam a texente tela succiditur*, '(more) than the web is cut by the weaver'. As the Hebrew original mentions only a 'weaver's shuttle' (ארג) in this stich, we may see in Jerome's addition of 'web' and 'cutting' an awareness of the play. For additional evidence of the Vulgate's awareness of polysemy see 9.9-11; 18.4-5; 19.9-11; 20.25; 21.12-13, 23-24; 22.5-6; 24.20-21; 30.7-8; 36.15-16 (2×), 27-28, and 39.10-11.

The Peshitta also demonstrates an awareness of Hebrew polysemes, translating them either with puns or by way of additions.[1] To illustrate the former, I once again utilize רחם, 'womb/rain', in 24.20 which the Syriac renders with מרבעא, 'womb'. I suggested above that this represents a play on רביעא and רבעי, 'early rain, spring rain'. Arguing in favor of this is the fact that the Peshitta could have translated with the

1. For an extremely brief discussion of the Syriac's treatment of Hebrew polysemy see Szpek, *Translation Technique in the Peshitta to Job*, pp. 178-83, 248-52. That word-play is not uncommon in Syriac texts can be seen by the *Odes of Solomon*. See, for example, J.H. Charlesworth, 'Paronomasia and Assonance in the Syriac Text of the Odes of Solomon', *Semitics* 1 (1970), pp. 12-26.

cognate רחם but did not. A similar situation obtains in 3.25 with יגרתי, 'I feared, I have striven, stirred', for which the Syriac uses זאע, 'fear/stir up, set in motion'. In 6.20 the Peshitta renders the two meanings of the root חפר, 'search/be ashamed', by way of addition: ומטו לקתה ואחפרו, 'they came to gaze steadfastly and they were ashamed'. For additional evidence of the Peshitta's recognition of polysemy see 9.9-11; 10.7-8; 13.22-23; 20.27-28 (2x); 21.12-13; 22.5-6; 28.9-10; 29.20-23; 30.5-6; 36.15-16, and 39.10-11.

Statistically speaking, of the total number of polysemes recognized in Job (49), it is the Targum which shows the greatest awareness, translating with cognates, puns, or additions in 24/49 cases. The LXX and Peshitta follow the Targum, showing an awareness in 14/49 cases each, and the Vulgate in only 13/49. It would appear that the cognate languages, as one might expect, possess a greater ability to capture polysemy than do the non-cognate languages.

The versions demonstrate an awareness of and attempt to render the polysemous passages of the Hebrew text, suggesting the need for a fresh examination of the LXX.[1] Typically, in order to explain instances of textual variance among the versions, especially in the LXX, a different *Vorlage* has been posited.[2] The evidence above suggests that in some cases the variance may be due to the translators' desire to preserve the sacred word by rendering it fully, that is, by capturing its polysemy. To cite just one example I return to חול, 'sand/Phoenix', in 29.18, which the LXX treated as στέλεχος φοίνικος, 'the stem of a palm tree'. Some scholars[3] assume that the cause of the variance was a *Vorlage* which read נחל, 'palm tree' (cf. Num. 24.6) instead of חול. However, the closeness between φοίνικος, 'palm tree', and φοῖνιξ, 'Phoenix', suggests that the LXX translators merely attempted to construe the polysemy.

Similarly, the Targum's propensity for paraphrase and textual additions might not represent variant traditions in every case. We have seen in 24.20, for example, how the Targumist's lengthy addition confronts the dual nuances of the Hebrew polyseme רחם, 'womb/rain'. This

1. The excellent work of the following scholars notwithstanding: M. Greenberg, 'Ancient Versions for Interpreting the Hebrew Text', in J.A. Emerton *et al.* (eds.), *Congress Volume: Gottingen, 1977* (VTSup, 29; Leiden: Brill, 1978, pp. 131-48; Heater, *A Septuagint Translation Technique in the Book of Job*; J. Ziegler, *Beiträge zum griechischen Iob* (Göttingen: Vandenhoeck & Ruprecht, 1985).

2. The best discussion on this remains Orlinsky, 'Job: Chapter I', pp. 53-74.

3. See, for example, Gordis, *The Book of Job*, p. 321.

observation also calls into question M. Goshen-Gottstein's opinion that the Targumic variants are from a didactic rather than an explanatory tradition.[1]

While the above does not imply that all problems of variance between the versions and the Masoretic Text can be explained in this way, it does suggest that an awareness of polysemy in the Hebrew text might shed light on a few textual problems.

4. *Other Implications*

Janus Parallelism within the Context of Biblical Word-Play

In addition to the literary and social contexts in which we must examine polysemous parallelism, there is the context of word-play in general into which we must place the device. Many types of word-play exist in the Bible, for which many different terms have been employed (such as antanaclasis, paronomasia and anagrams).[2] Of note, however, is the relationship between them: their shared characteristics of sound and meaning manipulation, internal hermeneutics, and the subverting of reader/ listener expectations.[3] While scholarly research tends to compartmentalize word-play into distinct and independent types, this approach blurs the interdependence of and interaction between the various kinds of wordsmithing.

The relationship, for instance, between antanaclasis and polysemy may be closer than presently recognized. To illustrate, I first refer to the multifarious use of the root קוה discussed above. Its use in the Janus parallelism in Job 7.6-7 has been established already. What has not been pointed out, however, is that every time we find the root being used with a different meaning, we are dealing essentially with antanaclasis.[4]

1. M. Goshen-Gottstein, *Fragments of Lost Targumim* (Ramat-Gan: Bar-Ilan University Press, 1983), p. 20.

2. For definitions of these and other terms see Sasson, 'Word-Play in the Old Testament', pp. 968-70; Greenstein, 'Wordplay, Hebrew', pp. 968-71.

3. See, for example, the similarity between Janus parallelism and what W.G.E. Watson ('The Pivot Pattern in Hebrew, Ugaritic and Akkadian Poetry', *ZAW* 88 [1976], pp. 239-53) calls the 'pivot pattern'. This observation was anticipated by Christensen, 'Anticipatory Paronomasia in Jonah 3.7-8 and Genesis 37.2', p. 261 n. 2, and perhaps also by the rabbis (cf. *y. ʿAbod. Zar.* 3.41c; *b. Yom.* 52a-b; and *Ber. R.* 80b).

4. See, for example, A.R. Ceresko, 'The Function of Antanaclasis (*mṣʾ* "to find"//*mṣʾ* "to reach, overtake, grasp") in Hebrew Poetry, Especially in the Book of Qoheleth', *CBQ* 44 (1982), pp. 551-69.

To demonstrate the interaction between the Janus phenomenon and paronomasia I point to Eliphaz's quip in Job 24.24-26a: 'If you regard precious ore (בצר) as dirt, Ophir-gold as stones (בצור) from the wadi; (let) Shaddai be your precious ore (בצריך) and precious silver for you when you seek the favor of Shaddai.' One cannot help but hear the similarity in sound between the lexemes in parentheses. What makes the relationship between paronomasia and polysemy so close here is the fact that Eliphaz's words provide Job with the materials for his Janus construction in 28.9-10 (see Chapter 3).

That anagrams are tied up with the polysemous parallels can be seen in Elihu's polysemous remark to Job in 36.15-16: 'He rescues (יחלץ) the lowly from their affliction, and opens their understanding through distress (בלחץ). Indeed he draws you from the mouth of distress/ confinement (צר).' Note how the words 'rescues' and 'distress' are different only in the metathesis of their consonants. It is this relationship between Job's 'rescue' and his 'distress' that Elihu underscores with his choice of words and which is brought out still further by the polyseme צר.

Extra-Biblical Janus Parallels and Other Types of Word-Play

The extra-biblical examples of polysemous parallelism listed in Appendix 2 also exhibit a close relationship to other types of word-play. The polysemous parallel from the Qur'an 55.5-6 is a case in point. The scholarly world has been aware of the play here for many years, but as an example of *tawriyya*, that is, a word-play which subverts the expectation of the hearer by providing two meanings for a word, the second of which is the intended meaning. The distinction between *tawriyya* and polysemous parallelism is purely a scholarly construct. Whether the reader understands a word as having two meanings, of which only one is 'correct' (*tawriyya*), or two simultaneous meanings (polysemous parallelism), depends on the reader's philosophical openness to multiplicity of meaning.

The connection between antanaclasis and Janus parallelism also adheres in some of the Akkadian examples discussed in Appendix 2. For example, in the *Descent of Ištar* lines 29-30 we find that the polysemous *ša-pat(ṭ)*, when read as 'lip', parallels *šapat*, 'lip', in the next stich.

Note also the combined use of polysemy and paronomasia in *Gilgameš* XI.25-26, where the polysemous phrase *makkura zērma* in line 26 appears after the paronomastic expression *muššir mešrê*, 'abandon wealth', and before the similarly alliterative *libbi* ^{giš}*elippi*, 'heart of the boat'. See also how *zēr*, '(living) being', in line 27 rehearses the polysemous *zērma* in line 26 and how *napšāti*, 'living things', is repeated (with some variation) in lines 25, 26, and 27.

Similarly, observe the repeated bilabial /*b*/ and liquids /*l*/ and /*r*/ at work in *Gilgameš* XI.14: *šakān abūbi ubla libbašunu ilāni rabûti*, 'the great gods determined to bring about (flood with) the deluge'.

The use of paronomasia in conjunction with polysemous parallelism can be seen also in the Baal and ʿAnat story from Ugarit. As noted in Appendix II, the pericope containing the polyseme *šbʿr*, 'shine/prepare a caravan', is bound together by paronomasia between *ʿr*, 'donkey' (line 14), and *šbʿr* (line 16), and between *ʾṯrt*, 'Asherah' (line 14), and *ʾṯrt*, 'march' (line 18).

Surah 55.5-6 of the Qur'an also combines polysemy with paronomasia. Note how the passage is both alliterative, repeating the sounds /*j*/, /*n*/, and /*m*/, but also assonantal, lulling the readers with both short and long /*u*/ and /*a*/ vowels, as well as a rhyme pattern.

Given the multiple possibilities for polysemy which a syllabic system offers, as opposed to a consonantal one, we should perhaps also see the origins of anagrammatic whimsy in the cuneiform writing. To illustrate the proclivity of such a system for anagrams we may utilize *Enuma Eliš* I.21-23. Here we find the polysemy revolving around the polyvalent *muš* sign, which can be read both as *ṣir* and *muš*. Specifically, *nāṣiršunu*, 'their guard(ian)', may be read *namuššūnu*, 'they surged back and forth'. That the sign *muš* may be read as a Sumerogram meaning *ṣerru*, 'serpent', a fitting creature to find imbedded in the creation epic, demonstrates the advantage which the cuneiform system has for creating polyvalent anagrams.

Consider also the polysemous *zikru*, 'man/idea/penis', in line 91 of the *Descent of Ištar*; one meets this word again in an anagram in Ereškigal's curse upon the *zikru* Aṣu-šunamir: 'Come Aṣu-šunamir, I will curse you (*luzirkā*) with a great curse' (line 103). One also hears in lines 103-104 anagrammatic plays between 'come' (*alkā*) and 'food' (*akali*/*akalkā*).

In presenting this evidence I am not suggesting that scholars should abandon altogether the various terms used to describe the numerous types of word-play, but rather that the interaction between the various types be recognized and systematically examined. The alternative, therefore, to atomizing word-play into unrelated and independent classes is not based on a change in terminology, but rather on a change in approach, an approach which sees the various kinds of word-play as existing on a continuum.

Janus Parallelism in Job and its Impact on Textual Criticism

The recognition of polysemy in the passages examined above also bears upon issues of textual criticism. In a few instances, the polyseme involved in the Janus usage appears as a spelling *defectiva*. Such difficulties incline some scholars to emend the text; however, it is precisely this non-normative orthography which permits multiple meanings. In 32.11, Elihu plays upon two meanings inherent in אזין, 'give ear' (from *ʾdn*) and 'weigh' (from *wzn*). However, to achieve the meaning 'give ear' one expects to find אאזין. For this reason the critical apparatus of the *Biblia Hebraica Stuttgartensia* proposes to add the *aleph*. Yet no emendation is warranted, for it is precisely this non-normative orthography that allows the poet to achieve his polysemy.

Similarly, the author of Job wrote מלתי in 32.18 without an *aleph* in order to exploit the ambiguity of such an orthography. By recording the word aphaeretically, the poet was able to convey two, possibly three meanings: 'speaking' (from מלל), 'squeezing' (from מלל [Aramaic]), and 'filling' (from מלא). Again, the recognition of polysemy negates the need to emend the text.

The same argument applies to polysemes which are consonantally normative, but which require different vocalizations. For example, יגרתי in 3.25 mixes the vocalizations of the roots יגר, 'fear', and גור, 'stir up'; יגל in 20.28 requires a different pronunciation whether it means 'wash over' or 'remove'. We may add to this list a few others: בצרות (28.10), יחלו (29.21), ידמו (28.10), and ישנו (29.22).

The same punful exploitation of non-normative orthography obtains in the extra-biblical texts containing polysemy. For example, in order to bear the meaning 'boat', *makkuru*, 'property', in *Gilgameš* XI.26 should be spelled *makuru*. Yet, as is pointed out in Appendix 2, such an orthography, though rare, is not unattested. The poet merely opted for the rarer spelling in order to achieve his polysemy. We see a similar use of non-normative orthography in line 5 of the tale of the *Poor Man of Nippur*. There it is 'silver' uniquely spelled *kàs-pa* (not the expected KÙ.BABBAR) which enabled the poet to obtain the meaning 'bodily exuberance' (*kazba*).

Such non-normative orthography, I would argue, is the poet's way of alerting the reader to hidden polysemy, and by extension, to concealed wisdom. In some cases, it is not the polyseme which is marked by unique orthography, but another word in the passage. For example, in the *Descent of Ištar*, the poet hints at the double meaning of *šuqi*, 'raise' and 'drink', by placing after it the Sumerograms SAG.MEŠ (lit. 'heads'). The so-called scribal error facilitates the polysemy by forcing the reader to question: 'Whose head, Aṣu-šunamir's or Ereškigal's?' That there is some confusion over the usage can be seen by the fact that Aṣu-šunamir must clarify the matter for Ereškigal: 'No my lady, let them give me the waterskin so that I may drink water from it' (line 99).

Similarly, the poet of the *Descent of Ištar* (line 104) alerted the reader to the double meaning of the crux ^{giš}APIN.MEŠ, 'garbage dump' and 'bakers', by attaching to it the determinative ^{giš}, a sign which forces upon the reader yet another and inappropriate meaning, 'plow'. The confusion causes the reader to pause and explore the various possibilities for its interpretation.

There are still other ways for a scribe to alert the reader to the presence of polysemy. In the *Commentary to the Assyrian Cultic Calendar*, the author caused the polysemy of the expression *tīk zāre*, 'drop of sprinkling' and 'muster of hatred', in line 11 to stick out by placing it out of calendrical order. The polysemes occur in day 26, which is placed quite oddly between days 23 and 24. It is only by placing the commentary on day 26 in such a position that the poet was able to create a polysemous parallel.

Composition and Form: Toward a Syntax of Janus Parallelism

Though a syntactical examination is outside the parameters of this study, it is important to note that the consistency in form exhibited by the polysemous constructions not only bespeaks a need for a more comprehensive examination of the syntagmas involved with the usage, but more importantly, it lends support to the argument that polysemous parallels were intended by the author of Job. Of the 70 total biblical Janus constructions examined in this work, 64 are symmetrical in form, that is, they are accomplished in three stichs. Of these 64, 20 place the polyseme at the head of the stich, 20 in the middle, and 24 at the end. This suggests that the primary concern was the placement of the polyseme in the second of three stichs, and only secondarily with its position within that stich. Similarly, of the 6 asymmetrical Januses, 3 place the polyseme at the head of the stich, 2 in the middle and 1 at the end.

As for the totals of the various types of polysemes in Job, the author shows a nearly equal propensity for polysemes which are both oral and visual as for strictly visual polysemes; there are 26 of the former and 23 of the latter.[1] Only 1 polyseme has not been included in these totals, due to a lack of certain etymological information (Job 29.18-20).

The Unity of the Book of Job

The difficulties which confront the form critic when reading Job, specifically with regard to its present structure, have been discussed thoroughly by many scholars. Apposite to our discussion is that in the third cycle of the debate (chs. 25–28) Bildad's speech seems too short (ch. 25), Zophar lacks a third speech, and Job's sentiments (26.5-14) appear to mirror the previous remarks of his three friends. The present structure has led some scholars to reconstruct Zophar's missing speech from Job's remarks in 26.5-14 and to see ch. 28, the so-called Hymn to Wisdom, as a secondary addition.

Also problematic are Elihu's speeches in chs. 32–37, which appear to interrupt an otherwise consistent pattern: Job never responds to Elihu, and in the epilogue, neither God nor the narrator acknowledges his presence in the debate. Indeed, some view his speeches as intrusive, delaying the smooth transition from Job's request that God appear to God's theophany and response. Others have noted that Elihu's speeches fail to provide the anticipated solution to the problem of evil raised by Job. This also has caused some to question whether Elihu's speeches are not the result of a clumsy author or later redactor.

God's speeches in chs. 38–41 have also passed through the treadmill of form criticism. Not only have they been divided into two separate speeches, each ending with a statement by Job, but some have seen in them support for Job's claim that God relies on power and not justice.

While some of the arguments for the above observations are compelling, my examination of the text of Job finds such atomistic concerns unwarranted.[2] The complex system of referencing which occurs in Job,

1. One should keep in mind, however, that Job's statement in 6.3 may imply phonemic blending for poetic purposes: 'For this reason I have spoken indistinctly'. Thus, the oral difference between the two or more lexemes contained in a polyseme may at times be negligible. (The excellent work by some scholars to the contrary notwithstanding; see, for example, J. Barr, 'St Jerome and the Sounds of Hebrew', *JSS* 12.1 [1967], pp. 1-36.)

2. See also M. Segal, ספר איוב, *Tarbiz* 13 (1942), pp. 73-91; J.C. Holbert, '"The Skies Will Uncover His Iniquity": Satire in the Second Speech of Zophar (Job XX)', *VT* 31 (1981), pp. 171-79; Y. Hoffman, 'The Relation between the Prologue and the Speech-Cycles in Job', *VT* 31 (1981), pp. 160-70; *idem*, 'Ancient Near Eastern Literary Conventions and the Restoration of the Book of Job', *ZAW*

especially with regard to polysemous usages and internal quotations,[1] often crosses chapter and section boundaries. The final references made by God in chs. 38–41, for example, connect both speeches together and also link them to chs. 18, 19, 20, 21, 22, 24, 28, 29, 30, 31, 32, and 36. References to polysemes also bind together the discourses of Job and his friends. For example, the polyseme גר, 'stranger/crater', in the Hymn to Wisdom (28.4) plays upon the nearly verbatim expression עשה גדלות אין חקר ונפלאות עד אין מספר (9.10). Such is also the case with בצרות, 'in the rocks/precious ore', in the Hymn (28.10) which refers back to 22.24-26 and ahead to 36.19. Such referencing suggests that the Hymn to Wisdom is original and integral to the text. It is for this reason that I view ch. 29, the Hymn to Wisdom, as a continuation of Job's speech in ch. 28.[2]

The remaining structural problems facing scholars also vanish upon closer scrutiny. We may explain the brevity of Bildad's discourse in ch. 25, for example, as the poet's way of expressing Bildad's frustration. He simply has talked himself dry of answers. He has tried to convince Job, but like his friends, he has failed. In ch. 25, he simply has little more to add. Thus, there is no reason why one should expect a longer discourse.

That Job's statements in 26.5-14 mirror the remarks of his friends should also come as no surprise. Such referencing, as demonstrated above, is the poet's way of lending realism to the debate. Moreover, one should not search for Zophar's missing speech in 26.5-14, because, like Bildad, Zophar has given up with Job. He has nothing more to add. In a real argument few would expect neat and consistent patterns of discourse. To expect such consistency in the Jobian debate only denies the poet's talent for realism. Indeed, Bildad's brevity and Zophar's silence prepare us for Elihu's speeches, for which the narrator provides an apposite preface: 'But when Elihu saw that the three men had nothing to reply, he was angry' (32.5).

103 (1991), pp. 399-411; D. Wolfers, 'The Speech-Cycles in the Book of Job', *VT* 43 (1993), pp. 385-402.

1. See, for example, Gordis, *The Book of God and Man*, pp. 169-208; M. Fishbane, 'The Book of Job and Inner-Biblical Discourse', in L.G. Perdue and W.C. Gilpin (eds.), *The Voice from the Whirlwind: Interpreting the Book of Job* (Nashville: Abingdon Press, 1992), pp. 86-98.

2 *Contra* Gordis, *The Book of Job*, p. 298, who though seeing it as penned by the author of Job, believes it to be 'not an integral part of the book of Job'. For additional references see Chapter 3.

That Elihu's speeches appear as intrusive should not deter us either, for he admits the same: 'I have but few years, while you are old; therefore I was too awestruck and fearful to hold forth among you. I thought, "let age speak; let advanced years declare wise things".' It is because of his youth that he adds little of consequence to the contents of the debate and fails to answer Job's theological dilemma. As Donald Gowan noted in his discussion of the scripting of wisdom literature:

> [Elihu] is not the hero of the story who resolves the dilemma by his superior gifts of wisdom. He really has nothing new to say; even his most distinctive contribution, suffering for disciplinary purposes, has already been anticipated by Eliphaz (5.17-18). All his words demonstrate that Job and his friends have in fact exhausted the resources of wisdom.[1]

Therefore, it is because of Elihu's lack of wisdom, and possibly also because of the ancient deference to and respect for elders, that we do not find this brash youngster in the epilogue.

While the above does not attempt to answer all the perplexing questions raised by the composition of the book of Job, much less the numerous lexical peculiarities, it does argue for a greater unity for the book of Job than recognized by most exegetes.[2]

1. D. Gowan, 'Reading Job as Wisdom Script', *JSOT* 55 (1992), p. 96.

2. The following note lists commentaries and articles on the book of Job which make little or no reference to word-play. I have made no attempt at an exhaustive list, but list only a selection in order to illustrate the lack of recognition of word-play by scholars. Please refer to the bibliography for complete entries. F. Andersen; St Thomas Aquinas; W.E. Aufrecht; K. Barth; J.R. Baskin; A.C.M. Blommerde; H. Bloom; St John Chrysostom; D.W. Cotter; K.J. Dell; Didymos of Alexandria; J.H. Eaton; J. Eisenberg; G. Fohrer; F.E. Gaebelein; J.C.L. Gibson; E.M. Good; M. Guinan; N.C. Habel; F. Hesse; G. Holscher; G.J. Janzen; A. Jepsen; Fl. Julian; O. Keel; V. Kubina; H. Lamparter; A. Lichtenstein; V. Maag; R. Martin-Achard; D.L. McKenna; Olympiodorus; J. van Oorschot; V.E. Reichert; H. Richter; C.S. Rodd; A.J. Rosenberg; H.J. Rowley; A. van Selms; D.J. Simundson; N.H. Snaith; P.P. Szczygiel; S.L. Terrien; M. Tsevat; C. Westermann; R.N. Whybray.

APPENDIX 1

HITHERTO UNRECOGNIZED EXTRA-JOBIAN JANUS PARALLELS

Hosea 1.6-7

כי לא אוסיף עוד ארחם את בית ישראל
כי נשא אשא להם
ואת בית יהודה ארחם

> For I will no longer have mercy on the House of Israel כי נשא אשא להם
> And/but I will have mercy on the House of Judah.

The phrase כי נשא אשא להם, as pointed out already by Ibn Ezra, may be understood both as 'I will certainly carry them off' and as 'I will certainly pardon them'. Though Ibn Ezra was the first to point out the double meaning, he appears to have been unaware of Janus parallelism. With the sense of 'carry off', the Janus root נשא echoes לא אוסיף עוד ארחם את בית ישראל, 'I will no longer have mercy on the House of Israel', in line 6. With the sense 'pardon' it anticipates ואת בית יהודה ארחם, 'But I will have mercy on the House of Judah'. With one sentence, Yahweh pronounces a dual judgment.

Hosea 2.8-9

לכן הנני שך את דרכך בסירים
וגדרתי את גדרה ונתיבותיה לא תמצא
ורדפה את מאהביה ולא תשיג אתם
ובקשתם ולא תמצא ואמרה אלכה

> Therefore I will hedge up your way with thorns, and I will fence her in, so that she cannot find her paths.
> She will pursue her lovers, but not תשיג them. She will seek them but will not find them. Then she will say: 'I will return to my first husband, for it was better with me then than now.'

The root סוג means both 'move away, turn away, backslide' and 'fence about'.[1] If we read ולא תשיג אתם as 'she will not fence them in' the stich echoes שך את דרכך בסירים, 'I will hedge up your way with thorns (and I will fence her in)' in the previous line. However, if we read the phrase as 'you will not turn to them' we see it as an anticipation of 'She will seek them but will not find them. Then she will say: "I will return to my first husband, for it was better with me then than now".' Though the pun is separated from its referents by more than a stich it is no less impactful or meaningful.

Hosea 4.2-3

אלה וכחש ורצח וגנב ונאף
פרצו ודמים בדמים נגעו
על כן תאבל הארץ ואמלל כל יושב בה

By swearing, and lying, and killing, and stealing, and committing adultery, they break out, and נגעו ודמים בדמים.

Therefore, the land will mourn, and every one who dwells in it will languish.

The words in the phrase ודמים בדמים נגעו, 'blood touches blood', may be derived from either דמה, 'bleed', or דמם, 'wail, lament'.[2] As 'blood', the phrase links to the heinous acts described in v. 2, especially to the killing; and as 'wailing' it is connected with the phrase in line 3 'the land will mourn'.

Hosea 4.7-8

כרבם כן חטאו לי
כבודם בקלון אמיר
חטאת עמי יאכלו ואל עונם ישאו נפשו

According to their increase, they sin against me, I will אמיר their honor for shame.

They devour the sins of my people, and for iniquity they lift up their appetite.

The Janus here revolves around the word אמיר, which means both 'exchange' and 'procure food'. As the former, אמיר shadows the reciprocal relationship between the sinners' increase of their sins and the

1. BDB, pp. 690-91.

2. These definitions are supported by BDB, pp. 198-99, and by an Akkadian cognate meaning 'wail'; *CAD* D, p. 59, s.v. *damāmu*.

increase of their population. We might well render the line 'I will exchange their honor for shame'. When read according to its other meaning, the stich becomes a fitting parallel for 'they devour the sins of my people, and for iniquity they lift up their appetite' in the next line. We may, therefore, also translate our Janus stich 'I will procure their honor with shame'.

Hosea 4.16-17

כי כפרה סררה סרר ישראל
עתה ירעם יהוה ככבש במרחב
חבור עצבים אפרים הנח לו

For as a backsliding heifer, Israel backslides,
Now Yahweh will ירעם as a lamb in a wide place,
Ephraim is joined to idols: let him alone.

As 'he will pasture' ירעם faces the preceding line in which a heifer is mentioned. As 'he will associate' it faces forward to חבור עצבים, 'joined to idols'. The connection is strengthened by the fact that חבור not only means 'joined' but also 'associate with, be a friend of'.[1]

Hosea 6.7-9

והמה כאדם עברו ברית שם בגדו בי
גלעד קרית פעלי און עקבה מדם
וכחכי איש גדודים חבר כהנים
דרך ירצחו שכמה כי זמה עשו

But they, like a man, have transgressed the covenant: there have they dealt treacherously against me.
Gilead[2] is a city of them that work iniquity, and which is עקבה in blood.
And as troops of robbers wait for a man, so the company of priests murder in the way by consent; for they commit lewdness.

Here the word עקבה, 'foot-tracked', also may be read as 'deceitful'.[3] The word is used in association with גדודים, 'troops', in Gen. 49.19. It is joined to 'treacherously' in the previous line by its meaning 'deceitful'.

1. BDB, p. 288.
2. Note the similar word-plays on 'Gilead', 'Gad', and 'troops' in Gen. 49.19.
3. Both readings are given in BDB, p. 784.

Hosea 7.16

ישובו לא על
היו כקשת רמיה
יפלו בחרב שריהם מזעם לשונם

They return not to the Most High, they are a קשת רמיה, their princes will fall by the sword from the insolence of their tongues.

Pertinent here is the phrase קשת רמיה, 'bow of deceit', which may also be read as 'bow which has shot (its arrow)'.[1] Connected to this is the phrase ישובו לא על, which also may be read as 'they do not return from going up'. As 'deceit' רמיה connects with מזעם, 'insolence', in the next verse. The verse may therefore be rendered 'they do not return (from) going up, they are (like) a bow which has shot (its arrow)' or as 'they do not return from the Most High, they are a bow of deceit'. We also may classify this polysemous parallel, therefore, as a double polysemy. It is interesting to note that Hosea might have alerted his readers to the presence of such word-plays (lest they go unnoticed) at the end of his prophecies in Hos. 14.10: 'He who is wise will consider these words; he who is prudent will take note of them.'

Song of Songs 1.7

הגידה לי שאהבה נפשי
איכה תרעה
איכה תרביץ בצהרים

Tell me, O whom my soul loves, where do you תרעה?
Where do you lie down (your flocks) at noon?

Of significance is the word תרעה. It may be derived either from רעה 'pasture', or from רעה (= רצה), 'desire'.[2] As 'pasture' the verb looks ahead to the question 'Where do you lie down (your flocks) at noon?'

1. Both the root רמה and the word לשון, 'tongue', are used elsewhere in connection with arrows: in Jer. 9.7, 'Their tongue (לשונם) is as an arrow shot out, it speaks deceit (מרמה)'; in Jer. 4.29 the root is used in reference to archers; and in Prov. 25.18, 'A man that bears false witness against his neighbor is a maul, and a sword, and a sharp arrow.'

2. As 'desire' it represents the Aramaic reflex ḍ >ʿ; see also Hos. 12.2, a text exhibiting IH and/or Aramaic features, and Ps. 9.7. For the latter see Rendsburg, *Linguistic Evidence for the Northern Origin of Selected Psalms*, pp. 19-20.

In its sense 'desire' it faces back to the phrase שאהבה נפשי, 'O whom my soul loves'. As further support for this reading it is important to note that the verb רצה also occurs parallel to the verb אהב, 'love', in Prov. 3.12.

Isaiah 14.11-13

הורד שאול גאונך המית נבליך
תחתיך יצע רמה ומכסיך תולעה
איך נפלת משמים הילל בן שחר
נגדעת לארץ חולש על גוים
ואתה אמרת בלבבך השמים אעלה
ממעל לכוכבי אל ארים כסאי

Your pride is brought down to She'ol, the sound of your harps; maggots are the bed beneath you, and worms are your covering.
How you are fallen, O הילל, Son of Dawn! How you are cut to the ground, you who have laid the nations low.
You said in your heart, 'I will ascend to Heaven; above the stars of Elohim, I will set my throne on high.'

The Janus occurs with the word הילל, 'Shining One'. In its meaning 'shine', the root הלל connects with 'the stars of Elohim' in the following verse. As 'Boastful One', it echoes גאונך, 'your pride', in the previous line.

Appendix 2

JANUS PARALLELS IN EXTRA-BIBLICAL SOURCES

The relative frequency with which the biblical writers employed Janus parallelism prompted me to look to other Near Eastern literatures for the existence of this phenomenon. Though I found paronomasia (sound-play) mentioned in books and articles with some frequency,[1] I found polysemy rarely noted and of course Janus parallelism mentioned even more rarely. (In fact, one case posited by Watson in Ugaritic turned out to be a poor example.[2]) Thus, below are examples of polysemous parallelism which I have discovered in ancient Near Eastern sources.

1. *Akkadian*

The Epic of Gilgameš XI.14[3]

> *šakān abūbi ubla libbašunu ilānī rabûti*
> the great gods set their hearts to *ubla* the deluge.

Here *ubla* means both 'want, desire, yearn for, determine',[4] in which case it anticipates *libbašunu*, 'their hearts',[5] and 'carry off, sweep away

1. See the works of the scholars listed below in the bibliography: Abusch, Alster, Artzi and Malamat, Astour, Biggs, Bottéro, Cavigneaux, Civil, Cooper, Eichler, Ellis, Foster, Foxvog, Geller, Güterbock, Hurowitz, Jacobsen, Kilmer, Kramer, Livingstone, Machinist and Tadmor, Nemet-Nejat, Neugebauer, Oberhuber, Oppenheim, Poebel, Sasson, Sauren, Sefati, Soll, Speiser, Stol, Tinney, Veldhuis, Wallenfels, van der Westhuizen, and von Wilcke.

2. See Noegel, 'A Janus Parallelism in the Baal and ʿAnat Story', pp. 91-94.

3. See Noegel, 'An Asymmetrical Janus Parallelism in the Gilgamesh Flood Story', pp. 10-12.

4. *CAD* A/1, pp. 21-22, s.v. *abālu*.

5. *libbu* frequently occurs as the subject of *abālu*. See *CAD* A/1, p. 21, s.v. *abālu*.

(said of water)',[1] in which case it relates back to *abūbi*, 'the deluge'.[2] That both readings are acceptable by context suggests that both were intended. This Janus is of the asymmetrical type, that is, it is not accomplished in three stichs, a type which is also known from the Bible.[3]

As noted by Anne Draffkorn Kilmer,[4] similar word manipulation is common and quite meaningful in the *Gilgameš Epic* and is often accompanied by clues given by the characters in the story. Accordingly, one wonders if such subtleties are alluded to in lines 9-10 of the same tablet by Utu-napištim when he proclaims *lupetkā* ^{d}*Gilgameš amat niṣirti u pirīšta ša ilāni kâša luqbīkā*, '"I will reveal to you, Gilgameš, a thing that is hidden, a secret of the gods I will tell you!"' Moreover, it should be noted that the verb *wabālu* occurs in XI.241: 'let him wash, throw away his pelts, let the sea carry (them) away' (*libil tâmtu*).[5]

The Epic of Gilgameš XI.16-20[6]

> *malikšunu quradu* ^{d}*Enlil*
> Their counsellor was the hero ^{d}Enlil.
> *guzalâšunu* ^{d}*Ninurta*
> Their Chairbearer was ^{d}Ninurta.
> *gugallâšunu* ^{d}*Ennugi*
> Their Canal Inspector was ^{d}Enuggi.

1. *CAD* A/1, pp. 16-17, s.v. *abālu*; *AHw*, pp. 145-1452, s.v. *w/babālu*. So A. Schott, 'Zu meiner Übersetzung des Gilgameš-Epos', *ZA* 42 (1934), p. 136.

2. Note that *šakānu* can also mean 'to inflict loss or calamity'; *CAD* Š/1, pp. 129, 130, 155, s.v. *šakānu*; *AHw*, p. 1138, s.v. *šakānu*.

3. For biblical examples see Gordon, 'Asymmetric Janus Parallelism', p. 80*, and '"This Time" (Genesis 2.23)', in M. Fishbane and E. Tov (eds.), *'Sha'arei Talmon': Studies in the Bible, Qumran, and the Ancient Near East Presented to Shemaryahu Talmon* (Winona Lake, IN: Eisenbrauns, 1992), pp. 50-51.

4. A.D. Kilmer, 'A Note on an Overlooked Word-Play in the Akkadian Gilgamesh', in G. Van Driel, Th.J.H. Krispijn, M. Stol and K.R. Veenhof (eds.), *Zikir Sumim: Assyriological Studies Presented to F.R. Kraus on the Occasion of his Seventieth Birthday* (Leiden: Brill, 1982), pp. 128-32; 'Les jeux de mots dans les rêves de Gilgamesh et d'Atraḫasis' (paper read at Universitaire des Sciences Humaines, Strasbourg, 1983), pp. 1-7; 'The Symbolism of the Flies in the Mesopotamian Flood Myth and Some Further Implications', in F. Rochberg-Halton (ed.), *Language, Literature, and History: Philological and Historical Studies Presented to Erica Reiner* (New Haven, CT: American Oriental Society, 1987), pp. 175-80.

5. For this see *CAD* A/1, p. 16b, s.v. *abālu*.

6. See also Noegel, 'Janus Parallelism Clusters in Akkadian Literature', pp. 33-34.

> *^{d}Nin-ši-kù ^{d}Ea ittīšunu ta-me(šib)-ma*
> *^{d}Niššīku, ^{d}Ea, ittīšunu tamēma (tašibma).*
> *amassunu ušannâ ana kikkīšu*
> So he repeated their words to the reed house.

Of interest here is line 19: *^{d}Nin-ši-kù ^{d}Ea ittīšunu ta-me-ma*, which contains no less than three polysemous elements: *niššīku*, which can be read as another name for ^{d}Ea and as a common noun meaning 'prince';[1] *ittīšunu*, both as 'with them' and 'their sign';[2] and *tamēma*, 'he swore an oath',[3] which can also be read *tašibma*, 'you [Utu-napištim] sat'.[4] Such polysemy imbues the composition with multiple possibilities for reading, including '^{d}Niššīku, ^{d}Ea, spoke a sign', or '^{d}Niššīku, ^{d}Ea, swore an oath with them', 'You [Utu-napištim] sat with the prince ^{d}Ea', and/or 'You [Utu-napištim] sat with the ^{d}Niššīku, ^{d}Ea.' Note how the the latter refers back to the answer to Gilgameš's question in XI.7: 'How is it that you have stood in the assembly of the gods and have found life?'

The type of triple polysemy here functions as a Janus parallelism. As '^{d}Niššīku, ^{d}Ea, swore an oath with them', the line points ahead to *amassunu ušannâ ana kikkīšu*, 'So he repeated their words to the reed house', and as 'You [Utu-napištim] sat with the prince ^{d}Ea' the line faces the previous list of occupations, i.e., *malikšunu*, *guzalâšunu*, and *gugallâšunu*. Note that as 'you sat' (*tašibma*) the line also parallels *guzalâšunu*, 'their Chairbearer', by reference to an item on which one sits. Moreover, if we read ^{d}Niššīku as a name of ^{d}Ea, it parallels ^{d}Ea which follows immediately upon it. Finally, a word must be said about *ittīšunu*, which when read as 'with them' parallels the list of gods present in the assembly, and when read as 'omen, sign' parallels 'their words' (*amassunu*) in the following line.

The Epic of Gilgameš XI.25-27[5]

> *muššir mešrê šê' napšāti*
> Abandon wealth! Seek life!

1. *CAD* N/2, pp. 282-83, s.v. *niššīku*; *AHw*, p. 796, s.v. *niššīku*.
2. *CAD* I, pp. 304-10, s.v. *ittu*; pp. 302-303, s.v. *itti*; *AHw*, p. 405, s.v. *itti*; p. 406, s.v. *ittu*.
3. *AHw*, pp. 1317-18, s.v. *tamû*. So also M.B. Rowton, 'The Permansive in Classic Babylonian', *JNES* 21 (1962), p. 275.
4. The sign *me* can also be read as *šib*. See R. Labat, *Manuel d'Epigraphie Akkadienne* (Paris: Librairie Orientaliste Paul Geuther, 1988), p. 219; *CAD* N/2, pp. 386-408, s.v. *wašābu*; *AHw*, pp. 1480-84, s.v. *(w)ašābu*.
5. Noegel, 'A Janus Parallelism in the Gilgamesh Flood Story', pp. 419-21.

makkura zērma napišta bulliṭ
makkura zērma! Living beings keep alive!
[*š*]*ulima zēr napšāti kalama ana libbi* *[giš]elippi*
Make all living beings go up into the boat!

While explaining the redaction of these lines from the text's *Vorlage*, the 'Atra-ḫasis Epic', H.A. Hoffner pointed out the polysemy of two words in line 26; the noun *makkura* and the verbal form *zērma*.[1] Although Hoffner was aware of the pun, he did not recognize the presence of Janus parallelism. His first observation was that *makkura*, aside from its more common meaning 'property', also means 'a kind of boat' (the word is borrowed from the Sumerian má-gur$_8$).[2] Although the doubled *k* is not the expected syllabic orthography for *ma*(*k*)*kuru*, 'ark', it is attested. Hoffner states:

> Indeed a doubling of the first consonant following *ma* in the Akk. form of the Sum. loanwords for boat types is not isolated: *makkitu* (má-gíd-da), *makkūtu* (má-gud$_4$-da), notably all examples contain the Sum. phoneme g.[3]

Thus, the word *makkura* signifies here both 'property' and 'boat'.

Now we turn our attention to the word *zērma*, usually translated 'spurn, shun', or the like. The initial sibilant in *ze-e-er-ma* may be either *s*, *ṣ*, or *z*, and as Hoffner remarked, 'neither the spelling nor the form indicate whether the verb used is *eṣēru*, *as/ṣ/zâru* or *s/ṣ/zerû*'.[4] While this allows a certain flexibility in rendering the line, one possibility may be ruled out by context. Our word cannot derive from *sêru*, 'to coat, besmear, cover', for as Hoffner noted, its uses in Akkadian are limited to plating a surface with 'a metal foil, liquid or paste, and not the construction of a roof'.[5] This leaves us with two possibilities, both equally plausible in the light of the polysemous use of *ma*(*k*)*kuru*. The word in question could be read as both *zērmā*, 'Spurn!', and *ṣêru*, 'Build, construct!' With the reading 'Property, spurn it!', line 26 connects with line 25, 'Abandon wealth!' With the understanding 'Construct a boat!',

1. H.A. Hoffner, 'Enki's Command to Atraḫasis', in B.L. Eichler *et al.* (eds.), *Kramer Anniversary Volume* (AOAT, 25; Neukirchen–Vluyn: Neukirchener Verlag, 1976), p. 244.
2. Hoffner, 'Enki's Command to Atraḫasis', p. 244.
3. Hoffner, 'Enki's Command to Atraḫasis', p. 244.
4. Hoffner, 'Enki's Command to Atraḫasis', p. 244. Hoffner cited *CAD* E, p. 349, s.v. *eṣēru*.
5. Hoffner, 'Enki's Command to Atraḫasis', p. 244.

the sentence alludes to the following line's *ana libbi* ^{giš}*elippi*, 'into the boat'.

The Epic of Gilgameš XI.129-30[1]

> *sibu ūma ina kašādi ittarak meḫu abūbu qabla*
> When the seventh day arrived, the storm was pounding, the flood was a battle
> *ša imdaḫṣu kīma ḫayyālti*
> which fought with itself like a *ḫayyālti*.
> *inūḫ tâmti ušḫarirma imḫullu abūbu iklū*
> Tamti calmed, fell still, (her) flood-waters ceased.

The word *ḫayyālti*, 'a woman in travail',[2] though an apt description of an intense battle, also can be read as if derived from *ḫāyl*, 'army, force'.[3] As the latter, it parallels *qabla*, 'battle', in the previous verse, and as 'woman in labor', it anticipates the description of the breaking of Tamti's birth-water.[4]

The Poor Man of Nippur 3-5

> *ina ālīšu Nippur*^{KI} *šunuḫiš ašibma*
> in his city Nippur, wearily he sat,
> *ul iši kàs-pa simat nišīšu*
> he had no *kàs-pa*, the pride of the people,
> *ḫurāṣa ul išā simat ba'ulāte*
> gold, he had none, the pride of humankind.

Appearing in line 4 is *kàs-pa*, an abnormal syllabic spelling for 'silver'. Normally, the lexeme is written with the ideogram KÙ.BABBAR. The non-normative orthography permits us to see this word as a polyseme. By reading *kaz* for *kàs*,[5] *bá* for *pa*,[6] and by reading *silat*, 'weakness',[7]

1. M. Malul, 'A Possible Case of Janus Parallelism in the Epic of Gilgamesh XI, 130', *Acta Sumerologica* 17 (1995), pp. 338-42, apparently espied this same Janus independently.

2. *CAD* Ḫ, p. 32, s.v. *ḫalû*: *abūbu qabla ša imdaḫṣu kīma ḫa-a-al-ti*, 'the flood which had struggled (?) like a woman in labor'. Cf. *AHw*, p. 2, s.v. *ḫiālum*.

3. *CAD* A/1, p. 226b, s.v. *ajalu*.

4. The imagery is common to ancient Near Eastern literature. See, for example, Job 3.1-10.

5. Though *kazbu* is unattested elsewhere as *kàs-bu*, a confusion between the phonemes *z* and *s* is not uncommon; for example, *kasāsu* = *kazāzu*; *CAD* K, p. 242, s.v. *kasāsu*, *CAD* K, p. 310, s.v. *kazāzu*.

6. Labat, *Manuel d'Epigraphie Akkadienne*, p. 135.

7. *CAD* S, pp. 263-64, s.v. *sili'tu*; *AHw*, p. 1043, s.v. *sili'tu*. It also is

for *simat*, 'appropriateness, pride, mark' (the same sign can be read as *mat* and *lat*[1]) we arrive at: 'he had no bodily exuberance (*kazba*), which is the weakness of the people'.[2] In its meaning *kazba*, 'bodily exuberance', the polyseme harks back to *šunuḫiš ašibma*, 'wearily he sat', in the previous line, and as *kaspa*, 'silver', it faces forward to *ḫurāṣa ul išā simat ba'ulāte*, 'gold, he had none, the pride of humankind', in line 5.[3]

The Poor Man of Nippur 127-30

bēli ina ekleti išallimū bulṭūya
my lord, in the dark, my remedies are completed,
[ašar šēpu parsat] ukkulat alakta
(a room) where entry is forbidden, a dark way,
ušeribšuma ina bīti ašar lā âri
he made him enter a room where there was no *âri*,
ašar ibri u tappu lā iraššušū rēmu
where friends and companions could not show him mercy.

Of interest here is the phrase *lā âri* (line 129). As an infinitive of *wâru*, 'go', it means (lit.) 'a place of not going', i.e., a private chamber that one could not access.[4] As the infinitive of *arû*, 'see, light', it means 'a place of not seeing, or lighting'.[5] That the stich is a polysemous parallel is brought out by the line above it which speaks of the darkness in which Gimil-Ninurta's remedies could only be effective, and the line below it, which concerns the inability of the mayor's friends to access the inner chamber in which the mayor was being beaten. The phrase in

possible that *siltu* derives from *siliʾāti*, 'lies, deception', as the form does occur. Cf. *CAD* S, p. 262, s.v. *siliʾāti*; *AHw*, pp. 1043-44, s.v. *silītu*. As such it would depict Gimil-Ninurta as appearing deceptively weak.

1. *CAD* S, pp. 278-83, s.v. *simtu*; *AHw*, p. 1043, s.v. *simtu*. For the alternative renderings see Labat, *Manuel d'Epigraphie Akkadienne*, pp. 115, 135, 169.

2. *CAD* K, p. 310, s.v. *kazbu* and p. 614, s.v. *kuzbu*; *AHw*, p. 519, s.v. *kuzbu*.

3. With *CAD* B, p. 183b, s.v. *baʾulāte*. For 'gold' and 'silver' as a word-pair see Avishur, *Stylistic Studies of Word-Pairs*, pp. 152, 579, 591-92, 599-600.

4. *AHw*, p. 961, s.v. *wâru*.

5. BDB, p. 21, s.v. *ʾōr*. The same word may occur in the *Annals of Sennacherib* 1.17-19: *dadmêšun izzibūma kīma sutinni* ^{mušen} *nigiṣṣi ēdiš ipparšu ašar lā âri*, 'leaving their homes and flying alone, like bats of the crevices to a place not lit'. Might this be related to *arû*, *CAD* A/2, p. 313, s.v. *arû*; *AHw*, p. 1473, s.v. (*w*)*arûm*, 'führen', i.e., 'light the way'?

the middle stich both comments on the preceding verse and anticipates the following verses.

The Descent of Ištar 29-30

kīma nikiš [giš]*bini ēriqu panīšu*
like a cutting of a tamarisk was her face,
kīma šapat kunini iṣlima šapātūša
like a *šapat kunini* were her lips.

That the Akkadian script makes no differentiation between voiced and unvoiced labials and dentals allows the poet to take witty advantage of the possible readings of *ša-pat*. When read as 'the lips (*šapāt*) of a bowl',[1] the phrase *kīma šapāt kunini* provides a simile with which to compare Ištar's lips. However, if read as 'like a bruised (*šabaṭ*) kunini-reed'[2] it parallels 'the cutting of a tamarisk' in the previous verse. Though typically the polysemous pivot word occurs at the beginning or end of a stich it will be noticed that the parallel for 'bruised kuninu reed', i.e., 'the cutting of a tamarisk', also occurs in the middle of line 29. It also may be that the preposition *kīma*, 'like', was understood to have less force or significance than nouns and verbs in a sentence, therefore making *šapat* the first 'real' word or referent of the sentence.

The Descent of Ištar 89-92

ittil eṭlu ina kummīšu
The young man lies in his chamber,
ittil ardatum ina aḫīša
The young woman lies in her *aḫīša*
[d]*Ea ina emqi libbīšu ibtani* [*zik*]*ru.*
Ea in the wisdom of his mind, made a *zikru*
ibnīma Aṣû-šunamir [lu]*assinnu*
He created Aṣû-šunamir, a castrated male servant.

Lines 90 and 91 of the *Descent of Ištar* contain a double polysemous parallelism. Both *zikru* and *aḫīša* can be read in two ways: the former as 'man' and 'penis'[3] and the latter as 'her quarters (lit. her side)' and 'her

1. *CAD* Š/1, pp. 483-86, s.v. *šaptu*; *CAD* K, p. 539b, s.v. *kuninnu*; *AHw*, p. 507, s.v. *kuni*(*n*)*nu*.
2. *CAD* Š/1, pp. 8-9, s.v. *šabāṭu*; *CAD* K, p. 539b, s.v. *kuninnu*; *AHw*, p. 507, s.v. *kuni*(*n*)*nu*.
3. *CAD* Z, pp. 110-12, 116-17; *AHw*, pp. 1526-27, s.v. *zikru*.

chaperones (lit. brothers)'.[1] The polysemes here allow the poet to charge the lines with allusion. As 'man' *zikru* is a fitting parallel for the preceding mention of *aḫīša* as 'her brothers'. As 'penis' *zikru* parallels *assinnu*, 'a castrated male servant',[2] in the following verse. Similarly, *aḫīša*, when read as 'her brothers', parallels *zikru* as 'man', but when read as 'her quarters' it parallels *kummīšu*, 'her chamber',[3] in the previous line. In addition, *zikru* may be read as 'idea',[4] suggesting the possibility of reading it, in parallel with *libbīšu*, as 'his mind', rather than as 'his heart'.

The Descent of Ištar 97-99

> *tummēšima nīš ilāni rabûti*
> Have her swear an oath by the great gods.
> *šuqi rēšīka ana* ^{kuš}*ḫalziqi uzna šukun*
> *šuqi* your head and direct your attention to the waterskin.
> *ē bēlti* ^{kuš}*ḫalziqi liddinuni mê ina lulāti*
> No my lady, let them give me the waterskin so that I may drink water from it.

At the head of line 98 we find the polysemous expression *šuqi rēšīka*, both 'lift your head' and 'let (your head) drink'.[5] As the former, the stich parallels *tummēšima nīš ilāni rabûti*, 'have her swear an oath by the great gods', specifically *nīš*, '(lit.) lifting'.[6] As 'let your head drink' the stich anticipates the next line's *ē bēlti* ^{kuš}*ḫalziqi liddinuni mê ina lulāti*, 'no my lady, let them give me the waterskin so that I may drink water from it'.

The significance of this pun lies in the fact that these lines become part of the ruse by which Aṣû-šunamir tricks Ereškigal.[7] Though she hears in

1. *CAD* A/1, pp. 195-210, s.v. *aḫu*; *AHw*, pp. 21-22, s.v. *aḫu*. For a similar pun with this lexeme see J.S. Cooper, 'Gilgamesh Dreams of Enkidu: The Evolution and Dilution of Narrative', in M. de Jong Ellis (ed.), *Memoirs of the Academy of Arts and Sciences, 19: Essays on the Ancient Near East in Memory of Jacob Joel Finkelstein* (Hamden, CT: Archon Books, 1977), p. 40.
2. *CAD* A/2, pp. 341-42, s.v. *assinnu*; *AHw*, pp. 75-76, s.v. *assinnu*. See also Kilmer, 'A Note on an Overlooked Word-Play in the Akkadian Gilgamesh', pp. 128-32.
3. *CAD* K, pp. 533-34, s.v. *kummu*; *AHw*, p. 506, s.v. *kummu*.
4. *CAD* Z, p. 116, s.v. *zikru*; *AHw*, pp. 1526-27, s.v. *zikru*.
5. *CAD* Š/2, pp. 19-24, s.v. *šaqû*; pp. 24-28, s.v. *šaqû*; *AHw*, p. 1180, s.v. *šaqû*; *AHw*, p. 1181, s.v. *šaqû*. A similar play on these roots may occur in *Enūma Eliš* I.92.
6. *CAD* N/2, p. 80, s.v. *našû*; *AHw*, p. 762, s.v. *našû*.
7. Similarly, see Ea's tricky words to Ereškigal, *ana mûti*, 'for death', by which

šuqi the meaning 'lift' he really means 'let your head drink'. This can be seen in Aṣû-šunamir's immediate correction: 'no my lady, let them give me the waterskin so that I may drink water from it'. Note also that the double meaning may again be signalled by non-normative orthography, specifically the plural use of SAG.MEŠ, 'heads'.

The Descent of Ištar 104-105

> *akali* (NINDA.MEŠ) ^{giš}*eppinet* (APIN.MEŠ) *āli lū akalkā*
> May the bread from the ^{giš}*eppinet* (APIN.MEŠ) be your food,
> ^{dug}*ḫabannat āli lū maltikā*
> May the catch-water of the city be your drink.

R.D. Biggs offered a new reading for the crux *giš*.APIN.MEŠ in line 104 of the Nineveh version of *The Descent of Ištar*, taking it as *tubkinnu*, 'garbage dump', instead of 'plow'.[1] M. Malul provided additional textual evidence in support of Biggs.[2] I would add to the observations of the above scholars and suggest that the difficulty behind the crux is due largely to the presence of a word-play. That *giš*.APIN.MEŠ can be read as *tubkinnu*, 'garbage dump', seems sufficiently demonstrated in the brief notes by Biggs and Malul and does not require comment here. What has not been mentioned, however, is an alternative reading for *giš*.APIN.MEŠ (*e-pi-<né>-et* in the Assur version), namely 'baker'.[3] Thus, the word *epinnet*, 'gutters', also may be read *apinnet*, 'bakers'. That the pun occurs after the mention of *akali*, 'food, bread', and before ^{dug}*ḫabannat āli lū maltitkā*, 'catch-water of the city', demonstrates its use as a polysemous parallelism.

Thus, there exists the possibility of interpreting the line as 'May the bread of the city bakers be your food'. A clue as to why the pun between 'baker' and 'garbage dump' occurs can be found in line 33 of *The Descent of Ištar* (lines 34-35 of the Assur version) in the mouth of

he intends *ana muti*, 'for the husband'. For reference and discussion see Bottéro, *Mesopotamia: Writing, Reasoning, and the Gods*, p. 245.

1. R.D. Biggs, 'Descent of Ištar, Line 104', *NABU* 74 (1993), pp. 58-59.
2. M. Malul, 'Eating and Drinking (One's) Refuse', *NABU* 75 (1993), pp. 82-83.
3. *AHw*, p. 231, s.v. *epû*; *CAD* E, pp. 247b, 248, s.v. *ēpu*. There may be an additional play on the *assinnu* involving ^{giš}.APIN as a sexual double entendre meaning 'the penis which plows'; an allusion familiar to Sumerian. Cf. B. Alster, 'Marriage and Love in Sumerian Love Songs', in M.E. Cohen *et al.* (eds.), *The Tablet and the Scroll: Near Eastern Studies in Honor of William W. Hallo* (Bethesda, MD: CDL Press, 1993), pp. 20-24.

Ereškigal: 'should I eat clay instead of bread (NINDA.MEŠ), drink muddied water instead of beer?'

The pun's connection to line 33 is also supported by the use of ^{dug}*ḫabanat* in the next line, which typically means 'a drinking vessel' when not attached to URU, 'city'.[1] In effect, Aṣû-šunamir is cursed with the very fate which Ereškigal mentioned earlier. Moreover, the curse which Ereškigal utters revolves around his looking at a waterskin (*kuš ḫal-zi-qi*) and his desire to drink from it in lines 98-99. Interestingly, as Aṣu-šunamir's trick involves polysemy in lines 97-99 above, so also does his curse. His punishment, therefore, is made commensurate with his crime.

So while the words of Ereškigal, according to Malul, employ 'a widespread topos attested in various ANE literary genres',[2] they do so with a clever twist on the topos.

Enūma Eliš I.21-23

> *innindūma atḫû ilāni*
> They were banded together, the allies, the gods;
> *ešû* ^{d}*Tiamat u nāṣiršunu ištappu*
> They *ešû* ^{d}Tiamat and *na-ṣir(muš)-šunu ištappu.*
> *dalḫunimma ša* ^{d}*Tiamat karassa*
> They troubled the mood of Tiamat.

Several lexemes in line 22 are polysemous parallels. *ešû* can be read as 'destroyed, rebelled', and as 'confused, troubled'.[3] The former meaning parallels the verb *emēdu*, 'unite, rebel',[4] in line 21 and the latter parallels the use of *dalāḫu*, 'confuse, roil',[5] in line 23. The word *naṣiršunu*, when read as 'their guard(ian)',[6] parallels *atḫû*, 'allies, brothers',[7] in line 21, and as 'they surged back and forth'[8] (reading *muš* for *ṣir* to form *namuššunū*[9]), it also parallels *dalāḫu* in line 23. *ištappu* is also polysemous,

1. CAD Ḫ, p. 7a, s.v. *ḫabannatu*; *AHw*, p. 302, s.v. *ḫabannatu*.
2. Malul, 'Eating and Drinking (One's) Refuse', p. 83.
3. *CAD* E, p. 364, s.v. *ešē'u*; *CAD* E, p. 378, s.v. *ešû*; *AHw*, pp. 259-60, s.v. *ešû*.
4. *CAD* E, p. 145, s.v. *emēdu*; *AHw*, pp. 211-13, s.v. *emēdu*.
5. *CAD* D, pp. 43-46, s.v. *dalāḫu*; *AHw*, pp. 152-53, s.v. *dalāḫu*.
6. *CAD* N/2, pp. 33-47, s.v. *naṣāru*; *AHw*, pp. 755-56, s.v. *naṣāru*.
7. *CAD* A/2, p. 493, s.v. *atḫû*; *AHw*, p. 86, s.v. *atḫū*.
8. *CAD* N/1, pp. 220-21, s.v. *namāšu*; *AHw*, p. 726, s.v. *namāšu*.
9. This interchange of signs may also play on the reading MUŠ = *ṣerru*, 'serpent', a well-known image suitable for a creation epic.

since it can be understood as 'glorified'[1] (from *apû*), in which case it parallels *ilāni*, 'gods', in line 21 and 'swell up and down' (from *šapû*),[2] in which case it parallels *dalāḫu*, 'confuse, roil', in line 23. The result is a liquid-like interpretation which challenges the reader.

Enūma Eliš IV.138-40

> *mišlušša iškunamma šamama uṣāllil*
> Half of her he set up and made as a cover (like) heaven.
> *išdud mašku maṣṣaru ušasbit*
> He stretched out the *maš-ku* and assigned watchmen.
> *meša lā šūṣa šunūti umtā'ir*
> He ordered them not to let her waters escape.

As Foster noted, *mašku*, 'hide',[3] in line 139 also may be read *parku*, 'dividing line'.[4] As 'hide' the polyseme faces back to lines 137-38 in which Tiamat's carcass is split and set up as the cover of heaven. As 'dividing line' *parku* anticipates the mention of boundaries which the watchmen are assigned to guard. The ambiguity set up by the pivotal orthography of *mašku/parku* permits the poet to equate the newly created horizon with Tiamat's hide. Additional support for the connection between a 'hide' and the 'heavens' comes from a Sumerian proverb: ^{d}Iškur an dar-dar-re kuš.a.gá.lá nu-dar-re, 'the storm splits the heavens but it does not split the waterskin'.[5]

Enūma Eliš V.53-56

> *iškun qaqqad*[*su*] *ina* [*UGU-šu šada*]*-a išpuk*
> He laid down her (lit. his) head, heaped [a mountain up]on it,
> *nagbu uptetta a<g>u ittasbi*
> Opened such a spring that a torrent could be drawn off,
> *iptēma ina IGI^{II}-ša Pur*[*atta*] *Idiglat*
> (Then) he opened her IGI^{II}, the Euphrates and the Tigris,

1. *CAD* A/2, pp. 202-203, s.v. *apû*; *AHw*, p. 62, s.v. *apû*.

2. *CAD* Š/1, p. 489, s.v. *šapû*; *AHw*, pp. 1176-77, s.v. *šapû*.

3. B.R. Foster, *Before the Muses: An Anthology of Akkadian Literature* (Bethesda, MD: CDL Press, 1993), pp. 377, 402; *CAD* M/1, p. 342a, s.v. *mašku*; *AHw*, pp. 627-28, s.v. *mašku*.

4. *AHw*, p. 834, s.v. *parku*. For the multiple reading of *maš* (= *par*) see Labat, *Manuel d'Epigraphie Akkadienne*, pp. 69-70.

5. B. Alster, 'Paradoxical Proverbs and Satire in Sumerian Literature', *JCS* 27 (1975), p. 208.

naḫīreša upteḫa x y etēzba
Closed up her nostrils, reserved [the water].

Though line 56 is partly broken, it is clear, as it is for line 53, that body parts are being described, specifically the head and the nostrils. The Janus pivot-word occurs in line 55, 'her spring', which also may be read as 'her eyes'. Though the *CAD* reads this line as 'He [Marduk] made the Euphrates and Tigris rivers flow from her [Tiamat's] eyes',[1] the line that immediately follows ('opened such a spring that a torrent could be drawn off'), suggests that IGI^{II} should be read as 'springs'. Though the two words 'eyes' and 'springs' are related etymologically, i.e., because they both provide water,[2] they typically are kept separate by context. Thus, that both contexts are provided in the lines preceding and following suggests that the poet wished to combine both ideas into one. Additional support for the connection comes from an ancient commentary on this text which elucidates this line: *Idiglat ēn imittiša Puratta ēn šumēliša*, 'her right eye is the Euphrates, her left eye the Tigris'.[3] Therefore, this example of polysemous parallelism is of the semantic and symmetrical types.

Atraḫasīs Epic III.viii.9-17
I turn now to yet another example of Janus parallelism in Akkadian, this time, in the Old Babylonian version of the *Atraḫasīs Epic* III.viii.9-17.[4]

kīma niškunu [*abūba*]
How we have brought about [the flood],
awīlum iblutu ina karašî
yet a man survived [the cataclysm].
attā mālik ilī rabûti
You, counsellor of the great gods,
tēretiš[*ka*]
at [your] command
ušabši [*qabla*]
I caused the [destruction].
šanittiška
For your *šanittiš*

1. *CAD* I/J, p. 154, s.v. *īnu*; *AHw*, p. 383, s.v. *īnu*.
2. See also, for example, עינים in Gen. 38.14, 21.
3. See this observation by E. Ebeling *apud* B. Landsberger and J.V. Kinnier Wilson, 'The Fifth Tablet of *Enuma Eliš*', *JNES* 20 (1961), p. 175.
4. I have adopted the numeration of W.G. Lambert and A.R. Millard, *Atraḫasīs: The Babylonian Story of the Flood* (Oxford: Clarendon Press, 1969), p. 105.

annīam zamāra
this song
lišmūma Igigi
let the Igigi-gods hear;
liṣṣirū narbîka
let them make famous your greatness!

As A.D. Kilmer notes,[1] the word *šanittiš* in line 14 is a pun which can mean both 'praise' (from *nadû*)[2] and 'hostile, inimical word or matter' (from *šanītu*).[3] As the former, the Janus pun faces ahead to *zamāra*, 'song', and *lišmūma Igigi liṣṣirū narbîka*, 'let the Igigi-gods hear; let them make famous your greatness!' As 'hostile word', *šanittiš* looks backwards to the 'flood', *abūbu*, 'cataclysm', *karašî*, and 'destruction', *qablu*. The Janus is reinforced by yet another pun on *narbû*, both 'greatness'[4] and 'softness/cowardice'.[5]

Other studies on word-play in the *Atraḫasīs Epic* have shown puns and paronomasia to serve emphatic or referential roles in the story.[6] Here both functions are at work. As the last lines of the poem, the puns underscore the ambiguity of Enlil's role in the story by referring the reader to a previous event in the poem. As Kilmer comments, the puns 'refer to Enlil's cowardice at the time of the worker god's rebellion and to the fact that he himself was apparently *in absentia* during the most terrifying part of the Flood'.[7] Thus, the Janus parallelism connects Enlil's hostile, yet cowardly, act with his follower's praise of his greatness.

Moreover, as Kilmer has also demonstrated, clues to the presence of the puns often appear in the text. Accordingly, we may wonder if the

1. Though she notes the presence of the puns discussed here, she did not catch the presence of a Janus parallelism. See A.D. Kilmer, 'Fugal Features of Atraḫasīs: The Birth Theme', in M.E. Vogelzang and H.L.J. Vanstiphout (eds.), *Proceedings of the Gronigen Group for the Study of Mesopotamian Literature, 2* (Lewiston: Edwin Mellen, 1995), p. 10.

2. *CAD* N/1, p. 101, s.v. *nadû*; *AHw*, p. 1319, s.v. *tanittu*.

3. *CAD* Š/1, p. 388, s.v. *šanītu*; *AHw*, p. 1164, s.v. *šanītu*.

4. *CAD* N/1, p. 351, s.v. *narbû*; *AHw*, p. 746, s.v. *narbû*.

5. *CAD* N/1, p. 350, s.v. *narbu*; *AHw*, p. 746, s.v. *narbu*.

6. See, for instance, Kilmer, 'A Note on an Overlooked Word-Play in the Akkadian Gilgamesh', pp. 128-32; 'Les jeux de mots dans les rêves de Gilgamesh et d'Atraḫasīs', pp. 1-7; S.A. Geller, 'Some Sound and Word Plays in the First Tablet of the Old Babylonian Atramḫasīs Epic', in B. Walfish (ed.), *Frank Talmage Memorial Volume I* (Haifa: University of Haifa Press, 1993), pp. 63-70.

7. Kilmer, 'Fugal Features of Atraḫasīs: The Birth Theme', p. 10.

poet has flagged the puns for us by emphatically concluding with an exhortation to 'listen!' (*šimā*).

The Poem of the Righteous Sufferer I.18-20

ikkaraṭma zamarma xx alittuš
Yet, he quickly shows mercy... [1] on the one who begets.
iddudma rīmaš[a] ukanni
He acts quickly and assigns (bad fortune) to *rīmaša*.[2]
u kî arāḫ būri ittanasḫara arkīšu
Yet, like a cow with a calf he keeps turning back to him.

The poet of *ludlul bēl nēmeqi* also shows an interest in the use of polysemy. His use of *rīmaša*, both 'his lover'[3] and 'his ox',[4] must be seen in the light of the Janus device. As 'his lover', *rīmaša* parallels the previous mention of *karāṭu*, 'mercy', in line 18. As 'his ox' the polyseme parallels both *araḫ*, 'cow',[5] and *būri*, 'calf',[6] in the next line. Such plays involving cows and love are found also in the incantation text 'Cow of Sin',[7] and a comparison of the two texts in the light of such similarities will perhaps prove fruitful. Yet, for the purpose of this study, suffice it to note the use of polysemous parallelism in the *Poem of the Righteous Sufferer*.[8]

The Rights of Egašankalamma Reverse 7-9

[qa]lāte ša GAR-*nu* DUL.DU *ana* AN.TA.MEŠ *kî qab[û]*
The burned parts which are produced go up to the upper regions,
as it is said.

1. For this reading see D.J. Wiseman, 'A New Text of the Babylonian Poem of the Righteous Sufferer', *Anatolian Studies* 30 (1980), pp. 105, 107.

2. Both Moran and Foster missed the pun here, the former holding to 'his lover' and the latter to 'his ox'. See W.L. Moran, 'Notes on the Hymn to Marduk in *Ludlul Bel Nemeqi*', *JAOS* 103 (1986), p. 260; B.R. Foster, '*tuktullu* "shiver, quake"', *RA* 75 (1981), p. 189.

3. *AHw*, pp. 986-87, s.v. *rîmu*.

4. *AHw*, p. 986, s.v. *rīmu*.

5. *CAD* A/2, p. 263, s.v. *arḫu*; *AHw*, p. 67, s.v. *arḫu*.

6. *CAD* B, pp. 341-42, s.v. *būru*; *AHw*, p. 141, s.v. *būru*.

7. See N. Veldhuis, *A Cow of Sin* (Library of Oriental Texts, 2; Gröningen: Styx Publications, 1991), pp. 17-27.

8. Foster noted the pun but did not recognize the presence of a Janus parallelism. See his *Before the Muses*, p. 311 n. 1.

[NU$^{?}$] ŠEŠ-*ka ša ina* KAŠ.MEŠ *ulabukū* SU ŠEŠ ÍL-*ni kî qab*[*û*]
[The image of] your brother which they soak in beer ÍL-*ni* the body of the brother, as it is said.
[*sa*] ^{d}KÁR.KÁR LÀL *šarkā*[*šu*]
Honey is the pus of the Kidnapped God.

In his commentary on this text Alasdair Livingstone remarked about ÍL-*ni* in line 8 that its translation 'could equally well be "carry off", not "lift up", thus setting the stage for the "Kidnapped God"'.[1] Livingstone, though aware of the double sense here, was unaware of the presence of a Janus parallelism. As 'lift up' ÍL-*ni* serves as a perfect parallel for DUL.DU *ana* AN.TA.MEŠ, 'go up to the upper regions', in line 7. As 'carry off', then, line 8 parallels the Kidnapped God in line 9. Perhaps it is such polysemy which is signalled in the last line of the text (line 20): '[Secret lore of the great gods. An initiate may] show it [to another initiate]; the uninitiated may not see it.'[2]

A Commentary to the Assyrian Cultic Calendar 10-14

UD-23-KÁM *taḫāzu šu uzuššu unīḫ*
The 23rd day is the battle; he calmed his ire.
[UD]-26-KÁM [*ša* DINGIR] *ana* É-KAŠ DU-*ku* É iḫru ^{d}*Anum ša tīk zāre*
The 26th day, when the god goes to the brewery, (is) where they dug Anu and which is called a *tīk zāre*
[DUG$_4$].GA-*ú dīki an*[*ūnti*]
stirring up bat[tle].
[U]D-24-KÁM *ša* LUGAL AGA ÍL-*u bēlum* GÚ ^{d}*Anum ikkisum*[*a*] [xxxx]
The 24th [day], when the king wears a crown, is (when) Bel slashed and [. . .] Anu's neck;
LUGAL-*tu kî ilqu* [A].MEŠ *irmuk nalbašu itt*[*albiš*]
Having assumed kingship, he bathed and donned the (royal) garb.

The polysemy in this text revolves around the expression *tīk zāre* which can be read 'drop of sprinkling' (*ti-ik zāre*)[3] or a 'muster of hatred' (*di-ik zēre*).[4] Marduk's bath after his wrath in line 14 provides a perfect

1. A. Livingstone, *Court Poetry and Literary Miscellanea* (State Archives of Assyria, 3; Helsinki: Helsinki University Press, 1989), pp. 97-89 n. 8; *CAD* N/2, p. 80, s.v. *našû*; *AHw*, p. 762, s.v. *našû*.

2. Cf. the last words of Hosea in 14.10 cited above.

3. *AHw*, pp. 1357-58, s.v. *tīku*; *CAD* Z, pp. 70-71, s.v. *zarû*; *AHw*, p. 1516, s.v. *zarû*.

4. *CAD* D, p. 140, s.v. *dīku*; *AHw*, p. 170, s.v. *dīku*; *CAD* Z, pp. 97-99, s.v. *zêru*; *AHw*, p. 1522, s.v. *zêru*.

parallel for *tīk zāre* as 'drop of sprinkling'. Moreover, the mention of Marduk's ire calming after his battle with Tiamat in line 10 affords a fitting parallel for the latter meaning. Thus, we have another example of a Janus parallelism. One wonders if the author of the commentary signalled the presence of the polysemy by placing the comments on day 26 out of order, that is, before day 24. Up to this point in the text, all days are in perfect sequence beginning with the 16th day and leading to the 26th. Only the 20th and 25th days are missing in the commentary, which is why the non-sequential placement of day 26 appears so unusual.

Since my initial discovery and publication of Akkadian examples of Janus parallelism, Jean-Georges Heintz, Wayne Horowitz, and Shalom Paul have suggested three additional examples.[1] As these authors provide ample evidence for their proposals in their brief notes, I will refrain from citing dictionaries and other documentation. Heintz's note appeared first, and so I will continue with his observation.

ARM XXVI 419.9′-21′

> *Ia-tam-ri-im ù ìr-meš-šu al-li-ik-ma*
> (without taking the time to inform) Atamrum and his servants, I went
> *i-na ṣa-bi-im ša be-lí-ia ṣí-ri-im-tam*
> into the army of my lord; I introduced the cutting tool and
> *aš-ku-un-ma 8 gi-ḫa bu-ur-t*[*a*]*-am ep-*[*t*]*e-*[*e-ma*]
> I opened a well 8 measures deep,
> *me-e ú-še-li-ma a-na a-tam-ri-im me-e*
> I made the water rise, and
> *ú-te*$_4$*-ḫi-ma a-tam-rum ma-di-iš iḫ-du*
> I supplied Atamrum with water, so that Atamrum is rejoicing greatly.
> *ù ki-a-am iq-bé-em um-ma-a-mi i-na qa-li-ka-m*[*a*]
> At that time he said to me: 'Certainly, by your care (alone)
> *i-na é dingir še-tu na-ra-am ša* [*be-l*]*í-ka*
> in this temple, there is a *nârum* of your lord.
> *a-na wa-ar-ki-it u*$_4$*-mi tu-*[*uš*]*-zi-iz*
> for all the days to come you have erected (it)!'
> *i-na-an-na mu-ú ša iš-tu ṣi-it ni-ši*
> Since the people left, the water

1. One might expect Horowitz and Paul's example from *Enūma Eliš* to be grouped with the other examples from that text above. However, since the publication of their observation appeared after the completion of the dissertation from which this book derives, I felt it more appropriate to place it at the end of this section.

i-na é dingir še-tu ú-ul i-ba-aš-šu-ú
in the temple had failed.
a$^{?}$-[*n*]*a*-[*k*]*u* [*ú-š*]*a-ab-ši ṣa-al-ma-am*
I myself have restored it. There (now) is a statue
[*ša be-lí-i*]*a a-na wa-ar-ki-it u*$_{4}$*-mi*
of my lord, for all the days to come,
[*i-na é* ^{d}*nè-iri*$_{11}$*-gal ša ḫu-ub-ša-lim*^{ki} *uš*]*-zi-iz*
(that) I have erected in the temple of Nergal of Hubšalum.

At least one text from Mari also exhibits Janus parallelism. According to Jean-Georges Heintz,[1] the term *nârum* can mean 'stele' or 'water-course'. As the former, it looks ahead to the *ṣalmun*, 'statue', which was erected in the temple of the god (lines 19′-21′), and as the latter, it mirrors the mention of *mû*, 'water' (lines 5′, 12′ [2x], 17′), and *bûrtum*, 'well', in line 11′.

What Heintz did not notice, however, is the presence of another Janus parallelism in lines 9′-11′. Here we read: ^{I}*A- tam-ri-im u ìr-meš-šu al-li-ik-ma i-na ṣa-bi-im ša be-lí-ia ṣí-ri-im-tam aš-ku-un-ma 8 gi-ḫá bu-ur-t*[*a*]*-am ep-*[*t*]*e-*[*e-ma*], which Fr. Joannès translates: '^{I}Atamrum et ses serviteurs, j'y suis allé; dans l'armée de mon Seigneur, j'ai introduit l'émulation et [j'ai ouvert] un pu[i]ts de 8 cannes de profondeur…'[2]

Of note here is *ṣí-ri-im-tam* in line 10′. While on the one hand we can read it with Joannès as a 'cutting tool' used for clearing debris from wells,[3] its appearance with *ṣabim*, 'army', in a military context in the Mari letter A.4627 suggests that we interpret *ṣirimtam* as '(military) endeavor, effort'.[4] That letter reads as follows: *Ha-am-mu-ra-bi ù A-tam-rum bi-ri-šu-nu iš-ta-lu-ma i-na ṣa-bi-šu-nu ṭà-ra-di-im ma-di-iš ṣí-ri-im-tam ir-šu-ú*, 'Hammurapi and Atamrum have consulted amongst themselves and they have made a rushed effort to send their armies'.

Moreover, the term *ṣabim* (line 10′), though clearly meaning 'army' in this context, can also mean 'waterwork, irrigation' (from *ṣabû*), especially when used with *šakānu* (as it is here), and is known to mean this elsewhere in the Mari corpus.[5] Thus, the phrase *i-na ṣa-bi-im ša be-lí-ia*

1. J.G. Heintz, 'Myth(olog)èmes d'époque amorrite et amphibologie en ARMT XXVI, 419, ll.3'-21'?', *NABU* 68 (1994), p. 59.

2. F. Joannès, *Archives épistolaires de Mari I/2* (Paris: Editions Recherche sur les Civilisations, 1988), p. 307.

3. *CAD* S, p. 315, s.v. *sirimtu*.

4. *CAD* Ṣ, p. 208, s.v. *ṣirmu*.

5. *CAD* Ṣ, p. 45, s.v. *ṣabû*, cites ARM VI, 3.11; *AHw*, p. 1082, s.v. *ṣapû*.

ṣí-ri-im-tam aš-ku-un-ma permits several interpretations:

I have set my (military) endeavor for the army of my Lord.
I have set my endeavor to the waterworks of my Lord.
I have set (to work) the cutting tool for the army of my Lord.
I have set (to work) the cutting tool to the waterworks of my Lord.

Here both polysemes also function as Janus parallelisms. As 'army', the term *ṣabim* reminds us of the military personnel in line 9′. As 'waterwork', it directs our attention ahead to the clearing of the well in line 11′. Likewise, as '(military) endeavor, effort', *ṣarimtum* faces back to *ṣabim* (as 'army'), and as 'cutting tool', it anticipates the *bûrtum*, 'well', in line 11′.

Šamaš Hymn 171-73

[d]laḫmū š[ūt tâm]ti ša malû puluḫta
The *laḫmū*-beings o[f the se]a who are filled with fearsomeness,
e-ri-ib tâ[m]ti ša apsâ iba'û
The *erib tâmti* which passes through the Deep,
mišriti nāri ša irteddû [d]Šamaš ina maḫrīk[a]
the abundance of the river which moves, O Šamaš, is before yo[u].

This is the first of the two cases of Janus parallelism spotted by Wayne Horowitz and Shalom Paul. In line 172 of this hymn the words *erib tâmti* can be read as 'gifts of the sea', which faces forward to *mišriti nāri*, 'the abundance of the river', and as 'locust of the sea (shellfish)', which looks back to '*laḫmū*-beings o[f the se]a'. According to the authors, the latter constitutes a merism including 'all the creatures of the sea, great and small...'[1]

Enūma Eliš I.99-102

ulluma ina ilāni šūtur lān[šu]
(He was) exalted among the gods, surpassing was [his] stature.
mešrêtūšu šutuḫā i-lit/li-ta šūtur
His limbs were long, he was surpassing as to his *i-lit/li-ta*.
ma-ri-ú-tu ma-ri-ú-tu
Māri'ūtu, Māri'ūtu,
māri [d]šamši ša ilāni
Son of the Sun, Sun of the gods.

1. Horowitz and Paul, 'Two Proposed Janus Parallelisms in Akkadian Literature', p. 12.

Horowitz and Paul founded their second instance of Janus parallelism on the word *i-lit/li-ta* in line 100 of the famous Akkadian creation epic. When read as *ilittu*, 'offspring', the lexeme faces forward to the repeated mention of Marduk as a *maru*, 'son'. When read as *ilītu*, 'upper part (of something)', here Marduk's upper body, the pun harks backwards to *šūtur lān*[*šu*], 'surpassing was [his] stature'.[1]

2. *Sumerian*

Enlil and Ninlil—The Marriage of Sud 152-54

> ^{d}nin-tu-re nin ù-tu nin dùg-bad mu-še$_{21}$ m[u-ri]-in-sa$_4$ ^{d}nin-tu$^{!}$ munus nu-ù-t[u]
>
> He gives her the name Nintu, the Lady-Who-Gives-Birth and the Lady-of-the-Open-Legs.
>
> [^{d}e]n-ba-tibira mùš-me mi-ni-in-sig$_7$ igi-x dím-[d]ím [^{d}en-ba$^{!}$-tibira$^{!}$ mùš-m[e]
>
> He makes beautiful Enbadtibira's mùš-me...
>
> [nam(?)-nu-gig-ga níg-nam munus-e]-ne [lú igi] nu-bar-re-dam [n]u-gig-ga níg-nam munus-e-ne lú igi nu-bar-re [xxx] níg-nam [ ]
>
> The [functions of the] nu-gig, everything pertaining to women that no man must see.

W.G. Lambert in his follow-up commentary to M. Civil's translation of this text noted the presence of an alternative rendering for line 153.[2] Though he did not cite the variant interpretation as an example of polysemy, the placement of the polyseme between two verses which parallel each of its suggested meanings points to its classification as a polysemous parallelism. Specifically, Lambert called attention to the use of mùš.me which corresponds to both Akkadian *būnu*, 'appearance',[3] thus alluding to the 'foetus', and *zīmu*, 'face'.[4] As 'foetus', mùš.me parallels the previous line's mention of ^{d}Nintu and her role as a giver of birth. As 'face' the polyseme anticipates the reference to 'eye' in the phrase lú igi nu-bar-re [xxx] nig-nam, 'that no man must eye'. Moreover, according

1. Horowitz and Paul, 'Two Proposed Janus Parallelisms in Akkadian Literature', p. 12.

2. M. Civil, 'Enlil and Ninlil: The Marriage of Sud', in J.M. Sasson (ed.), *Studies in Literature from the Ancient Near East by Members of the American Oriental Society Dedicated to Samuel Noah Kramer* (AOS, 65; New Haven, CT: American Oriental Society, 1984), pp. 65-66.

3. *CAD* B, pp. 320-22, s.v. *būnu*; *AHw*, p. 138, s.v. *būnu*.

4. *CAD* Z, pp. 119-22, s.v. *zīmu*; *AHw*, p. 1528, s.v. *zīmu*.

to Lambert, sig_7 can also mean 'make grow'. Thus, line 153 may be read: 'He makes grow Enbadtibira's foetus.' In this way the Janus effect is accomplished referentially by facing both ahead and behind.

Enlil and Ninlil—The Marriage of Sud 160-63

^{d}Iškur kù.gál ú-a-zu ḫé-im a ki-ta mi-ri-in-dé [ ]-gál ú-a-bi ḫé-me-en a ki-ta nag-nag

Let Iškur, the water master, be your provider, he will make water gush forth from the ground for you.

zag mu-a gu sag gibil-gibil-za še sag gibil-gibil-za [ ] še sag mú-mú-dè gu sag mú-mú-dè

The beginning of the year is in your new flax, in your new grain.

^{d}en-lil ^{d}nin-líl-bi KA.AN.NI.SI-a ḫé-mu-ni-[t]u-tu-[d]è-eš

Let Enlil and Ninlil procreate as kúrku-a.

lú li-bí-in-dug_4-ga-gu_{10} lú érim-mi ḫé-im $lirum_4$ un-bi tu-lu-ab [ ]-in-dug_4-ga-zu lú NE.DU-bi šà-nam $lirum_4$ un-bi dul-la-ab

Let the one I do not mention be your enemy, let the strength of his people diminish.

Another example of Sumerian polysemous parallelism occurs in the same text in line 162 with the word kúrku, 'desire, wish'. As Civil remarked in his commentary 'We have here a likely word play with *kurku* "(yearly) flood", and even possibly with *kurku* (ME.^{d}NIDABA)'.[1] That the two lines previous to line 162 refer both to gushing water and to grain suggests that the polysemy was intentional. Yet that the line following line 162 expresses Enlil's desire that his enemies' procreative abilities and agricultural yield diminish inversely to his own gains places line 163 in parallelism with line 162. Supporting this connection is the expressive use of the precative /ḫa-/ which rehearses Enlil's desire to bless his wife (cf. lines 150ff.). Moreover, the Sumerian bards seem to have enjoyed the polysemy which the word kúrku provided, using it punfully elsewhere in reference to Inanna.[2]

1. Civil, 'Enlil and Ninlil', p. 64.

2. J.J. Glassner, 'Inanna et les Me', in M. de Jong Ellis (ed.), *Nippur at the Centennial: Papers Read at the 35^{e} Rencontre Assyriologique Internationale, Philadelphia, 1988* (Occasional Publications of the Samuel Noah Kramer Fund, 14; Philadelphia: University Museum, 1992), p. 69.

3. *Hittite*

Hymn to Ištar KUB 24.7: II.9-12[1]

> TÚG.NÍG.LÁ[M-*ašma*(?)]*ašza* GIM-*an parkuwaia waššeskiši*
> When you put clean festive garments on them, you soil one,
> nu *kuin* [*pa*]*praḫti kuinmaza parkunpat arḫa piddalaši*
> and another you neglect even though he is *parkun*(!).
> *kuin uwateši nam* ^{giš}an.za.gàr-gim-*an parganuši*
> Another you bring and make him high like a tower.

Regarding the lexeme *parkun* in line 10, Hans Güterbock noted:

> Although *parkun*, strictly speaking, is from *parku*, 'high', the context here calls for *parkui*, 'clean, pure'. Mixing of the two adjectives is easy to assume; it would be the mistake of a scribe who thought of the verb *parganu*, 'to make high' of the next line.[2]

Though it would be easy to assume a scribal error at work here, in the light of the numerous examples of biblical and Akkadian polysemous parallels, it seems wiser to defer on the part of scribal whimsy. As 'clean', *parkun* echoes the mention of 'clean' and 'soiled' garments in line 9. As 'high', it anticipates ^{giš}AN.ZA.GÀR GIM-*an parganuši*, 'makes him high like a tower', in line 11. That the polyseme has referents in both the preceding and following stichs argues for its inclusion in the list of Janus parallels.

4. *Ugaritic*[3]

Baal and ʿAnat Cycle 51.IV.14-18

> *yštn.aṯrt.lbmt.ʿr*
> He sets Asherah on the back of an ass,
> *lysmsmt.bmt.pḥl*
> On the beautiful back of a donkey

1. The lack of Hittite concern for stichoi should not concern us here, though some Hittite hymns do possess them. See, for example, E. Reiner and H.G. Güterbock, 'The Great Prayer to Ishtar', *JCS* 21 (1967), pp. 255-66.
2. H.G. Güterbock, 'A Hurro-Hittite Hymn to Ishtar', in Sasson (ed.), *Studies in Literature from the Ancient Near East*, p. 162.
3. See, for example, Noegel, 'A Janus Parallelism in the Baal and ʿAnat Story', pp. 91-94.

qdš.yuḫdm.šbʿr.
Qadish seizes, he *šbʿr.*
amrr.kkbkb.lpnm
Even Amrar like a star before him
aṯr.btlt.ʿnt
Marches the virgin ʿAnat.

Of significance here is the lexeme *šbʿr* at the end of line 16. C.H. Gordon noted that the root *bʿr* may 'have a double meaning of "leading (a caravan)" and "shining (like a star)"'.[1] Both meanings are attested. As 'lead' we find the root *bʿr* in *Kret* 101, 190 and 1002.52; and as 'shine' in 125.80 and *ʿAnat* IV.70. The text above (51.IV.16) allows for both readings as it provides a context for each.[2] As 'lead (a caravan)' *šbʿr* parallels the caravan preparations which Qadish-and-Amrar makes in lines 14-15.[3] This connection is strengthened by a paronomasia between *šbʿr* and *ʿr*, 'donkey', in line 14.[4] As 'shines' the polyseme anticipates *amrr.kkbkb.lpnm*, 'even Amrar like a star before him', in line 17.[5]

The inherent ambiguity of *šbʿr* can be seen by the differences in the various translations. Though aware of the possibility of multiple readings Gordon opted to translate 'Qadish begins to light the way.'[6] J.C. de Moor, on the other hand, translated 'Qidshu took the lead.'[7] P. van Zijl, allowing for both possibilities, read it 'Qds began to lead (shine).'[8]

1. *UT*, p. 375. The root can also mean 'pillage; turn down; disappoint'.

2. M. Dietrich and O. Loretz ('Ugaritisch *bʿr* I "anzünden" und *bʿr* II "verlassen"', *UF* 22 [1990], pp. 41-54) appear to have overlooked the word-play here.

3. This usage is also supported by cognates from Modern South Arabian. See G. Rendsburg, 'Modern South Arabian as a Source for Ugaritic Etymologies', *JAOS* 107.4 (1987), p. 625.

4. Note also the paronomasia between *aṯrt*, 'Asherah', in line 18 and *aṯr*, 'marches', in line 14. For additional examples of Ugaritic paronomasia see B. Margalit, *A Matter of 'Life' and 'Death': A Study of the Baal-Mot Epic (CTA 4–5–6)* (AOAT, 206; Neukirchen–Vluyn: Neukirchener Verlag, 1980), pp. 40, 49. Margalit did not treat the present text but did cite several additional examples of word-play in Ugaritic; see pp. 71, 77, 80, 145-46, 173, 181.

5. There may be an additional play on *šbʿr* as 'pillage' since it immediately follows *yuḫdm*, 'he seizes', in line 16.

6. C.H. Gordon, 'Poetic Legends and Myths from Ugarit', *Berytus* 25 (1977), p. 93.

7. J.C. de Moor, *An Anthology of Religious Texts from Ugarit* (Leiden: Brill, 1987), p. 52. See his n. 231 on the same page: 'Others: "took a torch" or "kindled a torch".' H.L. Ginsberg (*ANET*, p. 133) translated similarly 'Qadesh proceeds to lead'.

8. P.J. van Zijl, *Baal: A Study of Texts in Connection with Baal in the Ugaritic*

5. *Arabic*

Qur'ān 55.5-6[1]

> *al-šamsu wal-qamaru biḫusbâni,*
> The sun and the moon (run their course) by a reckoning,
> *wal-najmu wal-šajaru yasjudâni*
> and the *najmu* and the trees bow in worship.

Though this quote from the Qurʾān has been cited as an example of the Arabic rhetorical device *tawriyya*,[2] it is more accurately speaking a polysemous parallel. The key word here is *najmu* which means both 'stars' and 'herbs'.[3] As 'stars' it echoes the previous mention of the sun and moon. As 'herbs' it anticipates what follows.

Interestingly, the *surah* continues its line of rhetorical questions by continually repeating the sentence 'which is it, of the favours of Allah, that you deny?', after which follows a series of items which are divided into pairs and then recognized as one. For example, 'he has loosed the two seas. They meet' (v. 19); 'there comes from both of them the pearl and the coral-stone' (v. 22); 'before him who fears standing before Allah there are two gardens' (v. 46); 'wherein are two fountains flowing' (v. 50); 'wherein is every fruit in pairs' (v. 52), etc. That this coupling alludes to the polysemy at the start of the pericope also finds support in the fact that the *surah* moves from a discussion of heaven and earth (i.e., suggestive of *najmu* as 'stars') to a description of the foliage of the two gardens (vv. 46-68), which is suggestive of *najmu* as 'herbs'.

Epics (AOAT, 10; Neukirchen–Vluyn: Neukirchener Verlag, 1972), p. 95.

1. Noted already by J. Finkel, 'An Interpretation of an Ugaritic Viticultural Poem', in A.G. Duker (ed.), *The Joshua Starr Memorial Volume: Studies in History and Philology* (Jewish Social Studies, 5; New York: Conference on Jewish Relations, 1953), p. 35; also noted by Paul, 'Polysensuous Polyvalency in Poetic Parallelism', p. 149.

2. D.F. Payne, 'Old Testament Exegesis and the Problem of Ambiguity', *ASTI* 5 (1967), pp. 49-50. For additional examples of word-play in Arabic see A. Hamori, 'Notes on Paronomasia in Abu Tammam's Style', *JSS* 12.1 (1967), pp. 83-90.

3. Wehr, *A Dictionary of Modern Written Arabic*, p. 945.

6. *Hieroglyphic Egyptian*[1]

Chester Beatty I.4.12–5.3[2]

wr sw n-i r t3 dmḏt
Greater is she to me, than the compendium.
wḏ3(t) p3y-s(t) ʿḳn bnr
(My) *wḏ3* is her entering from the outside.
ptr-st k3 snb
Seeing her, then, is health;
wn-s(t) irti-s(t) rnpyhʿt-i
She opens her eyes, rejuvenating my body.

The word *wḏ3*(*t*) is typically understood as 'the eye of Horus'[3] and therefore as an amulet-type medicine or compendium. However, that *wḏ3*(*t*) is written with the 'eye of Horus' symbol suggests that a visual play is at work with the expression *ptr-st*, 'seeing her', in 5.2.[4] According to Richard H. Wilkinson, the use of the eye of Horus as a protective device revolved around its pictorial representation as an eye.

1. For other word-plays in Egyptian literature see W.R. Dawson, 'The Number "Seven" in Egyptian Texts', *Aegyptus* 8 (1927), pp. 27-107; C.E. Sander-Hansen, 'Die Phonetischen Wortspielen des Ältesten Ägyptischen', *AcOr* 20 (1948), pp. 1-22; H. Grapow, *Der Stilistische Bau der Geschichte des Sinuhe* (Untersuchungen zur Ägyptischen Stilistik, 1; Berlin: Akademie-Verlag, 1952), pp. 44-47, 117; O. Firchow, *Grundzüge der Stilistik in den Altägyptischen Pyramidentexten* (Untersuchungen zur Ägyptischen Stilistik, 2; Berlin: Akademie-Verlag, 1953), pp. 215-35; R. Moftah, 'Ära-Datierungen, Regierungsjahre und Zahlwortspiele', *CdE* 39 (1964), pp. 44-60; E.S. Meltzer, 'A Possible Word-Play in Khamuas I?', *ZAS* 102.1 (1975), p. 78; S. Morenz, 'Wortspiele in Ägypten', in *Religion und Geschichte des alten Ägypten: Gesammelte Aufsätze* (Köln: Böhlau Verlag, 1975), pp. 328-42; W. Guglielmi, 'Eine "Lehre" für einen reiselustigen Sohn', *WO* 14 (1983), pp. 147-66; *idem*, 'Zu Einigen Literarischen Funktionen des Wortspiels', in *Studien zu Sprache und Religion Ägyptens* (Göttingen: Herbert & Co., 1984), pp. 491-506; H. Goedicke, '"Menna's Lament"', *REg* 38 (1987), pp. 63-80; C.J. Eyre, 'Yet Again the Wax Crocodile: P. Westcar 3, 123ff.', *JEA* 78 (1992), pp. 280-81.

2. Word-plays in the love poetry section of the Chester Beatty papyrus are quite common. See, for example, Guglielmi, 'Zu Einigen Literarischen Funktionen des Wortspiels', pp. 500-503.

3. A. Erman and H. Grapow, *Ägyptisches Handwörterbuch* (Hildesheim: Olms, 1961), pp. 401-402.

4. Erman and Grapow, *Ägyptisches Handwörterbuch*, pp. 564-65.

> Above all the eye was a protective device, and this is seen in the countless representations of the *wedjat* which are found in amulets and jewelry and on the protective plaques which were placed over the embalming incision on mummies. This protective aspect is probably at least part of the significance of the two eyes which were commonly painted on the left side of coffins during the First Intermediate Period and Middle Kingdom. Although the mummy was often placed on its left side in these coffins, suggesting that the eyes may have served as a 'window' onto the world of the deceased, a protective function also seems likely. In the same way, the Horus eyes painted on the bows of boats protected the vessels and 'saw' the way ahead.[1]

That a visual play was intended also can be seen by the poet's effort to amplify or rehearse the pun in 5.3: *wn-s*(*t*) *irti-s*(*t*) *rnpy ẖ*ʿ*t-i*, 'She opens her eyes, rejuvenating my body'.

Note how the Egyptian bard has prepared the reader for a play on *wḏ3*(*t*) by saturating the poem with references to 'seeing' (I.1, 2, 6; II.1, 3, 4, 7; III.1, 7; IV.2, 6), 'medicine' (I.8; III.3; IV.7, 8, 10), 'doctors' (IV.7, 8), 'diagnoses' (IV.8), and 'revival' (IV.9, 10). That the polyseme should connect 'seeing' and 'medicine', therefore, is quite fitting. Moreover, the poet has placed the polysemy in the seventh and final stanza.[2]

7. *Medieval Hebrew*

David Yellin in his תורת השירה הספרדית[3] gives several examples of polysemous parallelism as found in the medieval poets. Though he does not refer to the device as Janus parallelism, opting instead for the expression משנה ההוראה, he is nonetheless aware of the usage.[4] That the medievals demonstrate an awareness of polysemous parallelism has been discussed above in relation to the various biblical commentaries. Here we find this awareness put into poetic compositional practice. As Yellin provided ample lexical and dictionary support for his observations, I will not repeat it here, but rather refer the reader to his book.

1. R.H. Wilkinson, *Reading Egyptian Art: A Hieroglyphic Guide to Ancient Egyptian Painting and Sculpture* (London: Thames & Hudson, 1992), p. 43.

2. For the significance of the number seven to the Egyptians see Dawson, 'The Number "Seven" in Egyptian Texts', pp. 27-107.

3. D. Yellin, תורת השירה הספרדית (Jerusalem: Magnes Press, 1972), pp. 245-51.

4. Yellin appears to be the first to have discovered the device. See Chapter 2.

Samuel Hanagid (בן תהלים)

הכינתי כבר שירה ועתה
תהילה המאירה ככסילים

I already have established a song and now,
תהלה lights up as (the stars) of Orion.

As Yellin noted,[1] the lexeme תהילה can be read as 'praise' and as 'light'. As the former, תהילה parallels שירה, 'song', in the previous stich and as the latter, it parallels the following phrase המאירה ככסילים, 'lights up as (the stars) of Orion'. That the polyemous parallelism is not differentiated in speech and is accomplished in two stichs categorizes this example with the asymmetrical as well as oral and visual types.

Samuel Hanagid (בן תהלים)[2]

הכימים בחרתם במרדים
וכלילות חפצתם בבגדים
למען תלבשו מכלול ורקמה
ונסים על בנו מלבש חרדים

Have you chosen rebellion daily
And nightly, you desire בבגדים?
So that you are clothed with a garment and embroidery
And put upon his son clothes of trembling?

Samuel Hanagid's use of בגדים for both 'treachery' and 'clothes' also demonstrates his knowledge of the Janus usage. As 'treachery', בגדים harks back to מרדים, 'rebellion', in the previous stich and as 'clothes' it anticipates the repeated use of לבש as well as the nouns כלול and רקמה in the next stichs.

Judah Halevi (על הים הסוער)[3]

דבריו מתפתיו צוף מריקים
וניביו מעצי פריו קצובים

His words from his lips are honey from emptiness,
And his ניב cut off from his fruit trees.

1. Yellin, תורת השירה הספרדית, p. 246.
2. See Yellin, תורת השירה הספרדית, p. 247.
3. Yellin, תורת השירה הספרדית, p. 250.

As Yellin observes, the lexeme ניב means both ‘pleasant words’ (cf. Isa. 57.19) and ‘fruit’ (cf. Mal. 1.12). Thus he sees in this verse a polysemous parallel in which ניב as ‘pleasant words’ parallels דבריו מתפתיו in the previous stich, and as ‘fruit’ parallels מעצי פריו, ‘from his fruit trees’, which follows. That Yellin’s prooftext for the rendering ‘pleasant words’ (Isa. 57.19) occurs in a difficult text raises the question whether the passage there also refers to ‘fruit of the lips’. Nevertheless, a Janus usage, not noted by Yellin, may adhere in another derivation for ניביו, namely ‘hollow’ (derived from נבב). As such the polyseme parallels מריקים, ‘emptiness’, in the previous stich. Indeed, the proposed meanings are not mutually exclusive, and all could have been intended.

Appendix 3

JANUS PARALLELS PROPOSED BY OTHERS BUT REJECTED

Jeremiah 25.10-11

והאבדתי־רחים מהם קול ששון וקול שׂמחה קול חתן
וקול כלה קול רחים ואור נר.
והיתה כל הארץ הזאת לחרבה לשמה ועבדו
הגוים האלה את מלך בבל שבעים שנה.

I shall banish from among them the sound of mirth and joy, the voice of bridegroom and bride, the sound of the hand-mill and וארו נר.
The whole land shall be in ruin and desolation. And those nations shall serve the king of Babylon seventy years.

According to D. Grossberg,[1] the phrase ואור נר may be read as 'the light of the lamp' and as 'tilled land'.[2] While there is no major problem with reading אור as 'light',[3] the meaning 'land' is unsubstantiated. In addition, there is insufficient reason to assume that נר would not have interrupted the polysemous effect. Had נר a second meaning suitable to the context the existence of a Janus here might be more convincing. Moreover, as 'light' אור lacks a parallel in the previous stich (other than נר which is in too close proximity). Therefore, I refrain from viewing it as a polysemous parallel.

Isaiah 7.10-11

ויוסף יהוה דבר אל אחז לאמר
שאל לך אות מעם יהוה אלהיך העמק שאלה או הגבה למעלה

1. D. Grossberg, 'Pivotal Polysemy in Jeremiah XXV, 10-11a', *VT* 36 (1986), pp. 481-85.

2. There is no support from the dictionaries for reading נר as 'tilled'. See BDB, pp. 632-33; KB, p. 634; *HALAT*, III, pp. 682-83.

3. So BDB, p. 21; KB, p. 22; *HALAT*, I, p. 24; *HAHAT*[18], pp. 26-27.

> Yahweh spoke further to Ahaz saying:
> שאל for a sign from Yahweh your God, from the depths of Sheʾol to the sky above.

Paul wants to see here a Janus with the root שאל, reading it both as 'ask',[1] normative in biblical Hebrew, and as an allusion to שאלה, 'Sheʾol',[2] in the next stich. Though 'ask' would follow nicely upon the sentence 'Yahweh spoke further to Ahaz' it is nonetheless problematic for several reasons. First, the reference to Sheʾol in the following stich makes שאלה an example of antanaclasis, that is, a word-play which uses the same root twice, the second time with a different meaning. Thus, properly speaking, it is not a Janus parallel. Secondly, even if antanaclasis were indistinguishable from or an integral part of the Janus parallel construction,[3] Paul's example would require us to see the first of his three stichs as prose, which is unlikely given that this would be the only such example.[4] Thirdly, the root שאל does not bear more than one meaning, as is required of all Janus parallels. It only means 'ask', even if, as Paul reminds us, it is to ask profoundly or deeply. Thus, there is insufficient reason to include Isa. 7.11 in the list of Janus parallels.

Isaiah 19.9-10

ובשו עבדי פשתים שריקות וארגים חורי
והיו שתתיה מדכאים כל עשי שכר אגמי נפש

> The workers of combed flax will be ashamed, the weavers of white cotton.
> Those who are שתתיה will be crushed, and all who work for hire will be grieved.

Again, Paul's efforts to see in שתתיה both 'pillars, nobles'[5] and 'drinkers'[6] depends upon changing the text in some way; in this case, changing

1. So BDB, pp. 981-82; KB, pp. 936-37; *HALAT*, IV, pp. 1276-79.
2. None of the dictionaries reads it this way; BDB, pp. 982-83; KB, p. 935; *HALAT*, IV, pp. 1274-75.
3. There may be a relationship between the two types of word manipulation. See Chapter 4.
4. Ruth 1.21 occurs in direct speech and thus may be considered poetry within prose.
5. From שתה I. So BDB, p. 1059.
6. From שתה II. See KB, p. 1014; *HALAT*, IV, pp. 1537-39. BDB treats this root as שתה I; see BDB, p. 1059.

שתתיה, 'pillars, nobles', to שותיה in order to read it as 'drinkers'. This is not merely a change in the vocalization, but also in the consonantal text. While it can hardly be denied that the word שתתיה alludes to both meanings and that it has referents for these meanings both before and after it, it cannot be considered a Janus, primarily because the reading 'drinkers' for שתתיה is uncertain.[1] Perhaps it may be considered a portmanteau word, or simple allusion, but not a Janus.

Isaiah 57.18

דרכיו ראיתי וארפאהו
ואנחהו ואשלם נחמים לו ולאבליו

I have seen his ways, but I will heal him, ואנחהו and I will requite him with comfort.

Paul's suggestion of a Janus construction in Isa. 57.18 faces severe difficulties. Paul proposed that ואנחהו may be read both as 'I will lead him',[2] which would connect with דרכיו, 'his ways', in the previous stich, and as 'I will give rest, relief',[3] which would parallel prospectively the statement ואשלם נחמים לו ולאבליו, 'I will requite him with comfort'. Problematic with Paul's observation is seeing ואנחהו as the pivot word. If it were read as 'I will give rest, relief' it would possess not only a prospective referent but also a retrospective one in וארפאהו, 'I will heal him'. Though Paul briefly raises this issue, he does not appear to view it as problematic. Yet no other Janus parallel has such a construction, since the intention of such a pun is defeated if the meaning to which it is attempting to allude in the next stich already has been stated explicitly. Therefore, I hesitate to see Isa. 57.18 as an example of Janus parallelism.

Isaiah 60.5

אז תראי ונהרת
ופחד ורחב לבבך
כי יהפך עליך המון ים חיל גוים יבאו לך

Then תראי and you will be radiant, and your heart will fear and be enlarged.

1. Some read 'weavers'. See KB, p. 1014; *HALAT*, IV, p. 1537.
2. From נחה. So BDB, p. 635; KB, p. 606; *HALAT*, III, p. 647.
3. From נוח. For a general reference see BDB, pp. 628-29; KB, pp. 601-602; *HALAT*, III, pp. 641-42.

As noted by Paul, some manuscripts read תראי as 'you will see'[1] and others as תיראי, 'you will fear, be in awe'.[2] As the former, it echoes 'raise your eyes' in v. 4. As the latter, it leads to פחד, '(your heart) will fear'. While this is convincing on the surface, it will be noted that to read this as a Janus Paul must use as the prior referent 'raise your eyes', which is separated from the pivot word by three stichs. However, that the polysemous parallel must rely on variant readings in different manuscripts, rather than on a polysemy in the same manuscript, casts doubt on the presence of a Janus here.

Moreover, it is surprising that Paul did not view ונהרת, 'and you will be radiant', as the pivot pun. It more accurately constitutes a Janus parallel in Isa. 60.5. The root נהר possess two meanings, 'shine, beam' and 'flow, stream', both of which are employed in the Bible.[3] As 'you will shine, beam' it forms a word-pair with the root ראה which Paul sees as the pivot word.[4] If we read it as 'you will (over)flow' it anticipates in a typical Janus fashion the following line, not included in Paul's study: כי יהפך עליך המון ים, 'for the abundance of the sea will be turned upon you'. Therefore, we have reason to include Isa. 60.5 in the collection of Janus parallels, but not for the reasons which Paul has given.

Jeremiah 9.3

איש מרעהו השמרו ועל כל אח אל תבטחו
כי כל אח עקוב יעקב
וכל רע רכיל יהלך

> Trust not even his brother! For every brother עקוב יעקב, every friend is base in his dealings/slanders.

While Paul is undoubtedly correct in noting a subtle reference to Jacob, it must remain doubtful for two reasons whether the phrase עקוב יעקב constitutes a Janus parallel. First, it remains to be seen whether the roots עקב and אח form a word-pair. That Jacob is a brother of someone,

1. From ראה. BDB, pp. 906-909; KB, pp. 861-64; *HALAT*, III, p. 1079–IV, p. 1083.
2. From ירא. BDB, p. 431; KB, pp. 399-400; *HALAT*, II, pp. 413-14.
3. BDB, pp. 625-26.
4. While the root ראה is not parallel elsewhere in the Bible with the root נהר, it is parallel with the root נבט, 'see', in 1 Sam. 17.42; 2 Kgs 3.14, and elsewhere. As נבט is parallel with נהר in Ps. 34.6, we may infer that ראה and נהר comprise a word-pair.

namely Isaac, is insufficient evidence to call this a Janus parallel. We must see the two words or roots in a parallel relationship elsewhere. Secondly, such allusions, while undoubtedly intentional, are nonetheless word-plays of a different sort than Januses. In essence, they are literary and/or historical allusions which are more closely related to the midrashic interpretations of names as given in the Bible.[1] Therefore, there is little reason to see Jer. 9.3 as a Janus parallel.

Hosea 2.18-19

תקראי אישי ולא תקראי לי עוד בעלי
והסרתי את שמות הבעלים מפיה ולא יזכרו עוד בשמם

You will call me my husband, and no longer will you call me בעלי.
For I will remove the name of the Baᶜalim from their mouth.

In the study by Paul, there is no distinction made here between various types of literary techniques. Well-established and easily distinguishable literary devices are grouped together with Janus parallels. In Hos. 12.18-19 Paul rightly sees בעלי as both 'my husband' and 'my Baᶜal',[2] but the referent in the third stich of the construction contains the same root as the proposed Janus word בעל. Again, this is antanaclasis, as noted above in connection with Isa. 7.1. The difference between them is that in Janus parallelism, the referents of the Janus word do not contain the same root as the Janus word; in antanaclasis, the same root is repeated with a different meaning. This is what exists in Isa. 7.1 and Hos. 2.18-19, and though the two techniques may be related, or used in tandem, they should be distinguished.

Amos 1.11

על רדפו בחרב אחיו
ושחת רחמיו
ויטרף לעד אפו
ועברתו שמרה נצח

Because he pursued his brother with the sword, and destroyed רחמיו,
his anger seethed ceaselessly, and his fury raged incessantly.

1. They are both from עקב. BDB, p. 784; KB, p. 729; *HALAT*, III, p. 825; Garsiel, *Biblical Names*, pp. 134, 141.

2. Both from בעל. BDB, p. 127; KB, pp. 137-38; *HALAT*, I, pp. 137-38; *HAHAT*[18], pp. 162-63.

While it is quite possible, indeed intriguing, that merism may be utilized in the construction of a Janus, the example here as quoted by Paul is unconvincing. Though in theory there is no difficulty with reading רחמיו as 'his women'[1] and connecting it with אחיו, 'his brother', in the previous line, and with reading רחמיו as 'his mercy'[2] and linking it to אפו, 'his anger', and עברתו, 'his fury', in the following line, the supposition is devoid of substantiating evidence. For instance, one would like to see if the root רחם (or אשה) as 'woman' and אח, 'brother', are parallel elsewhere. Likewise, does the root רחם, 'mercy', parallel אף, 'anger', or עברה, 'fury', anywhere else in the Bible? Pending more evidence, the proposed Janus remains uncertain.

Nahum 3.6-7

והשלכתי עליך שקצים
ונבלתיך ושמתיך כראי
והיה כל ראיך ידוד ממך

I will throw loathsome things on you, I will disfigure you, And I will make you like ראי. All who see you will recoil from you.

If it may even be considered a word-play, Nah. 3.6-7 is again an example of antanaclasis, and not, as Paul conjectures, a Janus parallel. The word which Paul wants to see as a pivot, ראי, as meaning both 'spectacle'[3] and 'excrement', probably means only 'spectacle'. Though the meaning 'excrement' is common in postbiblical Hebrew in the forms ראי and רעי, it is not attested in the Bible, unless we count this passage. Thus, it is too speculative to label Nah. 3.6-7 a polysemous parallel.

Zephaniah 3.3

שריה בקרבה אריות שאגים
שפטיה זאבי ערב
לא גרמו לבקר

Her officials within her are roaring lions, her judges are wolves of ערב. They leave nothing until the morning.

1. As found in the Mesha stele line 17 and in Judg. 5.30. See KB, p. 886.
2. See BDB, p. 933; KB, pp. 885-86; *HALAT*, IV, pp. 1134-35.
3. From ראה. So BDB, p. 909; KB, p. 864; *HALAT*, IV, p. 1084.

The Janus parallel that Paul finds in Zeph. 3.3 revolves around the word ערב, which he reads as both 'evening'[1] and 'steppe'.[2] While both readings are equally plausible, there is a crucial problem in regarding this as a Janus parallel, namely that there is no referent in the first stich to which the meaning 'steppe' may be attached. One would expect to see a reference to land, hills, mountains, or some other topographical feature, but there is none. For this reason, though Zeph. 3.3 may contain a pun, I do not consider it a Janus parallel.

Lamentations 1.1

ישבה בדד העיר רבתי עם
היתה כאלמנה רבתי בגוים
שרתי במדינות היתה למס

> Lonely sits the city once great with people. She that was רבתי among the nations has become like a widow. The princess among the provinces has become a vassal.

Here Paul views רבתי as meaning both 'great' and 'princess'.[3] While this is convincing in itself, the word does not form a Janus parallel in Lam. 1.1. Though it nicely parallels שרתי, 'princess', in the next stich, its only referent in the previous stich is רבתי, which may or may not mean the same as 'princess'. In fact, this is splitting hairs, for the two meanings are related. So while it may possibly be another example of antanaclasis, it should not be considered a Janus parallel.

Lamentations 1.7-8

ראוה צרים שחקו על משבתיה
חטא חטאה ירושלם על כן לנידה היתה
כל מכבדיה הזילוה כי ראו ערותה

> Enemies looked on and gloated over her downfall. Jerusalem has sinned greatly. Therefore, she has become נידה. All who honored her despise her for they have seen her nakedness.

1. So BDB, pp. 787-88; KB, p. 732; *HALAT*, III, pp. 830-31.
2. As a by-form of ערבה. See BDB, p. 787; KB, p. 733; *HALAT*, III, pp. 831-32.
3. Both from רבב. BDB, pp. 912-13; KB, p. 868; *HALAT*, IV, pp. 1094-96.

One difficulty in seeing a Janus parallel in Lam. 1.7-8 is the fact that the pivot word לנידה is a *hapax legomenon*.[1] According to Paul, it may be interpreted as a 'derisive shaking of the head'[2] or like נדה as an 'unclean, or menstruating woman'.[3] Both meanings derive from the same root (נדד), suggesting that there is little or no semantic distinction between those things which are viewed as 'derisive' and those which are seen as 'unclean'. A fundamental characteristic of Janus parallelism is that a word must have more than one meaning, even within its own semantic range. In addition, it is unclear how 'a derisive shaking of the head' fits in this passage, since there appears to be no context for such a reading. It therefore seems wise to refrain from viewing Lam. 1.7-8 as a Janus construction.

I ʿAnat II.23-26

mid tmtḫṣn wtʿn
Hard did she fight and look;
tḫtṣb wtḥdy ʿnt
do battle and gloat did ʿAnat;
tǵdd kbdh bṣḥq ymlu
her belly swelled with laughter,
lbh bšmḫt...
her heart was filled with happiness.

This Ugaritic Janus parallelism, which was proposed by W.G. Watson,[4] sees the verb *ḥdy*, 'gaze', in the second line as parallel with *ʿny*, 'see', in the first line. In its meaning 'rejoice' it anticipates the mirth in the next verse. Despite the attempt, there is reason to reject *I ʿAnat* II.23-26 as an example of Janus parallelism because Watson apparently confused separate phonemes, *ḥ* and *ḫ*. The roots in question are *ḥdy*, 'gaze', and *ḫdy*, 'rejoice'. As the two phonemes are never confused either in pronunciation or in writing, it is doubtful whether one would allude to the other, other than by paronomasia. Thus, Watson's example cannot be included among the list of polysemous parallels.

1. However, in itself, this is not an insurmountable problem.
2. From נדד. BDB, p. 622; KB, p. 596; *HALAT*, III, p. 635.
3. BDB, p. 622; KB, pp. 596-97; *HALAT*, III, pp. 635-36.
4. Watson, *Classical Hebrew Poetry*, p. 159.

Appendix 4

WORKS ON PARONOMASIA

Please see bibliography for complete entries. H. Rechendorff (1909); E.S. McCartney (1919); E.A. Russell (1920); F. Bohl (1926); G. Böstrom (1928); D. Yellin (1929); K. Fullerton (1930); O.S. Rankin (1930); J. Fichtner (1956); A.F. Key (1964); A. Weiser (1964); A. Guillaume (1964); D.R. Driver (1967); D.F. Payne (1967); D. Lys (1969); J.F.A. Sawyer (1969); J.J. Glück (1970); W.L. Holladay (1970); J.H. Charlesworth (1970); L. Peeters (1971–72); I.H. Eybers (1971–72); P. Hugger (1972); M. Delcor (1973); M. Paran (1973); J. Fraenkel (1978); P.D. Miller (1979); P. Doron (1979–80); B. Beitzel (1980); B. Halpern and R.E. Friedman (1980); J.P. van der Westhuizen (1980); Y. Hoffman (1980); Y. Gitay (1980); W.G.E. Watson (1981); A.R. Ceresko (1982); G. Rendsburg (1982); J.N. Carreira (1982); E.D. Mallon (1983); D.L. Christensen (1983); L. Boadt (1983); L.I. Weinstock (1983); S. Segert (1984); W.G. Watson (1984); A. Wolters (1985); W. Farber (1986); R.B. Chisholm (1987); R.T. Cherry III (1988); A. Wolters (1988); H. Eilberg-Schwartz (1988); G. Rendsburg (1988); D.F. Pennant (1989); B.O. Long (1990); D. Marcus (1990); E.F. Davis (1990); P.R. Raabe (1991); A. Wolters (1991); E.A. Russell (1991); D. Stern (1991); N. Klaus (1991–92); J.B. Curtis (1992); C.G. den Hertog (1992); S.T. Lachs (1992); B.T. Arnold (1993); D. Bivin (1993); J.A. Fitzmeyer (1993); S. Fisher (1993); S. Storoy (1993); M. Garsiel (1993); E. Marino (1993); E. van Wolde (1994); K. Larkin (1994); M. Garsiel (1995).

BIBLIOGRAPHY

Abraham, C., 'The Pun on Peter', *BARev* 19.1 (1993), p. 68.

Abusch, Tz., 'Gilgamesh's Request and Siduri's Denial', in M.E. Cohen *et al.* (eds.), *The Tablet and the Scroll: Near Eastern Studies in Honor of William W. Hallo* (Bethesda, MD: CDL Press, 1993), pp. 1-14.

—'The Form and Meaning of a Babylonian Prayer to Marduk', in J. Sasson (ed.), *Studies in Literature from the Ancient Near East: by Members of the American Oriental Society Dedicated to Samuel Noah Kramer* (AOS, 65; New Haven, CT: American Oriental Society, 1984), pp. 3-15.

Ahl, F., *Metaformations: Soundplay and Wordplay in Ovid and Other Classical Poets* (Ithaca: Cornell University Press, 1985).

—'Ars Est Caelare Artem (Art in Puns and Anagrams Engraved)', in J. Culler (ed.), *On Puns: The Foundation of Letters* (Oxford: Basil Blackwell, 1988), pp. 17-43.

Ahrend, M.M., *Le commentaire sur Job de Rabbi Yoseph Qara': études des méthodes philologique et exégetique* (Hildesheim: Gerstenberg, 1978).

Alster, B., 'On the Interpretation of the Sumerian Myth "Inanna and Enki"', *ZA* 64 (1975), pp. 20-34.

—'Paradoxical Proverbs and Satire in Sumerian Literature', *JCS* 27 (1975), pp. 201-30.

—'The Sumerian Folktale of the Three Ox-Drivers from Adab', *JCS* 43–45 (1991–1993), pp. 27-38.

—'Marriage and Love in the Sumerian Love Songs', in M.E. Cohen *et al.* (eds.), *The Tablet and the Scroll: Near Eastern Studies in Honor of William W. Hallo* (Bethesda, MD: CDL Press, 1993), pp. 15-27.

Andersen, F.I., *Job: An Introduction and Commentary* (Downers Grove, IL: Inter-Varsity Press, 1976).

Aquinas, St T., *The Literal Exposition on Job: A Scriptural Commentary Concerning Providence* (ed. A. Domico; Atlanta: Scholars Press, 1989).

Arnold, B.T., 'Wordplay and Narrative Technique in Daniel 5 and 6', *JBL* 112.3 (1993), pp. 479-85.

Artzi, P., and A. Malamat, 'The Great King: A Preeminent Royal Title in Cuneiform Sources and the Bible', in M.E. Cohen *et al.* (eds.), *The Tablet and the Scroll: Near Eastern Studies in Honor of William W. Hallo* (Bethesda, MD: CDL Press, 1993), pp. 28-38.

Astour, M.C., 'Sparagmos, Omophagia, and Estactic Prophecy at Mari', *UF* 24 (1992), pp. 1-2.

Aufrecht, W.E. (ed.), *Studies in the Book of Job* (Waterloo, Ontario: W. Laurier University Press, 1985).

Avishur, Y., *Stylistic Studies of Word-Pairs in Biblical and Ancient Semitic Literatures* (AOAT, 210; Neukirchen–Vluyn: Neukirchener Verlag, 1984).
Bacher, W., 'Le Commentaire sur Job de R. Samuel B. Nissim d'Alep', *REJ* 21 (1890), pp. 118-32.
Barr, J., 'St. Jerome and the Sounds of Hebrew', *JSS* 12.1 (1967), pp. 1-36.
—'The Symbolism of Names in the Old Testament', *BJRL* 52 (1969–1970), pp. 11-29.
—'Hebrew Orthography and the Book of Job', *JSS* 30 (1985), pp. 1-33.
Barth, K., *Hiob* (Biblische Studien, 49; Neukirchen–Vluyn: Neukirchener Verlag, 1966).
Baskin, J.R., 'Rabbinic Interpretations of Job', in L.G. Perdue and W.C. Gilpin (eds.), *The Voice from the Whirlwind: Interpreting the Book of Job* (Nashville: Abingdon Press, 1992), pp. 101-10.
Basser, H., and B.D. Walfish (eds.), *Moses Kimḥi: Commentary on the Book of Job* (South Florida Studies in the History of Judaism, 64; Atlanta: Scholars Press, 1992).
Baum, P.F., 'Chaucer's Puns', *PMLA* 71 (1956), pp. 225-46.
Baumgartner, W., and L. Koehler (eds.), *Hebräisches und Aramäisches Lexicon zum Alten Testament*, I–IV (Leiden: Brill, 1967–1990).
Beaulieu, P.A., 'New Light on Secret Knowledge in Late Babylonian Culture', *ZA* 82 (1992), pp. 98-111.
Beitzel, B., 'Exodus 3.14 and the Divine Name: A Case of Biblical Paranomasia', *TrinJ* NS 1 (1980), pp. 5-20.
Berlin, A., 'Grammatical Aspects of Biblical Parallelism', *HUCA* 50 (1979), pp. 17-43.
—*The Dynamics of Biblical Parallelism* (Bloomington, IN: Indiana University Press, 1985).
—'Parallelism', in D.N. Freedman (ed.), *The Anchor Bible Dictionary* (Garden City, NY: Doubleday, 1992), V, pp. 155-62.
Beyer, K., *Die aramäischen Texte vom Toten Meer* (Göttingen: Vandenhoeck & Ruprecht, 1984).
Biggs, R.D., 'The Abū Ṣalābīkh Tablets', *JCS* 20 (1966), pp. 73-88.
—'Descent of Ištar, Line 104', *NABU* 74 (1993), pp. 58-59.
Bivin, D., 'The Pun on Peter Works Better in Hebrew', *BARev* 19.3 (1993), pp. 18-19.
Black, M., *An Aramaic Approach to the Gospels and Acts* (Oxford: Clarendon Press, 3rd edn, 1967), pp. 160-85.
Blau, J., 'Über Homonyme und Angeblich Homonyme Wurzeln', *VT* 6 (1956), pp. 242-48.
—*On Pseudo-Corrections in Some Semitic Languages* (Jerusalem: Israel Academy of Sciences and Humanities, 1970).
—'"Weak" Phonetic Change and the Hebrew Śîn', *HAR* 1 (1977), pp. 67-119.
—'On Polyphony in Biblical Hebrew', *Proceedings of the Israel Academy of Sciences and Humanities* 6 (1983), p. 3.
Blommerde, A.C.M., *Northwest Semitic Grammar and Job* (Rome: Pontifical Biblical Institute, 1969).
Bloom, H. (ed.), *The Book of Job* (New York: Chelsea House Publishers, 1988).
Boadt, L., 'Intentional Alliteration in Second Isaiah', *CBQ* 45 (1983), pp. 353-63.
Bohl, F., 'Wortspiele im Alten Testament', *JPOS* 6 (1926), pp. 196-212.

Böstrom, G., *Paranomasi iden äldre Hebreiska Maschalliteraturen med särsklid hänsyn till proverbia* (Lund: Gleerup, 1928).
Bottéro, J., 'Les noms de Marduk, l'écriture et la "logique" en Mésopotamie ancienne', in M. de Jong Ellis (ed.), *Memoirs of the Academy of Arts and Sciences, 19: Essays on the Ancient Near East in Memory of Jacob Joel Finkelstein* (Hamden, CT: Archon Books, 1977), pp. 5-28.
—'La creation de l'homme et sa nature dans le poème d'Atraḫasîs', in M.A. Dandamayev *et al.* (eds.), *Societies and Languages of the Ancient Near East: Studies in Honor of I.M. Diakonoff* (Warminster: Aris & Phillips, 1982), pp. 24-32.
—*Mesopotamia: Writing, Reasoning, and the Gods* (Chicago: University of Chicago Press, 1992).
Brown, J., 'Eight Types of Puns', *PMLA* 71 (1956), pp. 14-26.
Burns, J.B., 'Support for the Emendation *r^eḥōb m^eqōmô* in Job XXIV 19-20', *VT* 34.4 (1989), pp. 480-84.
—'Namtara and Nergal—Down but Not Out: A Reply to Nicolas Wyatt', *VT* 43 (1993), pp. 1-9.
Carey, P., J. Mehler, and T.G. Bever, 'Judging the Veracity of Ambiguous Sentences', *Journal of Learning and Verbal Behavior* 9 (1970), pp. 243-54.
—'When Do We Compute All the Interpretations of an Ambiguous Sentence?', in G.B. Flores d'Arcais and W.J.M. Levelt (eds.), *Advances in Psycholinguistics* (Amsterdam and London: North-Holland Publishing Company, 1970), pp. 61-75.
Carmichael, C.M., 'Some Sayings in Genesis 49', *JBL* 88 (1969), pp. 434-44.
Carreira, J.N., 'Kunstsprache und Weisheit bei Micha', *BZ* 26 (1982), pp. 50-74.
Casanowicz, I.M., *Paronomasia in the Old Testament* (Boston, 1894).
Cavigneaux, A., 'Aux sources du Midrash: l'herméneutique babylonienne', *AcOr* 5.2 (1987), pp. 243-55.
Ceresko, A.R., *Job 29–31 in the Light of Northwest Semitic: A Translation and Philological Commentary* (Rome: Biblical Institute Press, 1980).
—'The Function of Antanaclasis (*mṣ*ʾ "to find"//*mṣ*ʾ "to reach, overtake, grasp") in Hebrew Poetry, Especially in the Book of Qoheleth', *CBQ* 44 (1982), pp. 551-69.
—'Janus Parallelism in Amos's "Oracles Against the Nations" (Amos 1.3–2.16)', *JBL* 113 (1994), pp. 485-90.
Charlesworth, J.H., 'Paronomasia and Assonance in the Syriac Text of the Odes of Solomon', *Semitics* 1 (1970), pp. 12-26.
Cheneb, M. Ben, 'Tawriya', in H.A.R. Gibb, *et al.* (eds.), *Encyclopaedia of Islam* (Leiden: Brill, 1960), pp. 707-708.
Cherry, R.T. III, 'Paranomasia and Proper Names in the Old Testament: Rhetorical Function and Literary Effect' (PhD dissertation, Southern Baptist Theological Seminary, 1988).
Ching, M.K.L., 'The Relationship among the Diverse Senses of a Pun', *The Southeastern Conference on Linguistics Bulletin* 2.3 (Fall, 1978), pp. 1-8.
—'A Literary and Linguistic Analysis of Compact Verbal Paradox', in *idem, et al.* (eds.), *Linguistic Perspectives on Learning* (London: Routledge & Kegan Paul, 1980), pp. 175-81.
Chisholm, R.B., 'Word Play in the Eighth-Century Prophets', *BSac* 144 (1987), pp. 44-52.

Christensen, D.L., 'Anticipatory Paronomasia in Jonah 3.7-8 and Genesis 37.2', *RB* 90 (1983), pp. 261-63.

Chrysostom, St J., *Commentaire sur Job* (ed. H. Sorlin; Paris: Cerf, 1988).

Civil, M., 'Išme-Dagan and Enlil's Chariot', *JAOS* 88 (1968), pp. 3-14.

—'Review of Th. G. Pinches. *Cuneiform Texts from Babylonian Tablets in the British Museum*', *JNES* 28 (1969), p. 71.

—'The Anzu-Bird and Scribal Whimsies', *JAOS* 92 (1972), p. 271.

—'Enlil and Ninlil: The Marriage of Sud', in J.M. Sasson (ed.), *Studies in Literature from the Ancient Near East by Members of the American Oriental Society Dedicated to Samuel Noah Kramer* (AOS, 65; New Haven, CT: American Oriental Society, 1984), pp. 43-66.

—'Sumerian Riddles: A Corpus', *AcOr* 5.2 (1987), pp. 17-37.

—'On Mesopotamian Jails and their Lady Warden', in M.E. Cohen *et al.* (eds.), *The Tablet and the Scroll: Near Eastern Studies in Honor of William W. Hallo* (Bethesda, MD: CDL Press, 1993), pp. 72-78.

Clines, D.J.A., *Job 1–20* (WBC, 17; Dallas: Word Books, 1989).

Cooper, J.S., 'Gilgamesh Dreams of Enkidu: The Evolution and Dilution of Narrative', in M. de Jong Ellis (ed.), *Memoirs of the Academy of Arts and Sciences, 19: Essays on the Ancient Near East in Memory of Jacob Joel Finkelstein* (Hamden, CT: Archon Books, 1977), pp. 39-44.

Cotter, D.W., *A Study of Job 4–5 in the Light of Contemporary Literary Theory* (Atlanta: Scholars Press, 1992).

Course, J.E., *Speech and Response: A Rhetorical Analysis of the Introductions to the Speeches of Job (Chaps. 4–24)* (CBQMS, 25; Washington, DC: Catholic Biblical Association of America, 1994).

Crenshaw, J.L., 'Wisdom', in J.H. Hayes (ed.), *Old Testament Form Criticism* (San Antonio: Trinity University Press, 1974), pp. 225-64.

—*Studies in Ancient Israelite Wisdom* (New York: Ktav, 1976).

—*The Old Testament Wisdom: An Introduction* (Atlanta: John Knox, 1981).

—'The Book of Job', in D.N. Freedman (ed.), *The Anchor Bible Dictionary* (Garden City, NY: Doubleday, 1992), III, pp. 858-68.

Culler, J., 'The Call of the Phoneme: Introduction', in *idem* (ed.), *On Puns: The Foundation of Letters* (Oxford: Basil Blackwell, 1988), pp. 1-16.

Curtis, J.B., 'Word Play in the Speeches of Elihu (Job 32–37)', *Proceedings of the Eastern Great Lakes and Midwest Biblical Societies* 12 (1992), pp. 23-30.

Dahood, M., 'Some Northwest-Semitic Words in Job', *Bib* 38 (1957), pp. 306-20.

—'HÔL "Phoenix" in Job 29.18 and in Ugaritic', *CBQ* 36 (1974), pp. 85-88.

—'A Phoenician Word Pair in Psalm 72, 16', *Bib* 60 (1979), pp. 571-72.

—'Eblaite and Biblical Hebrew', *CBQ* 44 (1982), pp. 1-24.

Davis, E.F., 'A Strategy of Delayed Comprehension: Isaiah LIV 15', *VT* 40.2 (1990), pp. 217-20.

Dawson, W.R., The Number "Seven" in Egyptian Texts', *Aegyptus* 8 (1927), pp. 27-107.

Delcor, M., 'Homonymie et interpretation de l'Ancient Testament', *JSS* 43.1 (1973), pp. 40-54.

Dell, K.J., *The Book of Job as Skeptical Literature* (Berlin and New York: de Gruyter, 1991).

Dhorme, P.A., *Le Livre de Job* (Paris: Lecoffre, 1926).

—*A Commentary on the Book of Job* (ed. U. Hagedorn and D. Hagedorn; trans. H.J. Knight; London: Nelson, 1967).

Didymos of Alexandria, *Kommentar zu Hiob (Tura–Papyrus)* (Bonn: R. Habelt, 1968).

Dietrich, M., and O. Loretz, 'Die Sieben Kunstwerke des Schmiedegottes in KTU 1.4 I 23-43', *UF* 10 (1978), pp. 57-63.

—'Ugaritisch *bʿr* I "anzünden" und *bʿr* II "verlassen"', *UF* 22 (1990), pp. 41-54.

Dietrich, M., O. Loretz, and J. Sanmartín, 'Zur Ugaritischen Lexikographie (VII)', *UF* 5 (1973), pp. 79-122.

Dor, M., 'כנף רננים־עפרוני', *BM* 128.1 (1992), pp. 84-85.

Doron, P., 'Paronomasia in the Prophecies to the Nations', *Hebrew Abstracts* 20–21 (1979–80), pp. 36-43.

Driver, G.R., 'Confused Hebrew Roots', in B. Schindler (ed.), *Gaster Anniversary Volume* (Occident and Orient; London: Taylor's Foreign Press, 1936), pp. 73-82.

—'Problems in the Hebrew Text of Job', in M. Noth and D.W. Thomas (eds.), *Wisdom in Israel and in the Ancient Near East* (VTSup, 3; Leiden: Brill, 1960), pp. 72-93.

—'Playing on Words', in *Proceedings of the 4th World Congress of Jewish Studies: Papers* (Jerusalem, 1967), I, pp. 121-29.

Driver, S.R., *A Critical and Exegetical Commentary on the Book of Job, Together with a New Translation*, I–II (New York: Charles Scribner's Sons, 1921).

Eaton, J.H., *Job* (OTG; Sheffield: JSOT Press, 1985).

Eichler, B.L., 'mar-URU$_5$: Tempest in a Deluge', in M.E. Cohen *et al.* (eds.), *The Tablet and the Scroll: Near Eastern Studies in Honor of William W. Hallo* (Bethesda, MD: CDL Press, 1993), pp. 90-94.

Eilberg-Schwartz, H., 'Who's Kidding Whom? A Serious Reading of Rabbinic Word Plays', *JAAR* 55 (1988), pp. 765-88.

Eisenberg, J., *Job, ou, Dieu dans la Tempête* (Paris: Verdier, 1986).

Ellis, M. de Jong, 'Gilgamesh's Approach to Huwawa: A New Text', *AfO* 28 (1981–82), pp. 123-31.

Erman, A., and H. Grapow, *Ägyptisches Handwörterbuch* (Hildesheim: Olms, 1961).

Eybers, I.H., 'The Use of Proper Names as a Stylistic Device', *Semitics* 2 (1971–1972), pp. 82-92.

Eyre, C.J., 'Yet Again the Wax Crocodile: P. Westcar 3, 123ff.', *JEA* 78 (1992), pp. 280-81.

Farb, P., *Word Play* (New York: Knopf, 1973).

—*Word Play: What Happens When People Talk* (New York: Bantam, 1975).

Farber, W., 'Associative Magic: Some Rituals, Word Plays, and Philology', *JAOS* 106.3 (1986), pp. 447-49.

Fichtner, J., *Die altorientalische Weisheit in ihrer israelitisch-jüdischen Ausprägung* (BZAW, 62; Giessen: Töpelmann, 1933).

—'Die Etymologische Ätiologie in den Namengebungen der Geschichtlichen Bucher des Alten Testaments', *VT* (1956), pp. 372-96.

Finkel, J., 'An Interpretation of an Ugaritic Viticultural Poem', in A.G. Duker (ed.), *The Joshua Starr Memorial Volume: Studies in History and Philology* (Jewish Social Studies, 5; New York: Conference on Jewish Relations, 1953), pp. 29-58.

Firchow, O., *Grundzüge der Stilistik in den Altägyptischen Pyramidentexten* (Untersuchungen zur Ägyptischen Stilistik, 2; Berlin: Akademie-Verlag, 1953).

Fishbane, M., 'The Book of Job and Inner-Biblical Discourse', in L.G. Perdue and W.C. Gilpin (eds.), *The Voice from the Whirlwind: Interpreting the Book of Job* (Nashville, TN: Abingdon Press, 1992), pp. 86-98.

Fisher, S., 'How Many Angels Can Dance on the Head of a Pun?', *BARev* 19.3 (1993), pp. 19, 76.

Fitzmeyer, J.A., 'Reply to Charles Abraham's "The Pun on Peter"', *BARev* 19.1 (1993), pp. 68, 70.

Fohrer, G. *Studien zum Buche Hiob* (Berlin: de Gruyter, 1983).

Fordyce, C.J., 'Puns on Names in Greek', *Classical Journal* 28 (1932–33), pp. 44-46.

Foss, D.J., 'Some Effects of Ambiguity upon Sentence Comprehension', *Journal of Learning and Verbal Behavior* 9 (1970), pp. 699-706.

Foss, D.J., T.G. Bever, and M. Silver, 'The Comprehension and Verification of Ambiguous Sentences', *Perception and Psychophysics* 4 (1968), pp. 304-306.

Foster, B.R., 'Humor and Cuneiform Literature', *Journal of the Ancient Near Eastern Society of Columbia University 6: The Gaster Festschrift* (1974), pp. 69-85.

—'*tuktullu* "shiver, quake"', *RA* 75 (1981), p. 189.

—*Before the Muses: An Anthology of Akkadian Literature* (Bethesda, MD: CDL Press, 1993).

—'Self-Reference of an Akkadian Poet', in J. Sasson (ed.), *Studies in Literature from the Ancient Near East: by Members of the American Oriental Society Dedicated to Samuel Noah Kramer* (AOS, 65; New Haven, CT: American Oriental Society, 1984), pp. 123-30.

Fox, M.V., *The Song of Songs and the Ancient Egyptian Love Songs* (Madison, WI: University of Wisconsin Press, 1985).

—'Words for Wisdom', *ZAH* 6 (1993), pp. 149-69.

Foxvog, D., 'Astral Dumuzi', in M.E. Cohen *et al.* (eds.), *The Tablet and the Scroll: Near Eastern Studies in Honor of William W. Hallo* (Bethesda, MD: CDL Press, 1993), pp. 103-108.

Fraenkel, J., 'Paranomasia in Aggadic Narratives', *Scripta Hierosolymitana* 27 (1978), pp. 27-35.

Frances, I., ספר מתק שפתים, in H. Brody (ed.), *Hebraeische Prosidie von Immanuel Frances* (Krakau, 1892).

Frank, C., 'Zu den Wortspielen *kukku* und *kibāti* in Gilg. Ep. XI', *ZA* 36 (1925), p. 216.

Frank, R., 'Some Uses of Paranomasia in Old English Scriptural Verse', *Speculum* 47 (1972), pp. 207-26.

Frisch, A., 'ועניתם (I Reg 12,7): An Ambiguity and its Function in the Context', *ZAW* 103 (1991), pp. 415-18.

Fullerton, K., 'Double Entendre in the First Speech of Eliphaz', *JBL* 49 (1930), pp. 320-74.

Gaebelein, F.E. (ed.), *The Expositor's Bible Commentary: With the New International Version of the Holy Bible* (Grand Rapids: Zondervan, 1976).

Gammie, J., *et al.* (eds.), *Israelite Wisdom: Theological and Literary Essays in Honor of Samuel Terrien* (Missoula: Scholars Press, 1978).

Gard, D.H., *The Exegetical Method of the Greek Translator of the Book of Job* (Philadelphia: Society of Biblical Literature, 1952).

Garrett, M.F., 'Does Ambiguity Complicate the Perception of Sentences?', in G.B. Flores d'Arcais and W.J.M. Levelt (eds.), *Advances in Psycholinguistics*

(Amsterdam and London: North-Holland Publishing Company, 1970), pp. 48-60.

Garsiel, M., 'Wit, Words, and a Woman: 1 Samuel 25', in Y.T. Radday and A. Brenner (eds.), *On Humor and the Comic in the Hebrew Bible* (JSOTSup, 92; Sheffield: Almond Press, 1990), pp. 161-68.

—*Biblical Names: A Literary Study of Midrashic Derivations and Puns* (Ramat-Gan: Bar-Ilan University Press, 1991).

—'Homiletic Name-Derivations as a Literary Device in the Gideon Narrative: Judges VI–VIII', *VT* 43.3 (1993), pp. 302-17.

—'Puns upon Names: Subtle Colophons in the Bible', *JBQ* 23 (1995), pp. 182-87.

Geller, S.A., 'Some Sound and Word Plays in the First Tablet of the Old Babylonian Atramḫasīs Epic', in B. Walfish (ed.), *Frank Talmage Memorial Volume I* (Haifa: University of Haifa Press, 1993), pp. 63-70.

Geyer, J.B., 'Mythological Sequence in Job XXIV 19–20', *VT* 42 (1992), pp. 118-20.

Gibson, J.C.L., *Job* (Philadelphia: Westminster Press, 1985).

Gilbert, M. (ed.), *La Sagesse de l'Ancien Testament* (Gembloux: Duculot; Leuven: Leuven University Press, 1979).

Gitay, Y., 'Deutero-Isaiah: Oral or Written?', *JBL* 99.2 (1980), pp. 185-97.

Glassner, J.J., 'Inanna et les Me', in M. de Jong Ellis (ed.), *Nippur at the Centennial: Papers Read at the 35e Rencontre Assyriologique Internationale, Philadelphia, 1988* (Occasional Publications of the Samuel Noah Kramer Fund, 14; Philadelphia: University Museum, 1992), pp. 55-109.

Glück, J.J., 'Paronomasia in Biblical Literature', *Semitics* 1 (1970), pp. 50-78.

Goedicke, H., 'Adam's Rib', in A. Kort and S. Morschauser (eds.), *Biblical and Related Studies Presented to Samuel Iwry* (Winona Lake, IN: Eisenbrauns, 1985), pp. 73-76.

—'"Menna's Lament"', *REg* 38 (1987), pp. 63-80.

Good, E.M., *In Turns of Tempest: A Reading of Job, with a Translation* (Stanford, CA: Stanford University Press, 1990).

Goodman, L.E., *The Book of Theodicy: Translation and Commentary on the Book of Job by Saadiah ben Joseph Al-Fayyumi* (New Haven, CT: Yale University Press, 1988).

Gordis, R., *The Book of God and Man: A Study of Job* (Chicago: University of Chicago Press, 1965).

—*The Book of Job: Commentary, New Translation and Special Studies* (New York: Jewish Theological Seminary, 1978).

Gordon, C.H., *Ugaritic Textbook* (AnOr, 38; Rome: Pontifical Biblical Institute, 1965).

—'New Light on the Hebrew Language', *Hebrew Abstracts* 15 (1974), pp. 29-31.

—'Poetic Legends and Myths from Ugarit', *Berytus* 25 (1977), pp. 5-133.

—'New Directions', *Bulletin of the American Society of Papyrologists* 15 (1978), pp. 59-66.

—'Asymmetric Janus Parallelism', *EI* 16 (*Harry M. Orlinsky Volume*) (1982), pp. 80-81*.

—'On Making Other Gods', in A. Kort and S. Morschauser (eds.), *Biblical and Related Studies Presented to Samuel Iwry* (Winona Lake, IN: Eisenbrauns, 1985), pp. 77-79.

—'"This Time"' (Genesis 2.23)', in M. Fishbane and E. Tov (eds.), *'Sha'arei Talmon': Studies in the Bible, Qumran, and the Ancient Near East Presented to Shemaryahu Talmon* (Winona Lake, IN: Eisenbrauns, 1992), pp. 50-51.

Gordon, C.W., 'Qetûl Nouns in Classical Hebrew', *Abr-Nahrain* 29 (1991), pp. 83-86.

Gordon, E.I., *Sumerian Proverbs: Glimpses of Everyday Life in Ancient Mesopotamia* (Philadelphia: University Museum, 1959).

Gordon, R.P., 'The Meaning of the Verb *ŠWY* in the Targum to I Samuel V–VI', *VT* 42 (1992), pp. 395-97.

Goshen-Gottstein, M., *Fragments of Lost Targumim* (Ramat-Gan: Bar-Ilan University Press, 1983).

Gowan, D., 'Reading Job as Wisdom Script', *JSOT* 55 (1992), pp. 85-96.

Grabbe, L.L., *Comparative Philology and the Text of Job: A Study in Methodology* (SBLDS, 34; Missoula, MT: Scholars Press, 1977).

Grapow, H., *Der Stilistische Bau der Geschichte des Sinuhe* (Untersuchungen zur Ägyptischen Stilistik, 1; Berlin: Akademie-Verlag, 1952).

Gray, J., 'The Massoretic Text of the Book of Job, the Targum and the Septuagint Version in the Light of the Qumran Targum (11 QtargJob)', *ZAW* 86 (1974), pp. 331-50.

Greenberg, M., 'Ancient Versions for Interpreting the Hebrew Text', in J.A. Emerton *et al.* (eds.), *Congress Volume: Gottingen, 1977* (VTSup, 29; Leiden: Brill, 1978), pp. 131-48.

Greenfield, J.C., 'Lexicographical Notes 1', *HUCA* 29 (1958), pp. 203-28.

—'Lexicographical Notes 2', *HUCA* 30 (1959), pp. 141-51.

—'The Cluster in Biblical Poetry', *maarav* 55–56 (1990), pp. 159-68.

—'Philological Observations on the Deir 'Alla Inscription', in J. Hoftijzer and G. van der Kooij (eds.), *The Balaam Text from Deir 'Alla Re-evaluated* (Leiden: Brill, 1991), pp. 109-20.

Greenstein, E.L., 'Two Variations of Grammatical Parallelism in Canaanite Poetry and their Psycholinguistic Background', *Journal of the Ancient Near Eastern Society of Columbia University 6: The Gaster Festschrift* (1974), pp. 87-105.

—'Wordplay, Hebrew', in D.N. Freedman (ed.), *The Anchor Bible Dictionary* (Garden City, NY: Doubleday, 1992), VI, pp. 968-71.

Grossberg, D. 'Pivotal Polysemy in Jeremiah XXV 10-11a', *VT* 36 (1986), pp. 481-85.

Grossfeld, B., 'The Translation of Biblical Hebrew פקד in the Targum, Peshitta, Vulgate and Septuagint', *ZAW* 96 (1984), pp. 83-101.

Guglielmi, W., 'Eine "Lehre" für einen reiselustigen Sohn', *WO* 14 (1983), pp. 147-66.

—'Zu Einigen Literarischen Funktionen des Wortspiels', in *Studien zu Sprache und Religion Ägyptens* (Göttingen: Hubert & Co., 1984), pp. 491-506.

Guillaume, A., 'The Arabic Background of the Book of Job', in F.F. Bruce (ed.), *Promise and Fulfillment: Essays presented to S.H. Hooke* (Edinburgh: T. & T. Clark, 1964), pp. 106-27.

—'Paronomasia in the Old Testament', *JSS* 9 (1964), pp. 282-90.

—*Studies in the Book of Job* (Leiden: Brill, 1968).

Guinan, M., *Job* (Collegeville, MN: Liturgical Press, 1986).

Güterbock, H.G., 'A Hurro-Hittite Hymn to Ishtar', in J. Sasson (ed.), *Studies in Literature from the Ancient Near East: by Members of the American Oriental*

Society Dedicated to Samuel Noah Kramer (AOS, 65; New Haven, CT: American Oriental Society, 1984), pp. 155-64.

Habel, N.C., *The Book of Job: A Commentary* (Philadelphia: Westminster Press, 1985).

Halpern, B., and R.E. Friedman, 'Composition and Paronomasia in the Book of Jonah', *HAR* 4 (1980), pp. 79-92.

Hamori, A., 'Notes on Paronomasia in Abu Tammam's Style', *JSS* 12.1 (1967), pp. 83-90.

Hartley, J.E., *The Book of Job* (Grand Rapids, MI: Eerdmans, 1988).

Hatch, E., and H.A. Redpath (eds.), *A Concordance to the Septuagint and Other Greek Versions of the Old Testament*, I–II (Graz: Akademische Druck/Universitäts-Verlagsanstalt, 1954).

Heater, H., *A Septuagint Translation Technique in the Book of Job* (Washington, DC: Catholic Biblical Association, 1982).

Heintz, J.G., 'Myth(olog)èmes d'époque amorrite et amphibologie en ARMT XXVI, 419, ll.3'-21'?', *NABU* 68 (1994), p. 59.

Held, M., 'Marginal Notes to the Hebrew Lexicon', in A. Kort and S. Morschauser (eds.), *Biblical and Related Studies Presented to Samuel Iwry* (Winona Lake, IN: Eisenbrauns, 1985), pp. 93-103.

Hertog, C.G. den, 'Ein Wortspiel in der Jericho-Erzählung (Jos. 6)?', *ZAW* 104 (1992), pp. 99-100.

Herzberg, W., 'Polysemy in the Hebrew Bible' (PhD dissertation, New York University, 1979).

Hesse, F., *Hiob* (Zürich: Theologischer Verlag, 1978).

Hoffman, Y., 'The Use of Equivocal Words in the First Speech of Eliphaz (Job IV–V)', *VT* 30 (1980), pp. 114-19.

—'The Relation between the Prologue and the Speech-Cycles in Job', *VT* 31 (1981), pp. 160-70.

—'Ancient Near Eastern Literary Conventions and the Restoration of the Book of Job', *ZAW* 103 (1991), pp. 399-411.

Hoffner, H.A., 'Enki's Command to Atraḫasis', in B.L. Eichler, *et al.* (eds.), *Kramer Anniversary Volume* (AOAT, 25; Neukirchen–Vluyn: Neukirchener Verlag, 1976), pp. 241-45.

Hoftijzer, J.J., *Dictionnaire des Inscriptions Sémitique de l'Ouest* (Leiden: Brill, 1965).

Holbert, J.C., 'The Function and Significance of the "Klage" in the Book of Job with Special Reference to the Incidence of Formal and Verbal Irony' (PhD dissertation, South Methodist University, 1975).

—'"The Skies Will Uncover His Iniquity": Satire in the Second Speech of Zophar (Job XX)', *VT* 31 (1981), pp. 171-79.

Holladay, W.L., 'Form and Word-Play in David's Lament Over Saul and Jonathan', *VT* 20 (1970), pp. 153-89.

Holscher, G., *Das Buch Hiob* (Tübingen: Mohr, 1952).

Horowitz, W., and Sh. Paul, 'Two Proposed Janus Parallelisms in Akkadian Literature', *NABU* 70 (1995), pp. 11-12.

Hugger, V.P., 'Die Alliteration im Psalter', in J. Schreiner (ed.), *Wort, Lied, und Gottesspruch: Beiträge zu Psalmen und Propheten. Festschrift für Joseph Ziegler* (Würzburg: Katholisches Biblewerk, 1972), pp. 81-90.

Hurowitz, V.A., 'Some Literary Observations on the Sitti-Marduk Kudurru (BBSt. 6)', *ZA* 82 (1992), pp. 39-59.

Hurvitz, A., 'The Date of the Prose-Tale of Job Linguistically Reconsidered', *HTR* 67 (1974), pp. 17-34.

—'לדיוקו של המונח "אמון" בספר משלי ח/ל', המקרא בראי מפרשו ספר זיכרון לשרה קמין (ed. S. Japhet; Jerusalem: Magnes Press, 1994), pp. 647-50.

Irwin, W.H., 'Syntax and Style in Isaiah 26', *CBQ* 41 (1979), pp. 240-61.

Jacobsen, Th., 'Abstruse Sumerian', in M. Cogan and I. Eph'al (eds.), *Ah, Assyria: Studies in Assyrian History and Ancient Near Eastern Historiography Presented to Hayim Tadmor* (Scripta Hierosolymitana, 33; Jerusalem: Magnes Press, 1991), pp. 279-91.

Janzen, J.G., *Job* (Atlanta, VA: John Knox, 1985).

Japhet, S., 'The Nature and Distribution of Medieval Compilatory Commentaries in the Light of Rabbi Joseph Kara's Commentary on the Book of Job', in M. Fishbane (ed.), *The Midrashic Imagination: Jewish Exegesis, Thought, and History* (Albany, NY: State University of New York Press, 1993), pp. 98-130.

Jastrow, M., *A Dictionary of the Targumim, the Talmud Babli and Yerushalmi, and the Midrashic Literature* (New York: Judaica Press, 1989).

Jepsen, A., *Das Buch Hiob und seine Deutung* (Berlin: Evangelische Verlagsanstalt, 1963).

Joannès, F., *Archives épistolaires de Mari I/2* (Paris: Editions Recherche sur les Civilisations, 1988).

Johnston, R.K., *The Christian at Play* (Grand Rapids: Eerdmans, 1983).

Joseph, S. ben, *The Book of Theodicy: Translation and Commentary on the Book of Job* (New Haven: Yale University Press, 1988).

Julian, Fl., *Der Hiobkommentar des Arianers Julian* (ed. D. Hagedorn; Berlin and New York: de Gruyter, 1973).

Kaufman, S.A., 'The Classification of the North West Semitic Dialects of the Biblical Period and Some Implications Thereof', in *Proceedings of the Ninth World Congresss of Jewish Studies, Panel Session: Hebrew and Aramaic Languages* (Jerusalem: World Union of Jewish Studies, 1988), pp. 55-56.

—'The Job Targum from Qumran', *JAOS* 93.3 (1973), pp. 317-27.

Keel, O., *Jahwes Entgegnung an Ijob* (Göttingen: Vandenhoeck & Ruprecht, 1978).

Kelly, L.G., 'Punning and the Linguistic Sign', *Linguistics* 66 (1970), pp. 5-11.

Key, A.F., 'The Giving of Proper Names in the Old Testament', *JBL* 83 (1964), pp. 55-59.

Kilmer, A.D., 'A Note on an Overlooked Word-Play in the Akkadian Gilgamesh', in G. Van Driel, Th.J.H. Krispijn, M. Stol and K.R. Veenhof (eds.), *Zikir Sumim: Assyriological Studies Presented to F.R. Kraus on the Occasion of his Seventieth Birthday* (Leiden: Brill, 1982), pp. 128-32.

—'Les jeux de mots dans les rêves de Gilgamesh et d'Atraḫasis' (paper read at the Universitaire des Sciences Humaines, Strasbourg, 1983), pp. 1-7.

—'The Symbolism of the Flies in the Mesopotamian Flood Myth and Some Further Implications', in F. Rochberg-Halton (ed.), *Language, Literature, and History: Philological and Historical Studies Presented to Erica Reiner* (New Haven, CT: American Oriental Society, 1987), pp. 175-80.

—'Appendix C: The Brick of Birth', *JNES* 46 (1987), pp. 211-13.

—'Fugal Features of Atraḫasīs: The Birth Theme', in M.E. Vogelzang and H.L.J. Vanstiphout (eds.), *Proceedings of the Gronigen Group for the Study of Mesopotamian Literature*, II (Lewiston: Edwin Mellen, 1995), pp. 127-39.

Klaus, N., 'משחקי־לשון במקרא', *BM* 129 (1991–92), pp. 170-81.

Kökeritz, H. 'Rhetorical Word-Play in Chaucer', *PMLA* 69 (1954), pp. 937-52.

Kramer, S.N., 'Gilgamesh and the Land of the Living', *JCS* (1947), pp. 3-46.

Kramer, S.N., and J. Maier, *Myths of Enki, the Crafty God* (New York: Oxford University Press, 1989).

Kubina, V., *Die Gottesreden im Buche Hiob* (Freiburg im Breisgau: Herder, 1979).

Kugel, J.L., *The Idea of Biblical Poetry: Parallelism and its History* (New Haven, CT: Yale University Press, 1981).

Labat, R., *Manuel d'Epigraphie Akkadienne* (Paris: Librairie Orientaliste Paul Geuther, 1988).

Lachs, S.T., 'Sexual Imagery in Three Rabbinic Passages', *JSJ* 23.2 (1992), pp. 244-48.

Lambert, W.G., and A.R. Millard, *Atraḫasīs: The Babylonian Story of the Flood* (Oxford: Clarendon Press, 1969).

Lamparter, H., *Das Buch der Anfechtung: das Buch Hiob* (Stuttgart: Calwer Verlag, 1979).

Landsberger, B., and J.V. Kinnier Wilson, 'The Fifth Tablet of *Enuma Eliš*', *JNES* 20 (1961), pp. 154-79.

Larkin, K., *The Eschatology of Second Zechariah: A Study of the Formation of a Mantological Wisdom Anthology* (Kampen: Kok, 1994).

Laymon, C.M. (ed.), *Wisdom Literature and Poetry: A Commentary on Job, Psalms, Proverbs, Ecclesiastes, the Song of Solomon* (Nashville: Abingdon Press, 1983).

Lichtenstein, A., 'Toward a Literary Understanding of the Book of Job', *Hebrew Abstracts* 20–21 (1979–80), pp. 34-35.

Lieberman, S.J., 'A Mesopotamian Background for the So-Called *Aggadic* "Measures" of Biblical Hermeneutics?', *HUCA* 58 (1978), pp. 157-225.

Limet, H., 'Le secret et les écrits: aspects de l'ésotérisme en Mésopotamie ancienne', *Homo Religiosus* 13 (1986), pp. 243-54.

Lindblom, J. 'Wisdom in the Old Testament Prophets', in M. Noth and D.W. Thomas (eds.), *Wisdom in Israel and in the Ancient Near East* (VTSup, 3; Leiden: Brill, 1960), pp. 192-204.

Lindenberger, J., *The Aramaic Proverbs of Aḥiqar* (Baltimore: Johns Hopkins University Press, 1983).

Livingstone, A., *Mystical and Mythological Explanatory Works of Assyrian and Babylonian Scholars* (Oxford: Clarendon Press, 1986).

—*Court Poetry and Literary Miscellanea* (State Archives of Assyria, 3; Helsinki: Helsinki University Press, 1989).

Long, B.O., 'Reflections', in S. Niditch (ed.), *Text and Tradition: The Hebrew Bible and Folklore* (SBL Semeia Studies; Atlanta, GA: Scholars Press, 1990), pp. 225-28.

Loretz, O., 'Ugaritische und Hebräische Lexikographie', *UF* 12 (1980), pp. 279-86.

Lubetski, M. 'The Utterance from the East: The Sense of *hwt* in Psalms 52.4, 9; 91.3', *Rel* 20 (1990), pp. 217-32.

Lys, D., 'Notes sur le Cantique', in J.A. Emerton *et al.* (eds.), *Congress Volume: Rome, 1968* (VTSup, 17; Leiden: Brill, 1969), pp. 170-78.

Maag, V., *Hiob: Wandlung und Verarbeitung des Problems in Novelle, Dialogdichtung und Spatfassungen* (Göttingen: Vandenhoeck & Ruprecht, 1982).

Machinist, P., and H. Tadmor, 'Heavenly Wisdom', in M.E. Cohen, *et al.* (eds.), *The Tablet and the Scroll: Near Eastern Studies in Honor of William W. Hallo* (Bethesda, MD: CDL Press, 1993), pp. 146-51.

MacKay, D.G., and T.G. Bever, 'In Search of Ambiguity', *Perception and Psychophysics* 2 (1967), pp. 193-200.

Mahood, M.M., *Shakespeare's Wordplay* (London: Methuen, 1957).

Mallon, E.D., 'A Stylistic Analysis of Joel 1.10-12', *CBQ* 45 (1983), pp. 537-48.

Malul, M., 'A Possible Case of Janus Parallelism in the Epic of Gilgamesh XI, 130', *Acta Sumerologica* 17 (1995), pp. 338-42.

—'Eating and Drinking (One's) Refuse', *NABU* 75 (1993), pp. 82-83.

Mangan, C., *The Targum of Job* (The Aramaic Bible: The Targums, 15; Collegeville, MN: Michael Glazier, 1991).

Marcus, D., '"Lifting up the Head": On the Trail of a Word Play in Genesis 40', *Prooftexts* 10.1 (1990), pp. 17-27.

—*From Balaam to Jonah: Anti-Prophetic Satire in the Hebrew Bible* (BJS, 301; Atlanta, GA: Scholars Press, 1995).

Margalit, B., *A Matter of 'Life' and 'Death': A Study of the Baal-Mot Epic (CTA 4–5–6)* (AOAT, 206; Neukirchen–Vluyn: Neukirchener Verlag, 1980).

Marino, E., *Etimologia o paronomasia? Il significato dei nomi del libro della Genesi* (Lugio, 1993).

Martin-Achard, R., *Et Dieu crée le ciel et la terre: trois études, Esaie 40, Job 38–42, Genese 1* (Geneva: Labor & Fides, 1979).

McCartney, E.S., 'Puns and Plays on Proper Names', *CJ* 14 (1919), pp. 343-58.

McKenna, D.L., *The Communicator's Commentary, Job* (Waco, TX: Word Books, 1986).

Mehler, J., and P. Carey, 'Role of Surface and Base Structure in the Perception of Sentences', *Journal of Learning and Verbal Behavior* 6 (1967), pp. 335-38.

—'The Interaction of Veracity and Syntax in the Processing of Sentences', *Perception and Psychophysics* 3 (1968), pp. 109-11.

Meltzer, E.S., 'A Possible Word-Play in Khamuas I?', *ZAS* 102.1 (1975), p. 78.

Meyer, D.R., *Hebräisches und Aramäisches Handwörterbuch über das Alte Testament* (Berlin: Springer-Verlag, 18th edn, 1987).

Michel, W.L., *Job in the Light of Northwest Semitic* (BibOr, 42; Rome: Pontifical Institute Press, 1987).

Miller, P.D., 'Poetic Ambiguity and Balance in Psalm XV', *VT* 29.4 (1979), pp. 416-24.

Miqra'ot Gedolot (New York: Pardes Publishing House, 1957).

Moftah, R., 'Ära-Datierungen, Regierungsjahre und Zahlwortspiele', *CdE* 39 (1964), pp. 44-60.

Moor, J.C. de, *An Anthology of Religious Texts from Ugarit* (Leiden: Brill, 1987).

Morag, Sh., 'On the Historical Validity of the Vocalization of the Hebrew Bible', *JAOS* 94 (1974), pp. 307-15.

Moran, W.L., 'Rib-Hadda: Job at Byblos?', in A. Kort and S. Morschauser (eds.), *Biblical and Related Studies Presented to Samuel Iwry* (Winona Lake, IN: Eisenbrauns, 1985), pp. 173-81.

—'Notes on the Hymn to Marduk in *Ludlul Bel Nemeqi*', *JAOS* 103 (1986), pp. 255-60.

Morenz, S., 'Wortspiele in Ägypten', in *Religion und Geschichte des alten Ägypten: Gesammelte Aufsätze* (Köln: Böhlau Verlag, 1975), pp. 328-42.

Moriarty, F.L., 'Word as Power in the Ancient Near East', in H.N. Bream, *et al.* (eds.), *A Light Unto My Path: Old Testament Studies in Honor of J.M. Myers* (Philadelphia: Temple University Press, 1974), pp. 345-62.

Nel, P.J., 'The Talion Principle in Old Testament Narratives', *JNSL* 20 (1994), pp. 21-29.

Nemet-Nejat, K.R., 'A Mirror Belonging to the Lady of Uruk', in M.E. Cohen, *et al.* (eds.), *The Tablet and the Scroll: Near Eastern Studies in Honor of William W. Hallo* (Bethesda, MD: CDL Press, 1993), pp. 163-69.

Neugebauer, O., 'Unusual Writings in Seleucid Astronomical Texts', *JCS* 1 (1947), pp. 217-18.

Noegel, S.B., 'A Janus Parallelism in the Gilgamesh Flood Story', *Acta Sumerologica* 13 (1991), pp. 419-21.

—'An Asymmetrical Janus Parallelism in the Gilgamesh Flood Story', *Acta Sumerologica* 16 (1994), pp. 10-12.

—'A Janus Parallelism in the Baal and ʿAnat Story', *JNSL* 21 (1995), pp. 91-94.

—'Another Janus Parallelism in the Atra-Ḫasīs Epic', *Acta Sumerologica* 17 (1995), pp. 342-44.

—'Another Look at Job 18.2, 3', *JBQ* 23 (1995), pp. 159-61.

—'Janus Parallelism Clusters in Akkadian Literature', *NABU* 71 (1995), pp. 33-34.

Noth, M., and D.W. Thomas (eds.), *Wisdom in Israel and in the Ancient Near East* (VTSup, 3; Leiden: Brill, 1960).

O'Connor, M., 'Semitic **mgn* and its Supposed Sanskrit Origin', *JAOS* 109 (1989), pp. 25-32.

Oberhuber, K., 'Ein Versuch zum Verständnis von Atra-Hasis I 223 und I 1', in G. Van Driel, Th.J.H. Krispijn, M. Stol and K.R. Veenhof (eds.), *Zikir Sumim: Assyriological Studies Presented to F.R. Kraus on the Occasion of his Seventieth Birthday* (Leiden: Brill, 1982), pp. 279-81.

Olympiodorus, *Kommentar zu Hiob* (ed. U. Hagedorn and D. Hagedorn; Berlin and New York: de Gruyter, 1984).

Oorschot, J. van, *Gott als Grenze: Eine literar- und redaktionsgeschichtliche Studien zu den Gottesreden des Hiobbuches* (Berlin and New York: de Gruyter, 1987).

Oppenheim, A.L., *The Interpretation of Dreams in the Ancient Near East* (Philadelphia, 1956), p. 241.

Orlinsky, H.M., 'Studies in the Septuagint of the Book of Job: Chapter I', *HUCA* 28 (1957), pp. 53-74.

—'Studies in the Septuagint of the Book of Job: Chapter II', *HUCA* 29 (1958), pp. 229-71.

—'Studies in the Septuagint of the Book of Job: Chapter III', *HUCA* 30 (1959), pp. 153-67.

—'Studies in the Septuagint of the Book of Job: Chapter III (Continued)', *HUCA* 32 (1961), pp. 239-68.

—'Studies in the Septuagint of the Book of Job: Chapter IV', *HUCA* 33 (1962), pp. 119-51.

—'Studies in the Septuagint of the Book of Job: Chapter V', *HUCA* 35 (1964), pp. 57-78.

—'Studies in the Septuagint of the Book of Job: Chapter V', *HUCA* 36 (1965), pp. 37-47.

Orzech, C.D., 'Puns on the Humane King: Analogy and Application in an East Asian Apocryphon', *JAOS* 109.1 (1989), pp. 17-24.

Palmer, R.C., *et al.* (eds.), *Oxford Latin Dictionary* (Oxford: Clarendon Press, 1968–82).

Paran, M., 'למשנה הוראה במקרא', *Beersheva* 1 (1973), pp. 151-61.

Parpola, S., 'The Assyrian Tree of Life: Tracing the Origins of Jewish Monotheism and Greek Philosophy', *JNES* 52 (1993), pp. 161-208.

Patterson, J., *The Wisdom of Israel* (London: Lutterworth; Nashville: Abingdon Press, 1961).

Paul, Sh., 'A Technical Expression from Archery in Zechariah IX 13a', *VT* 39 (1989), pp. 495-97.

—'Polysensuous Polyvalency in Poetic Parallelism', in M. Fishbane and E. Tov (eds.), *'Sha'arei Talmon': Studies in the Bible, Qumran, and the Ancient Near East Presented to Shemaryahu Talmon* (Winona Lake, IN: Eisenbrauns, 1992), pp. 147-63.

Payne, D.F., 'Characteristic Word-Play in "Second Isaiah": A Reappraisal', *JSS* 12.2 (1967), pp. 207-29.

—'Old Testament Exegesis and the Problem of Ambiguity', *ASTI* 5 (1967), pp. 48-68.

Payne Smith, J., *A Compendious Syriac Dictionary* (Oxford: Clarendon Press, 1979).

Peeters, L., 'Pour une interpretation du jeu de mots', *Semitics* 2 (1971–72), pp. 127-42.

Pennant, D.F., 'The Significance of Root Play, Leading Words and Thematic Links in the Book of Judges' (PhD dissertation, Council for National Academic Awards, 1989).

Ploeg, J.P.M. van der, *Le Targum de Job de la grotte XI de Qumrân* (Leiden: Brill, 1993).

Poebel, A., 'The Sumerian Genitive Element', *AJSLL* 51.3 (1935), pp. 145-76.

Pope, M., 'Notes on Ugaritic *ndd-ydd*', *JCS* 1 (1947), pp. 337-41.

—*Job* (AB, 15; Garden City, NY: Doubleday, 1965).

Raabe, P.R., 'Deliberate Ambiguity in the Psalter', *JBL* 110.2 (1991), pp. 213-27.

Rabinowitz, I., *A Witness Forever* (Bethesda, MD: CDL Press, 1993).

Rad, G. von, 'Hiob xxxviii und die altägyptische Weisheit', in M. Noth and D.W. Thomas (eds.), *Wisdom in Israel and in the Ancient Near East* (VTSup, 3; Leiden: Brill, 1960), pp. 293-301.

—*Wisdom in Israel* (Nashville and New York: Abingdon Press, 1972).

Rankin, O.S., 'Alliteration in Hebrew Poetry', *JTS* 31 (1930), pp. 285-91.

Ratner, R., 'The "Feminine Takes Precedence" Syntagm and Job 19, 15', *ZAW* 102 (1990), pp. 238-51.

Rechendorff, H., *Über Paronomasie in den semitischen Sprache: Ein Beitrag zur allgemeinen Sprachwissenschaft* (Giessen: Töpelmann, 1909).

Redfern, W., *Puns* (Oxford: Basil Blackwell, 1984).

Reichert, V.E., *Job: Hebrew Text and English Translation* (London and New York: Soncino Press, 1946).

Reiner, E., and H.G. Güterbock, 'The Great Prayer to Ishtar', *JCS* 21 (1967), pp. 255-66.

Reinink, G.J., and H.L.J. Vanstiphout (eds.), *Dispute Poems and Dialogues in the Ancient and Mediaeval Near East: Forms and Types of Literary Debates in Semitic and Related Literatures* (ALBO, 42; Leuven: Peeters, 1991).

Rendsburg, G., 'Janus Parallelism in Gen. 49.26', *JBL* 99 (1980), pp. 291-93.

—'Double Polysemy in Genesis 49.6 and Job 3.6', *CBQ* 44 (1982), pp. 48-51.

—'Hebrew RḤM = "Rain"', *VT* 33.3 (1983), pp. 357-62.

—'Modern South Arabian as a Source for Ugaritic Etymologies', *JAOS* 107.4 (1987), pp. 623-28.

—'Bilingual Wordplay in the Bible', *VT* 38 (1988), pp. 354-57.

—*Linguistic Evidence for the Northern Origin of Selected Psalms* (SBLMS, 43; Atlanta, GA: Scholars Press, 1990).

—'*Kabbîr* in Biblical Hebrew: Evidence for Style-Switching and Addressee-Switching in the Hebrew Bible', *JAOS* 112 (1992), pp. 649-51.

—'Notes on Genesis XV', *VT* 42.2 (1992), pp. 266-72.

—'The Dialect of the Deir ʿAlla Inscription', *Bibliotheca Orientalis* 3.4 (1993), pp. 309-30.

Rendsburg, G., and S.L. Rendsburg, 'Physiological and Philological Notes to Psalm 137', *JQR* 83.3-4 (1993), pp. 385-99.

Renkema, J., 'The Meaning of the Parallel Acrostics in Lamentations', *VT* 45 (1995), pp. 379-82.

Richard, E., 'Expressions of Double Meaning and their Function in the Gospel of John', *NTS* 31 (1985), pp. 96-112.

Richler, B., 'Rabbeinu Tam's "Lost" Commentary on Job', in B. Walfish (ed.), *Frank Talmage Memorial Volume I* (Haifa: University of Haifa Press, 1993), pp. 191-202.

Richter, H., *Studien zu Hiob: Der Aufbau des Hiobbuches, dargestellt an den Gattungen des Rechtslebens* (Berlin: Evangelische Verlagsanstalt, 1959).

Rignell, L.G., 'Notes on the Peshiṭta of the Book of Job', *ASTI* (1973), pp. 98-106.

Rignell, L.G., and Peshitta Institute, *Vetus Testamentum Syriace*, Pt 2, Fasc. 1a (*Liber Iob*) (Leiden: Brill, 1982).

Rodd, C.S., *The Book of Job* (Philadelphia: Trinity Press, 1990).

Rosenberg, A.J. (ed.), *Job: A New English Translation* (*Translation of Text, Rashi and Commentary by A.J. Rosenberg*) (New York: Judaica Press, 1989).

Rowley, H.H., *Job* (Grand Rapids, MI: Eerdmans, 1980).

Rowton, M.B., 'The Permansive in Classic Babylonian', *JNES* 21 (1962), p. 275.

Russell, E.A., *Paronomasia and Kindred Phenomena in the New Testament* (Leipzig: W. Drugulin, 1920).

—'Some Reflections on Humour in Scripture and Otherwise', *IBS* 13 (1991), pp. 199-210.

Sander-Hansen, C.E., 'Die Phonetischen Wortspielen des Ältesten Ägyptischen', *AcOr* 20 (1948), pp. 1-22.

Sasson, J.M., 'Word Play in the Old Testament', *IDBSup* (Nashville: Abingdon Press, 1976), pp. 968-70.

—'Albright as an Orientalist', *BA* 56.1 (1993), p. 3.

—'The Divine Divide: re FM 2.71.5', *NABU* 67 (1994), pp. 39-40.

Sauren, H., 'Nammu and Enki', in M.E. Cohen, *et al.* (eds.), *The Tablet and the Scroll: Near Eastern Studies in Honor of William W. Hallo* (Bethesda, MD: CDL Press, 1993), pp. 198-206.

Sawyer, J.F.A., 'The Place of Folk-Linguistics in Biblical Interpretation', *Proceedings of the Vth World Congress of Jewish Studies* (Jerusalem: World Union of Jewish Studies, 1969), pp. 109-13.

Schökel, L.A., *A Manual of Hebrew Poetics* (Subsidia Biblica, 11; Rome: Editrice Pontificio Istituto Biblico, 1988).

Schott, A., 'Zu meiner Übersetzung des Gilgames-Epos', *ZA* 42 (1934), pp. 92-143.

Sefati, Y., 'An Oath of Chastity in a Sumerian Love Song (*SRT* 31)?', in J. Klein and A. Skaist (eds.), *Bar-Ilan Studies in Assyriology Dedicated to Pinhas Artzi* (Ramat-Gan: Bar-Ilan University Press, 1990), pp. 45-63.

Segal, M., ספר איוב, *Tarbiz* 13 (1942), pp. 73-91.

Segert, S., 'Paronomasia in the Samson Narrative in Judges XIII–XVI', *VT* 34.4 (1984), pp. 454-61.

Seidel, H., 'Hiob, der Patron der Muziker', in J. Hausmann and H.J. Zobel (eds.), *Alttestamentliche Glaube und Biblische Theologie: Festschrift für Horst Dietrich Preuss zum 65 Geburtstag* (Stuttgart: Kohlhammer, 1992).

Selms, A. van, *Job: A Practical Commentary* (Grand Rapids, MI: Eerdmans, 1985).

Simundson, D.J., *The Message of Job: A Theological Commentary* (Minneapolis, MN: Augsburg, 1986).

Skehan, P., *Studies in Israelite Poetry and Wisdom* (Washington, DC: Catholic Biblical Association of America, 1980).

Slotki, I.W., 'A Study of רעם', *AJSLL* 37 (1920–21), pp. 149-55.

Snaith, N.H., *Notes on the Hebrew Text of Job I–VI* (Study Notes on Bible Books; New York: Abingdon Press, 1945).

Snell, B., *The Discovery of the Mind: The Greek Origin of European Thought* (New York: Harper, 1960).

Soden, W. von, 'Zum Hebräischen Wörterbuch', *UF* 13 (1981), pp. 157-64.

Sokoloff, M., *A Dictionary of Jewish Palestinian Aramaic of the Byzantine Period* (Ramat-Gan: Bar-Ilan University Press, 1990).

—*The Targum to Job from Qumran Cave XI* (Ramat-Gan: Bar-Ilan University Press, 1974).

Soll, W.M., 'Babylonian and Biblical Acrostics', *Bib* 69 (1988), pp. 305-22.

Speiser, E.A., 'Word Plays on the Creation Epic's Version of the Founding of Babylon', in L.J. Finkelstein and M. Greenberg (eds.), *Oriental and Biblical Studies: Collected Works of E.A. Speiser* (Philadelphia: University of Pennsylvania Press, 1967), pp. 53-61.

Stec, D.M., *The Text of the Targum of Job: An Introduction and Critical Edition* (AGJU, 20; Leiden: Brill, 1993).

Stern, D., *Parables in Midrash: Narrative and Exegesis in Rabbinic Literature* (Cambridge, MA: Harvard University Press, 1991).

Stol, M., 'Biblical Idiom in Akkadian', in M.E. Cohen *et al.* (eds.), *The Tablet and the Scroll: Near Eastern Studies in Honor of William W. Hallo* (Bethesda, MD: CDL Press, 1993), pp. 246-49.

Storoy, S., 'On Proverbs and Riddles: Polar Word Pairs and Other Poetical Devices, and the Words for "Poor and Needy" in the Book of Proverbs', *SJOT* 7 (1993), pp. 270-84.

Strus, A., *Nomen Omen* (Rome: Pontifical Institute, 1978).

Sulzberger, M., 'Onoma Eponymon: Les noms propres chez Homère et dans la mythologique Grecque', *Revue des études grecques* 183 (1926), pp. 381-447.

Szczygiel, P.P., *Das Buch Job* (Heilige Schrift des Alten Testamentes, 5.1; Bonn: Peter Hanstein, 1931).

Szpek, H.M., 'The Peshitta on Job 7.6: "My Days Are Swifter than an ארג" ', *JBL* 113 (1994), pp. 287-90.

—*Translation Technique in the Peshitta to Job: A Model for Evaluating a Text with Documentation from the Peshitta to Job* (SBLDS, 137; Atlanta: Scholars Press, 1992).

Terrien, S.L., *Job* (Neuchâtel: Delachaux & Niestlé, 1963).

Thiselton, A., 'The Supposed Power in Words in the Biblical Writings', *JTS* 25 (1974), pp. 289-99.

Thom, J.C., '"Don't Walk on the Highways": The Pythagorian *Akousmata* and Early Christian Literature', *JBL* 113 (1994), pp. 93-112.

Tinney, S., '^{d}en-gi$_{6}$-du-du: muttarû rubē: A note on Erra I 21', *NABU* 1 (1989), pp. 2-4.

Tsevat, M., 'The Meaning of the Book of Job', *HUCA* 37 (1966), pp. 73-106.

—*The Meaning of the Book of Job and Other Biblical Studies: Essays on the Literature and Religion of the Hebrew Bible* (New York: Ktav, 1980).

Tsumura, D.T., 'Janus Parallelism in Nah. 1.8', *JBL* 102 (1983), pp. 109-11.

Tur-Sinai, N.H., *The Book of Job: A New Commentary* (Jerusalem: Kiryath Sepher, 1967).

Ulmer, G. 'The Puncept in Grammatology', in J. Culler (ed.), *On Puns: The Foundation of Letters* (Oxford: Basil Blackwell, 1988), pp. 164-89.

Veldhuis, N., *A Cow of Sin* (Library of Oriental Texts, 2; Gröningen: Styx Publications, 1991).

Villa-Amil, Ms. (ed.), *Targum de Job* (Madrid: Consejo Superior de Investigaciones Cientificas, Instituto Francisco Suarez, 1984).

Wallenfels, R., 'Zodiacal Signs among the Seal Impressions from Hellenistic Uruk', in M.E. Cohen *et al.* (eds.), *The Tablet and the Scroll: Near Eastern Studies in Honor of William W. Hallo* (Bethesda, MD: CDL Press, 1993), pp. 281-89.

Ward, W., 'Comparative Studies in Egyptian and Ugaritic', *JNES* 20 (1961), pp. 31-40.

Watson, W.G.E., 'Archaic Elements in the Language of Chronicles', *Bib* 53 (1972), pp. 191-207.

—'The Pivot Pattern in Hebrew, Ugaritic and Akkadian Poetry', *ZAW* 88 (1976), pp. 239-53.

—'Hebrew "To Be Happy"—an Idiom Identified', *VT* 31 (1981), pp. 92-95.

—'Reversed Rootplay in Ps. 145', *Bib* 62 (1981), pp. 101-102.

—'Allusion, Irony and Wordplay in Mic 1,7', *Bib* 65 (1984), pp. 103-105.

—*Classical Hebrew Poetry: A Guide to its Techniques* (JSOTSup, 26; Sheffield: JSOT Press, 1984).

Wehr, H., *A Dictionary of Modern Written Arabic* (Ithaca, NY: Cornell University Press, 1976).

Weinstock, L.I., 'Sound and Meaning in Biblical Hebrew', *JSS* 28 (1983), pp. 49-62.

Weiser, A., 'משנה הוראה בס' ישעיהו', *BM* 20 (1964), pp. 25-32.

Weiss, R., התרגום הארמי לספר איוב (Tel Aviv: Tel Aviv University Press, 1979).

Westbrook, R., *Studies in Biblical and Cuneiform Law* (Cahiers de la *Revue biblique*, 26; Paris: Gabalda, 1988).

Westermann, C., *Der Aufbau des Buches Hiob* (Tübingen: Mohr, 1956).

Westhuizen, J.P. van der, 'Assonance in Biblical and Babylonian Hymns of Praise', *Semitics* 7 (1980), pp. 81-101.

Whybray, R.N., *Two Jewish Theologies: Job and Ecclesiastes* (Hull: University of Hull Press, 1980).

Wieder, A. 'Ugaritic-Hebrew Lexicographical Notes', *JBL* 84 (1965), pp. 160-64.

Wilcke, C. von, 'Formale Gesichtspunkte in der sumerischen Literatur', in S.J. Lieberman (ed.), *Sumerological Studies in Honor of Thorkild Jacobsen on his Seventieth Birthday, June 7, 1974* (Assyriological Studies, 20; Chicago: University of Chicago Press, 1976), pp. 205-316.

—'ku-li', *ZA* 59 (1969), pp. 65-99.

Wilkinson, R.H., *Reading Egyptian Art: A Hieroglyphic Guide to Ancient Egyptian Painting and Sculpture* (London: Thames & Hudson, 1992).

Wiseman, D.J., 'A New Text of the Babylonian Poem of the Righteous Sufferer', *Anatolian Studies* 30 (1980), pp. 104-107.

Wolde, E. van, 'A Text Semantic Study of the Hebrew Bible, Illustrated with Noah and Job', *JBL* 113 (1994), pp. 19-35.

Wolfers, D., 'The Speech-Cycles in the Book of Job', *VT* 43 (1993), pp. 385-402.

Wolters, A., 'Ṣopîyyâ (Prov. 31.27) as a Hymnic Participle and Play on *Sophia*', *JBL* 104 (1985), pp. 577-87.

—'The Riddle of the Scales in Daniel 5', *HUCA* 57 (1991), pp. 155-77.

—'Untying the King's Knots: Physiology and Wordplay in Daniel 5', *JBL* 110 (1991), pp. 117-22.

—'Wordplay and Dialect in Amos 8.1-2', *JETS* 31.4 (1988), pp. 407-10.

Wood, J., *Wisdom Literature* (London: Gerald Duckworth, 1967).

Yellin, D., איוב-חקרי מקרא (Jerusalem, 1927).

—'משנה ההוראה בתנ'ך', *Tarbiz* 5 (1933), pp. 1-17.

—תורת השירה הספרדית (Jerusalem: Magnes Press, 1972).

York, A.D., 'A Philological and Textual Analysis of the Qumran Job Targum (11QtgJob)' (PhD dissertation, Cornell University, 1973).

Zacuto, A., ספר יוחסין (ed. H. Filipowski; Frankfurt: M.A. Wahrmann, 1924).

Zadok, R., 'Notes on the West Semitic Material from Emar', *AIOU* 51.2 (1991), pp. 114-37.

Ziegler, J., *Beiträge zum griechischen Iob* (Göttingen: Vandenhoeck & Ruprecht, 1985).

Zijl, P.J. van, *Baal: A Study of Texts in Connection with Baal in the Ugaritic Epics* (AOAT, 10; Neukirchen–Vluyn: Neukirchener Verlag, 1972).

Zuckerman, B., 'A Fragment of an Unstudied Column of 11QtgJob: A Preliminary Report', *Newsletter of the Comprehensive Aramaic Lexicon* 10 (1993), pp. 1-7.

—'The Targums to Job', in D.N. Freedman (ed.), *The Anchor Bible Dictionary* (Garden City, NY: Doubleday, 1992), III, pp. 868-69.

Zurro, E., 'Disemia de brḥ y paralelismo bifronte en Job 9,25', *Bib* 62 (1981), pp. 546-47.

INDEXES

INDEX OF REFERENCES

OLD TESTAMENT

OTHER JEWISH AUTHORS

OTHER ANCIENT SOURCES

INDEX OF AUTHORS